Armin Trost

Below Expectations

Why performance appraisals fail
in the modern working world
and what to do instead

Translated by
Emily Plank

© 2016 Armin Trost
Im Keltergarten 29
72070 Tübingen
Germany
http://www.armintrost.de
Twitter: @armintrost
mail@armintrost.de

All Rights reserved

Book title of the original German version:
Unter den Erwartungen.
Warum das jährliche Mitarbeitergespräch
in der modernen Arbeitswelt versagt.
2015 Wiley-VCH Verlag & Co. KGaA

Translator: Emily Plank, E-Translations
Cover-Design: Armin Trost
Coverfoto: fotolia #101786868
Business black man with a tablet

To Elena

Preface

The first project of my career as an HR professional involved introducing an annual performance appraisal at SAP AG. I actively participated in countless project meetings and workshops on the topic, and attended numerous information events for employees and managers. As an employee, I was the victim of the performance appraisal, and as a manager, the perpetrator. In the back of my mind was a constant nagging feeling that something about the whole matter just wasn't right. It was more a vague impression, fuelled by less-than-euphoric reactions from the parties in question. But what could be wrong with the idea that managers set targets with their employees at least once a year, discuss their development, and provide structured feedback?

Years later, I became a professor. In this capacity, coupled with my role as academic, advisor and coach, I held many controversial discussions with HR professionals, managers and MBA students who had designed or experienced this instrument during their careers. The dilemma still remained. What appeared so simple and well intended in theory proved to be a highly complex, multi-faceted concept in practice. Naivety appeared to be the last thing anyone would want here.

In 2012, more out of acute despair than anything else, I dedicated one of my columns in the German version of the Harvard Business Review to this topic. The article was, admittedly, highly polarising, even cynical. The first day after it was published, it received more than 10,000 hits. This was then followed by a deluge of comments and opinions, most of which were sent to me by email. The topic had evidently caused quite a stir. But there was still no solution in sight. Some saw it one way, others saw it another way.

In 2013, I then began gradually collating relevant information. I studied tomes of literature, developed models, and sought out discussions with HR professionals, managers and students. Things eventually started making more sense, and I feel I am now in a position to provide more clarity and structure to this issue. Before embarking on this book project, I engaged in extensive dialogue with relevant figures from the real world. I would like to take this opportunity to sincerely thank them. If their feedback hadn't been so positive, I would not have written this book. I believe the ideas raised in it are highly relevant to practice, and hope it can serve as a source of guidance and consolidation for anyone having to deal with annual performance appraisals.

Tübingen/Germany, 31/1/2016

Armin Trost

Content

1. Introduction 11
2. **The annual performance appraisal system** **20**
   It's a system 21
   We allay world hunger 33
3. **What? For whom? And why?** **40**
   From benefit to design 41
   The usual intended Benefits 47
   Performance appraisal customers 61
   Internal positioning 72
   Objective relevance 77
4. **Framework conditions** **84**
   Task environment 88
   Leadership role 102
   Organisation 122
   Hierarchical world – agile world 141
5. **Possibilities and limits** **149**
   Rewarding the best 150
   Addressing the weak 157
   Identifying talent 167
   Establishing internal suitability 178
   Employee development 186

Offering prospects 192
Learning through feedback 201
Managing companies 211
Motivating by objectives 218
Retaining employees 225
Interim conclusion 231

6. Alternatives **237**
Responsibility 240
Openness and diversity 248
Networked thinking 256
Sorted formats, content, times and players 261
Letting go 268
What now? 273

7. Conclusion and final remarks **284**

Bibliography **288**

1. Introduction

Every year, the same old scene plays out at almost every industry around the world, including Steven's. Steven is a sales manager at an international automotive supplier. While at the airport waiting to board yet another plane, he checks his emails again. As always, there are too many. One comes from his HR manager, the so-called "HR Business Partner", responsible for the International Sales division. Subject: Annual performance appraisal. The mailing list is long. It seems all the managers in his area have received the email. Steven can guess what is coming. "Dear manager, I wish to advise you that, as is the case every year, the annual performance appraisals are due to be conducted over the next few weeks. The link below will take you to the relevant forms for your staff members. It is important that all appraisals be completed by the end of January. Please also find attached some guidelines on conducting the annual performance appraisal". This is followed by the usual motivational phrases about the appraisal's great relevance in terms of leadership quality, performance culture, professionalism in dealings with employees, and the future of the company. Steven is already familiar with the guidelines from a compulsory training course for all managers. They state that goals must be formulated "SMARTly"[1], that feedback be given objectively, always starting with the positives, and so on. As he makes his way to his plane, Steven's mind is racing. His diary is nearly booked up. Yes, appraisals are important. But what's the purpose of it all? Has it really been a year already? It'll be a bit difficult with Peter (one of his staff). It's going to be a lot of work, but I'll get through it, etc. As he takes his seat on the aeroplane, he quickly sends off an email to his assistant: "Hi Rita, please make one-hour appointments with all 17 staff from our team during the second half of January. Subject: Performance appraisal. More to follow. Thanks and regards, Steven. PS: Don't forget that you and I also need an appointment ;-)".

The annual performance appraisal is undoubtedly one of the most common management tools worldwide. For many HR professionals, it is a fixed, integral component of professional HR management. Yet, at the same time, hardly any other management tool is as heavily criticised or at least as controversially discussed by affected employees and managers. But what could be wrong with a performance appraisal? Who could have anything against a manager taking time to speak to his/her employee about the past, future and possible developments once or twice a year? What is the problem if the content and results of this appraisal are noted down? It is first necessary to simply convey the idea of a performance appraisal at companies. As the responsible HR manager seeking to introduce the appraisal, you won't face many objections to start with. But reality soon proves to be less than smooth sailing.

---

[1] specific, measurable, appealing, realistic time-bound

For some, the annual performance appraisal is a tedious exercise which just needs to be "got through" to satisfy the HR staff – a case of "Don't mess with HR". Employees and managers often tend to share this view, and together they work out an easy way of conducting the appraisal without actually doing it. Last year's appraisal form is re-used and altered slightly, with both parties agreeing on which boxes to tick. And that's it. Everyone is happy and satisfied – including the HR department.

For others, the annual performance appraisal is the most important meeting of the year. Both parties – the employee and the manager – prepare for it knowing that this particular conversation will set the course for the coming months or even the employee's entire career. Working life without annual performance appraisals is inconceivable to all persons involved, or would at least be a significant problem.

In my lectures, I like to ask experienced MBA students from all over the world the following question: On a scale of zero to ten, how useful have you found annual performance appraisals to be in your career? Where zero is "absolute nonsense, pointless", and ten is "extremely important, essential". While virtually all students have encountered this tool, their opinions are often completely different. The spread could not be greater – a phenomenon I have observed consistently for many years. This is interesting, given that other Human Resource Management (HRM) tools tend to receive clearer ratings – one way or another. Employer branding, employee referral programmes, and action learning for junior employees are concepts generally viewed positively. But there are other HR schemes which rate just as controversially as performance appraisals, particularly among students with long-time professional experience. These primarily include employee surveys and management models. But why is the annual performance appraisal such a contentious issue?

There are of course the usual answers to this question, the most common presumably being: "Managers are not mature or competent enough to perform the appraisals properly. They need to be trained in the implementation of leadership principles". A common argument here is that managers who are unable or perhaps do not wish to conduct the appraisals are not fit to be managers. In other words, the misgivings are aimed more at the managers than the tool itself. This is probably also why the literature is full of guides for managers, coupled with the hordes of usually freelance advisors who teach them how to conduct these appraisals. The managers learn, for example, that they must always start a performance appraisal positively, then add the criticism, before once again concluding on a positive note. They also learn how to approach inefficient employees and gently break their problem to them, particularly when these employees appear to be satisfied with their performance. Another common view is that annual performance appraisals are ill-received because of poor communication to managers and employees, because staff have not been properly told why this HR measure is so important. Once again, it's not about the tool itself here.

Things are somewhat more complex than they first seem. It is certainly always positive when a manager speaks with his/her employees. But the question of whether the annual performance appraisal is a suitable tool cannot be answered with a flat "yes". In some situations, performance appraisals can even be toxic for a company, and harm a previously good management culture. In order to better understand the benefits and dynamics associated with annual performance appraisals, it is necessary to conduct a detailed examination – something frequently neglected by many companies. It is common for HR departments to find themselves in an undesirable position as a result of introducing a performance appraisal, their activism once again revealing how far removed they are from real working conditions. Naivety takes precedence over professional expertise. What was initially well intended ends in disaster. And the reasons for this are often never known, even after years of, in some cases, painful experiences.

Naivety or a "press on regardless" mentality seems to be the last thing likely to help here. In actual fact, the history of HR has seen many years of unprecedented unworldliness, in almost all areas. Variable salary systems were introduced based on the assumption that employees could be motivated by money. In the end, it became apparent that the approach had backfired, and had actually discouraged efficient employees. We conducted employee surveys every year because we thought measuring employee satisfaction, coupled with the structured integration of all employees, would gradually put a company in a better position. Reality proved to be rather disappointing. We developed leadership principles, and used every opportunity to communicate these to employees and managers in all available channels. Management quality was the last thing which improved. Having realised that diversity is important, we started managing it through KPIs, targets, directives, policies and continuous education, but failing to see that it must first be allowed to exist. Dual career paths were invented to ensure efficient employees not fit or able to be managers were not disadvantaged. These experts were given many privileges, often resulting in a farce. We devised intricate competence models to test future managers, only to later find out that we were running the risk of eliminating the true talent. I don't even want to imagine the damage caused in the past by well intended HR management, but believe one of the key causes of this is the naivety with which HR managers often approach real challenges. Many of the implicit or explicit assumptions on which an HR policy is based are debatable or just plain false. And it gets worse: the relevant persons responsible at their respective companies are not even aware of them.

This is largely also the case for annual performance appraisals. We want managers to speak to their employees more so as to enable mutual trust, and force all managers to conduct an appraisal based on a set model. We don't realise that this approach is particularly harmful to the mutual trust of the managers who, before introducing performance appraisals, displayed a high level of management quality. We want to employ or develop staff according to their skills, and rely on managers being suitable to validly assess these skills. Citing the notion that this is a key management task, we have for decades insisted on this form of staff appraisal, even though science has clearly shown, for at least the same amount of time, that this approach is not at all likely to achieve the desired success (e.g. Culbertson, Henning & Payne, 2013). As easy, obvious and respectful as the annual performance appraisal may seem at first glance, it is equally fraught with problems. Naivety and good faith are particularly dangerous when it comes to this widespread tool.

This book aims to help readers understand and frame the issue of performance appraisals more systematically – from a neutral perspective. I am neither for nor against it, but instead ask questions which I then attempt to answer: Which type of annual performance appraisal is recommended and when? When is it not? What can be achieved through performance appraisals and how? In which conditions and circumstances? When does the tool reach its limits? What are some relevant framework conditions? What are some possible alternatives in order to achieve the goals usually pursued through performance appraisals? And when is it better to give this tool a wide berth?

Why do we need another book on this topic? Looking at the literature on performance appraisals, employee assessment, target agreements and performance management, it soon becomes clear that there are currently three types of books. The first are those discussing the issue of how to conduct annual performance appraisals. These are guides which do not question the benefit of such appraisals, instead automatically assuming their worth in an almost naive, sometimes dogmatic manner. Among other things, they state that good preparation and catering to employees is important. The second category of books is of a scientific nature (e.g. Murphy & Cleveland, 1995), usually vividly describing what is done in actual practice. What are the methods? What benefit is observed? But the main scientific focus lies on the validity of evaluation processes, which are all viewed critically from a scientific perspective, meaning most of this literature lacks practical implications. The third category tends to demonise performance appraisals just as dogmatically as supporters defend it (e.g. Culbert, 2010; Coens & Jenkins, 2000). It includes authors who, often in a very inspiring manner, question everything relating to classic business management in order to instead market their own consultancy approach. They refer to new, modern corporate worlds which break with the old rules. A number of these authors' ideas are drawn on here.

This book does not fit into any of these three categories, least of all the guidebook literature. It picks up on scientific findings, and is inspired by the more critical literature. What makes this book special is the fact that it examines in detail the desired benefits of annual performance appraisals in relation to different contexts. The conditions in which certain benefits can be achieved using classic components of performance appraisal, and circumstances in which alternatives should be considered. Those engaging with this book's content will critically reflect on annual performance appraisals, and see things from new perspectives. Indeed many views will be turned on their head. Not only does the book put this popular HR tool to the test and break it down into its parts, it also serves as a practical reference point for readers.

But the most important reason to read this book lies in the changing working world. Most books on annual performance appraisals are written based on a traditional view of organisations – a perspective of increasingly little relevance to modern-day reality. They are implicitly or explicitly based on a static, hierarchical organisational structure, coupled with a traditional understanding of management. Goals and strategies are defined at the top, and then broken down. The top is about thinking, the bottom about actions. Requirements and processes are set by superordinate meta-intelligence. Once described and comprehensively examined, the organisation runs much like clockwork. Management essentially revolves around one central question: How can I get employees to do what I, as a manager, want them to? This line of thinking starts to crumble, particularly due to the increasing complexity of the corporate and business world, the heightened dynamics, and the rapid changes, both internally and externally. In light of this, much of what has been said, written and done in relation to annual performance appraisals in recent years is losing importance. And many HR professionals, managers or CEOs are noticing this. At least that's the impression I get. The aim of this book is to address, in a structured manner, the general unease manifesting in practice.

Chapter 2 initially describes the common notion of annual performance appraisals, and the understanding on which this book is based. Among other things, it shows that performance appraisals are much more than just a conversation between an employee and his/her manager. The typical content and intended benefits are discussed in this context. Chapter 3 illustrates that, when examining the issue of performance appraisals, the desired benefit must always serve as the starting point. It thus warns against adopting approaches too focused on the tool itself. Chapter 4 then deals with the relevant framework conditions, including the relationship between managers and employees, and the dynamics/precariousness of the tasks and working environment in which the affected players operate. The organisational context is also examined, and aspects such as employees' professional independence, their autonomy, and the degree of collaboration play a key role. This chapter states that introducing a textbook-like approach to performance appraisals at companies is, without question, the wrong path to take. It finishes by distinguishing between a traditionally hierarchical and an agile business reality. Chapter 5 draws on the benefit categories of performance appraisals briefly outlined in Chapter 3. Using different, contrasting corporate worlds, it illustrates where and how performance appraisals can fit in, comparing the hierarchical context with the agile one. The conclusion will ultimately be that, regardless of the situation, an annual performance appraisal can never solve all the problems associated with professional management. More modern alternatives prove to be worth considering, particularly at highly fluid companies. Chapter 6 then compares all relevant setup options in both the hierarchical and agile context, demonstrating practical alternatives which may potentially be viable in a modern, more fluid working world.

In summary

- The annual performance appraisal is one of the most common HR management tools used around the world.
- The annual performance appraisal is highly controversial among the affected employees and managers.
- The reasons for the opposition to annual performance appraisals relate less to the affected parties and more to the system itself.
- The annual performance appraisal is an extremely complex, multi-layered phenomenon. Acting naively can be very dangerous.

2. The annual performance appraisal system

I have been attending HR conferences or speaking with HR professionals about their approaches for many years, and I frequently get the sinking feeling that I have heard everything being presented 100 times before. One in ten presentations will stimulate me and allow me to discover something really new: Wow, that company has broken new ground. That's courageous. Respect. In some cases, it is the nature of the HR community to gear themselves around the practices of others. It creates an element of security. HR managers at SMEs in particular rarely have sparring partners on the same level as them at their company. So it's no wonder that, to a certain extent, people try to achieve what others have already attempted. Science also tends to lag behind practice, rather than provide groundbreaking inspiration. Many consultancy companies have for years been adopting the same old HR approaches at a wide range of businesses. This increases their own security and sense of routine, and yields the desired profit margin. Given this rather unfortunate state of affairs, the only choice is for the HR world to very definitively gear itself around a few, barely distinguishable best practices. Although companies may differ in the manner in which they conduct their annual performance appraisals, there is a prototype variant approximating practice as a whole. If we look at what random businesses are doing in terms of the annual performance appraisal, it may come as a surprise to see how similar the approaches are. It thus seems appropriate to start with the *traditional* annual performance appraisal described below.

It's a system

If an HR manager says they have "introduced performance appraisals at their company", it means they have implemented a system. It's not about Mr Smith talking with Ms Jones, but rather about all managers regularly conducting specific evaluations together with all employees, and making certain decisions. This system is governed by special rules and standards, usually defined by the HR department. The judgements and decisions then serve as the basis for many HR activities.

The annual performance appraisal is a cycle

The idea behind the annual performance appraisal is quite simple. Once a year, an employee and his/her manager sit down and discuss the past twelve months. The employee receives an evaluation of his/her performance, skills and any potential. The coming twelve months are then discussed, which essentially entails a target agreement, focusing on performance and development targets. What should the employee achieve over the next year, and how should he/she improve his/her skills? The latter ends up becoming something of a development plan for the coming year, while the performance goals are based on overarching targets. In general, this is a cyclical process which repeats itself every year (see Figure 1).

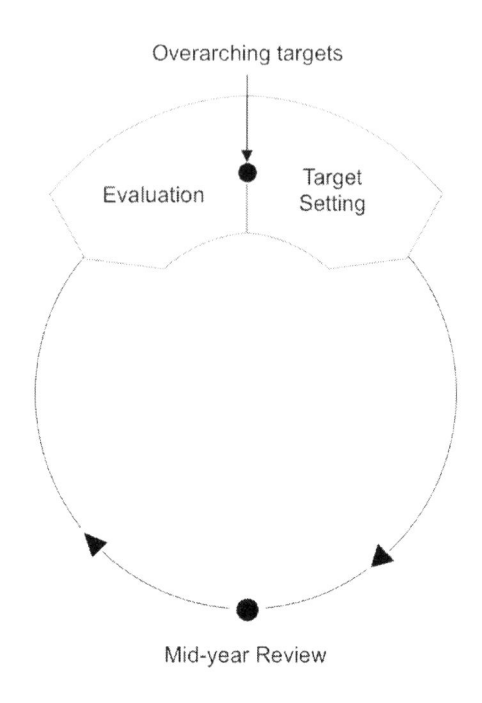

Figure 1:
Annual performance appraisals are usually cyclic.

At many companies, this cycle is supplemented with a half-yearly appraisal in which an interim review is conducted after six months. The results and evaluations discussed are usually either recorded in designated forms, or entered into a suitable IT system.

In practice, the content of performance appraisals reveals certain differences, but more commonalities. Performance evaluations and target agreements are part of the standard. We can also observe numerous other aspects which are addressed here, such as the concrete planning of development measures, the relevance of a talent programme, and the risk of employee turnover, just to name a few. The following section explores the wide range of content discussed at annual performance appraisals in more detail.

Uniformity in all areas, and at all levels

If companies conduct performance appraisals, they tend to do so at *all levels*, although the methods often differ greatly. Particularly when it comes to agreeing on targets, many companies endeavour to break these down in cascade-like fashion. The CEO first conducts performance appraisals with the managers directly below him/her, who then conduct appraisals with their direct subordinates and so forth. The cascade ends with the employees on the lowest rung of the ladder.

We also commonly observe attempts to conduct annual performance appraisals the same way at all areas, meaning the same standards apply in the sales, production or R&D divisions. The system applied in France is similar to that used in Germany and every other country. As far as the HR department is concerned, anything else would become impossibly complex. Above all, however, they don't want to have to keep re-teaching this tool to managers and staff who move areas internally or who are promoted. And last but not least, adopting different methods and content would involve considerable time and effort, both in terms of procedure and technology.

To ensure better comparability and capacity for standardisation, practice continues to be dominated by structured, quantitative evaluation approaches, which apply both to assessing skills and evaluating individual performance. The need for or relevance of so-called forced distribution or forced ranking remains a hotly disputed aspect here.

A focus on the individual

Another feature of performance appraisals is the fact that the focus is on the *individual employee*, not teams or entire departments. Targets and evaluations usually relate to the individual employee, and are technically filed away as personal information, e.g. in personnel records.

Other forms are, of course, also possible, as will be demonstrated throughout this book. Depending on the working environment, they may even be more appropriate. For instance, it is becoming increasingly common for companies to adopt collaborative, social approaches to performance evaluations and target agreements. In practice, however, these alternatives are rarely connected with the concept of performance appraisal.

Manager conducts the appraisal

There is an assumption that performance appraisals are conducted by an employee's respective *manager*, who is usually the initiator. It is hard for most managers or HR professionals to imagine a situation in which an employee approaches his/her boss, alerts him/her to the annual appraisal, and then conducts it: "Hi boss, please come to my office next Monday. The performance appraisal is coming up. Please be prepared. I have a lot of things to discuss with you." This alone shows that traditional forms of performance appraisal require a specific, often hierarchical management structure. It's about a manager's expectations of his/her employees. And it is usually also the managers who make judgements of the employee during the appraisal. Even if some companies claim employees can or should also provide their managers with feedback in this situation, this is more of a secondary aspect, and is an exception.

Performance appraisals are compulsory

At most companies, the annual performance appraisal is *compulsory*. There are clear expectations, at least for the managers who, as mentioned, are responsible for conducting it. The appraisals are usually monitored centrally by the HR departments. I know of companies in which employees and managers have to confirm in writing that the appraisal has been performed. Other companies monitor them by getting the HR department to collect the results in writing via relevant forms or IT systems. It seems that having an annual performance appraisal as an optional support service for employees or managers is more the exception.

Interfaces to affiliated HR processes

Examining publications from the last few decades of the 20th century on the topic of performance appraisal reveals that the focus indeed was on one-on-one conversation between the employee and his/her manager. They discussed bases of communication or directive versus non-directive communication. A wide range of performance evaluations have existed simultaneously for many centuries. It has only been in recent years that the idea of discussing an employee's performance with the person in question has become popular, resulting in performance appraisals. This tool has increasingly transformed into the linchpin of numerous HR instruments. A performance appraisal is thus much more than just talks between an employee and his/her manager. It is a *system*. It is institutionalised, formal, follows fixed rules, and displays clearly defined interfaces to affiliated HR concepts and processes. At least that's what most companies who employ this system claim. For instance, there are interfaces to the salary management system:

Variable salary components are calculated based on the performance evaluation and the achievement of agreed targets. The performance evaluation also has direct relevance to the identification of so called high potentials, as well as to the layoff of certain employees, depending on the evaluation result. The employees' goals are shown on a balanced scorecard, describing the overarching aims (cf. Kaplan & Norton, 1996). The skills evaluation details further steps to be taken as part of advanced professional training or in relation to workforce planning. The list can go on and on (see Figure 2).

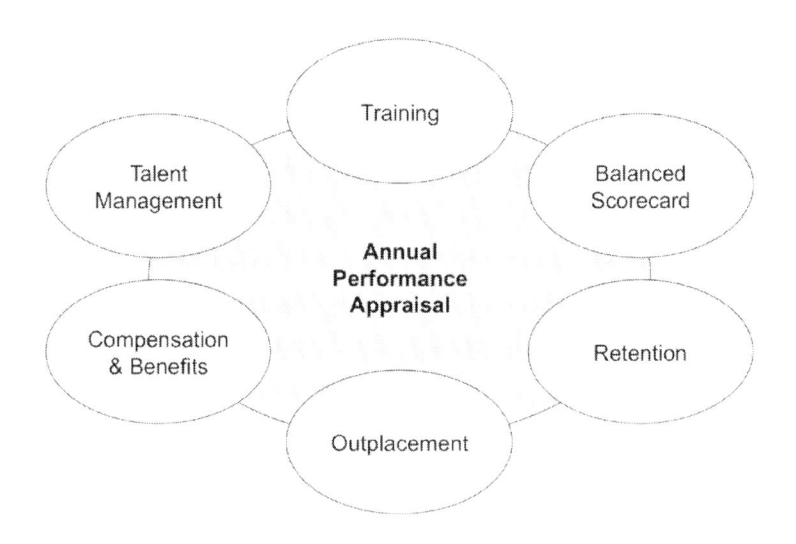

Figure 2:
The performance appraisal and its interfaces.

The individual purposes and interfaces will be explored in more detail throughout this chapter. So when we now think of performance appraisals in the context of HR management, it involves much more than just a "talk" between two people.

Modern HR professionals instead see them as being often highly complex, integrated systems with co-ordinated processes, sub-processes and interfaces, supported by corresponding IT systems which combine all relevant HR processes, and where relevant information is automatically exchanged. In doing so, data accumulated in one area is used in an affiliated process. Whether this vision has ever been successfully implemented at any company is questionable.

Formal, institutionalised and following fixed rules

Annual performance appraisals are conducted according to standardised rules in terms of times, content, documentation and the roles of the participating players. So if an employee and his/her manager have a meeting, this certainly does not make it a performance appraisal. Performance appraisals are of a formal nature, and cannot be compared with the usually informal communication between an employee and his/her manager during everyday work. Formal discussions and meetings, e.g. as part of project management, do not fall into this category either. Employees and managers tend to hold these discussions at their discretion, at self-appointed times, with self-defined content. Even if a manager asks an employee to come and see him/her (or vice versa) to clarify a general matter outside of daily business, such as lacking performance, conflicts or similar, this has nothing to do with the notion of an annual performance appraisal. This is an aspect frequently ignored in many publications on performance appraisals. Other types of formal performance appraisal are similarly widespread, and usually case-based, such as the return-to-work interview following an illness.

Decisions and judgements as the result

While the annual review in itself is of course a key component of performance appraisals, the latter are, in actual fact, more about decisions and assessments made at fixed times for usually specific purposes, in accordance with set, clearly described rules. In this respect, performance appraisals are certainly comparable with other systems, though these are usually labelled differently. For example, many companies have budgeting processes which also follow annual cycles, and which of course involve one-on-one reviews/interviews. No respectable managing director or HR manager would have anything against one-on-one reviews/interviews, because communication is rarely harmful – especially between managers and employees. All too often, we see performance appraisals being introduced so that managers can (finally) speak more with their staff. But the question is not whether such talks are good; it's whether the system is suitable for achieving the relevant goals with the judgements and decisions stipulated within it.

No annual performance appraisal without HR

Where there's a system, there's a system owner, an authority responsible for its design, setup and operation. This authority is almost always the HR department. At small businesses, it may also be the management, though this is rarely the case. Managers of course also speak with their employees when there is no HR department expressly expecting this. These talks are sometimes conducted in a structured, professional manner, if this is what is desired and practised by the respective managers. But a standard, company-wide annual performance appraisal format which follows set rules requires someone to monitor this uniformity and the rules, and indeed set these.

This implies that annual performance appraisals are inconceivable without HR: if there's no HR, there's no performance appraisal – a concept which particularly comes into focus later in this book. Because, as we can already sense, annual performance appraisals, at least in their classic form, require a strong HR element. Without this, a functional performance appraisal system is deemed completely impossible.

Summary and alternatives

Most companies which conduct performance appraisals will more or less identify with what has been detailed above. But I would suspect that very few have designed their annual performance appraisals exactly as outlined in the previous sections. Every time I present this prototypical description of traditional performance appraisals during a lecture, I find many people who disagree with various aspects. For the moment, it will suffice to assume that traditional performance appraisals are largely conducted as described here, even though there may be the odd difference here and there. Figure 3 shows a summary of the suggested elements, coupled with possible alternatives (cf. also Markle, 2000).

Element	Traditional performance appraisal	Alternative
Frequency	Annually	Monthly – Case-based
Obligation	Compulsory	Voluntary
Focus	Employee	Team
Responsibility	Manager	Employee/Team
Assessor	Manager	Peers/Self/Team
Evaluation format	Quantitative	Qualitative
Evaluation dimensions	Structured	Open
Forced distribution	Yes	No
Target setting	Top-down	Bottom-up
Results advised	Yes	No
Documentation	Centrally	None/Confidential
Central monitoring	Yes	No

Figure 3:
Elements of a traditional performance appraisal and alternatives.

The left-hand side of Figure 3 describes the annual performance appraisal as commonly found in practice. A subsequent chapter will address the potential alternative approaches – shown on the right – in relation to various benefit categories and framework conditions. Depending on objective (see Chapter 3) and framework conditions (Chapter 4), it may also be wise to consider basic alternatives to the annual performance appraisal. As will be demonstrated later on, modern, agile working environments characterised by a high level of dynamism, uncertainty and continuous change particularly require these alternative approaches.

Examining the alternatives on the right in more detail reveals the entire spectrum of possible options: Performance appraisals are voluntary and may be conducted several times a year, whenever the employees or their teams desire it. The focus is on the team itself. The team autonomously decides on the content of the appraisal, with the results usually adopting a qualitative nature. The manager plays the role of moderator – a role he/she can also delegate to specific team members. The content is performance-related, but also incorporates aspects of employer appeal. The targets are defined by the team, in a purely bottom-up manner. The results are only documented in part, and never leave the team, meaning they are never passed onto HR, nor entered into an IT system.

When I outline both ends of the spectrum in presentations or at workshops with HR professionals, and ask which side most accurately reflects the approach adopted at their company, it is extremely rare that anyone ever says the right-hand side. In fact, it seems to me that most HR managers only want to imagine one side. On the other hand, there are an increasing number of consultants or usually self-proclaimed management thinkers who become fixated on the right-hand column, often in an equally dogmatic fashion. Both parties claim that "that won't work". There are examples of success stories on both sides of the fence, which is why this book is not about giving preference to one particular alternative. It instead seeks to address what can be achieved with each in certain conditions. The matter is more complex than it first appears.

When it comes to conducting the annual performance appraisal, there appears to be a shift from traditional forms to a variant outlined in the right-hand column of the figure above. Even before performance appraisals became popular, there were structured staff evaluations which often involved very extensive, aspect-focused classification processes. Breisig (2005), for example, reports of practices which send even hard-nosed old-school HR professionals into a spin: Employees are classified based on 50 or more aspects and along set scales. Being able to speak with the employees about the manager's classification was virtually out of the question. So the introduction of institutionalised reviews was significant progress. Most companies have gradually moved away from endlessly convoluted processes, which tend to be more reminiscent of tax returns, and instead shifted towards simpler methods. Target setting became target agreements. Unilateral employee evaluations became dialogues on competence or development. Quantitative evaluation aspects have increasingly made room for qualitative alternatives. In this respect, I would go so far as to say that the above comparison doesn't just reflect two opposite poles, but rather a general trend in conducting annual performance appraisals (see also Murphy& Cleveland, 1995).

In summary

- The annual performance appraisal is far more than just a review/interview. It is a system with many different interfaces to other HR processes.
- The annual performance appraisal is cyclic, usually standardised, and is performed according to set rules, with pre-defined content. It is compulsory, and is primarily conducted by the managers.
- The annual performance appraisal requires a system owner – usually HR. Without HR, there would be no annual performance appraisal.
- We can observe trends towards more agile approaches, dominated by teams, personal responsibility and openness.

We allay world hunger

If a company is considering introducing a performance appraisal or related processes, it would do well to first get a clear idea of what it actually wants to achieve. Which decisions and judgements does it need when, from whom, and for what? It's a matter of the benefits and purposes pursued by performance appraisal. Once the objectives are clear, it often turns out that the task of evaluating an employee or making certain decisions is not to be assigned to a manager in the manner originally thought. So below we will go into more detail about the common decisions and judgements made as part of a classic annual performance appraisal. The following ideas will become relevant by the time this book addresses suitable performance appraisal methods and alternatives based on objectives and intended benefit later on.

Performance evaluation

The *performance evaluation* is of course usually a key component of annual performance appraisals. One very common approach involves dividing employees into three categories: A, B and C. A-players are the top performers, the employees whose performance is constantly above expectations. B-players make up the broad midfield, while C-players are the underperforming employees. In this context, there are often discussions about the extent to which certain percentages should be applied here – so-called forced distribution, which will be examined more closely later in the book. Most companies conduct performance evaluations in order to better ascertain which employees should be nominated for talent management programmes, so as to systematically prepare them for key positions. Performance evaluations play a role in determining variable salary components, or in deciding which employees should receive a pay increase and which shouldn't. C-players are identified in order to take suitable performance-boosting measures

– within the company or outside of it. It is often claimed that performance evaluations are a form of feedback designed to encourage employee learning and tell employees "where they currently stand".

Competence evaluation

Competence evaluations are not quite as common, but still very prevalent. Employees are usually assessed using predefined dimensions, with typical competencies being customer focus, team-working ability, willingness to learn, adaptability and leadership skills (Breisig, 2005). Similar to the performance evaluation (A, B and C), there are generally set levels: Beginner, Advanced, Experienced, Expert. These in turn feature behavioural anchors which use sample behaviour patterns to objectively illustrate what the individual levels mean. Many companies then conduct their evaluations based on a comparison between the employee's current profile and a previously defined, job-specific target profile, also known as a competence model. On the one hand, this skills evaluation seeks to determine an employee's need for development, and on the other, establishes his/her suitability for other possible tasks within the company. Last but not least, however, it's also about giving the employee feedback in order to – like performance evaluation – encourage learning.

Some companies even use competence evaluations to generally assess the availability of strategically relevant competencies as part of corporate management. This may, for example, be a factor when a company is focused on international growth, and wants to know how many employees can speak adequate English. An IT company switching to mobile applications may want to see whether enough software developers are in a position to programme mobile apps.

Performance and development target setting

The *target setting* is another very common component, and a distinction must be made here between agreements on performance targets and development targets. The former are established to act as a guide for employees: What will be expected of you in future? What should you focus your energies on – and what not? There is also an implicit hope of creating transparent mutual expectations between the employee and manager. Performance targets can serve as motivation under certain conditions. They are also agreed on to focus the employee's performance on an overarching goal in the sense of top-down cascading: "The sales target in Germany is X. That means Y for this region, Z for the local team, and 500,000 Euros for you in the next twelve months". Performance targets are ultimately established to facilitate the previously described appraisal component – the performance evaluation. Only by agreeing on targets beforehand is it possible to later determine the extent to which these have been achieved.

Development targets are usually established in addition to the performance targets. Building on from the competence evaluation, the manager discusses with the employee what his/her competence profile should look like in twelve months' time. These development targets in turn form the basis of a highly concrete development plan. In practice, we are constantly reminded that training is just one possibility – and rightly so, as other measures can include: challenging projects, international secondments, mentoring or coaching. Similar to the performance targets, the aim of development targets is also to help guide employees, so they know the areas they need to invest in.

Potential evaluation and clarification of career preferences

In addition to the performance evaluation, many companies expect their managers to assess their employees' development potential, also known as a *potential assessment*: To what extent does an employee have the drive and talent necessary to significantly improve over the next few years? Performance evaluations and potential assessments are combined when identifying promising talent (often referred to as "high potentials"). According to this logic, all employees treated as possible "high potentials" are ultimately those who not only put in an above-average performance on the day, but who also display considerable potential for development (Silzer & Church, 2009).

Discussions of the employee's *career preferences* are somewhat less prevalent than the components described so far. Previously, it was still common to hear the typical job interview question of where the employee sees himself/herself in ten years' time. Managers presumably only ask this question until they hear the response "Sitting in your chair". But the general content has endured, even though some companies ask more detailed questions. Key aspects include the employee's willingness to assume more responsibility, and spend extended periods abroad. Employees are asked about their willingness to potentially invest time in talent management programmes (in addition to their regular work). These talks increasingly set the course for a career as a general manager, expert or project manager (Trost, 2014).

Assessing the turnover risk

Some companies allow the employees to decide on aspects of their *work conditions.* For example, every two years, staff from Stuttgart-based company Trumpf are given the opportunity to decide how many hours per week they wish to work. Questions such as these can of course also be clarified at the annual appraisal. This aspect usually seeks to keep employees at the company. As the issue of employee retention is gaining importance in times of talent shortages, more and more companies are moving towards assessing an employee's *turnover tendencies* as part of an annual performance appraisal. An employee's turnover risk is rated high not only if he/she is thought to change jobs frequently, but also if he/she is a high potential or holds a key position. Depending on the result, this assessment serves as a catalyst for initiating suitable retention measures.

Figure 4 shows a summary of the conventional components of an annual performance appraisal, as well as its intended purpose.

Component	Intended use/purpose
Performance evaluation	Nomination for talent management programmes
	Defining variable salary components
	Pay-rise decision
	Initiating development measures
	Organising outplacement
	Promoting learning
Competence evaluation	Determining need for development
	Establishing internal suitability
	Promoting learning through feedback
	Determining company-wide skills
Target agreement (performance goals)	Orientation and focus
	Boosting motivation
	Creating transparency regarding expectations
	Focusing on overarching goals
	Enabling performance evaluation
Target agreement (development goals)	Meeting development requirements
	Orientation and focus
	Planning development measures

Potential assessment	Nomination for talent management programmes
Career preferences	Nomination for talent management programmes
	Planning development measures
	Determining career path
Assessing turnover risk	Adjusting work conditions
	Initiating retention measures

Figure 4:
Common components and intended purposes.

The right-hand column of Figure 4 illustrates that different components of annual performance appraisals are designed to pursue similar purposes. For example, performance evaluations, potential assessments and career preferences all contribute to talent management programme nominations. The following chapter once again draws on these benefit categories so as to then explore the question of the extent to which traditional annual performance appraisals are actually suitable for achieving said goals, in light of varying framework conditions.

Even here, we start seeing small indications that, at many companies, annual performance appraisals have a wide range of purposes. It's as if we want to allay world hunger with annual performance appraisals. They are seen as a key instrument in all kinds of business processes, such as corporate management and HR development. At least that is what is frequently claimed. If an instrument is interwoven into other processes to this extent, it is simply impossible to imagine a world without annual performance appraisals. In any case, that's what many HR professionals believe. At the same time, we see the dramas which result if this instrument is not properly accepted by the affected employee and managers – and this happens quite frequently. As already mentioned, failure in using this system is predominantly attributed to the management's lack of skill and willingness. But reality suggests otherwise. *Performance appraisals fail at many companies because they are set up incorrectly as a system.* This is a central assumption adopted in this book. We always need to start by asking why a performance appraisal is being implemented. Based on this, we can derive the necessary content, processes and responsibilities, whereby the corporate framework conditions must also be carefully examined. The following chapter will address this in greater detail.

In summary

- Annual performance appraisals in their traditional, most common form cover many different components, such as target setting, performance evaluations, competence assessments, potential evaluations, development plans, and turnover risk assessments.
- Annual performance appraisals also seek to achieve a wide range of goals and intended purposes.

3. What? For whom? And why?

HR management gives rise to what is probably one of the most niggling questions ever: *Why are we doing what we're doing, and for whom?* CEOs or managers are advised to direct this question to their HR managers whenever there are HR activities or measures looming. The answers are particularly exciting when it comes to the annual performance appraisal. You could also ask the more specific question here of: Who would have a problem if we didn't do it? You would receive a response listing a whole number of points. And who benefits? "Somehow, everyone does. The employees, the managers, the company". It is common for these sorts of answers to be met with caution. At the end of the last chapter, the goals and purposes usually associated with annual performance appraisals were briefly outlined. This chapter will now pick up on these and discuss them in more detail. The benefit categories play a key role in the general argument raised by this book. It becomes clear that any thoughts regarding implementation must start with the intended benefit. Later in the book, I attempt to illustrate that, depending on the framework conditions at the company, alternative approaches may even seem a more appropriate way of achieving the benefits explored below.

From benefit to design

We'll start with a somewhat exaggerated description of how performance appraisals are introduced at many companies, followed by a proposed alternative highlighting how things could potentially be improved.

Thinking in instruments

It is a well known fact that HR professionals love instruments and systems. At least that has been my observation over many years. People think in these categories in HR because they want to provide solutions for *everything* and *everyone*. Their everyday work frequently involves dealing with numerous, often acute problems. New problems arise every day. An employee writes off his/her company car. What do you do? You're looking for a new factory manager in Shanghai. What do you do? A team is crippled by a conflict between two colleagues. What do you do? The sales team wants training tailored to their special needs. What do you do? A good HR professional is someone who is able to solve a number of problems as quickly as possible. So it's rational to implement instruments and systems which are effective, and which increase managers' and employees' accountability.

The annual performance appraisal is one such system/instrument. However, if implementation starts with a decision for or against this instrument, the first big mistake has already been made. Approaches commonly adopt the logic illustrated in Figure 5.

Instrument! → Design → Context → Benefit?

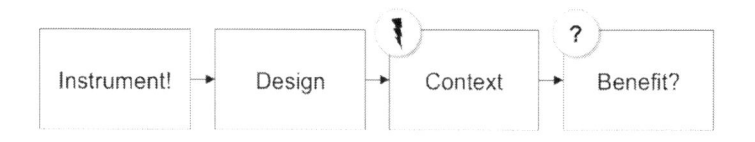

Figure 5:
The instrument as the starting point.

This logic has been known for many years in relation to another HR instrument, the employee *survey*. People decide to conduct an employee survey for all sorts of reasons. They then think about what they should ask whom, to whom the results will be sent, and how. First comes the instrument, then the design, and then finally the question of why all this is being done anyway. Although this description somewhat exaggerates actual reality, many companies will be able to identify with it, if they allow themselves to.

It's a similar story for many companies when it comes to annual performance appraisals. First comes the decision to implement the annual performance appraisal. And of course this decision doesn't appear out of thin air. It may be motivated by a number of different, sometimes bold reasons:

- The new HR manager is familiar with the instrument from his/her previous company, and wants to bring his/her experiences to the new environment.
- A company has become aware of its deficient leadership, and wants its managers to discuss fundamental issues with its staff in a sensible, structured manner at least once a year.
- The performance appraisal is seen by all as a key component of professional, modern HR management.
- The performance appraisal is needed for subsequent or affiliated processes, such as talent management or compensation management.

If a decision is made to introduce a performance appraisal, the next consideration is how it will be conducted. What should be addressed in the appraisal? Forms, guidelines, IT systems and management training courses are developed and rolled out, with employees and workers' councils simultaneously being involved and informed.

By the time the actual appraisal takes place, many companies, particularly the HR departments, have experienced a rude awakening. The appraisals are not conducted to the anticipated extent or at the anticipated level, or not in the format stipulated in the guidelines. There is overt and covert resistance. While some conduct the appraisal correctly and honestly, others take it less seriously and approach it in a creative manner. We see a colourful array of responses which are not only unexpected, but often even disappointing for those responsible. What's going on? The performance appraisal system conflicts with the company's framework conditions, the context. For many managers, the procedure is pointless. They either completely or partly fail to see the benefit. Relevant players sometimes simply find performance appraisals "silly", to use layman's speech. The framework conditions include aspects of organisation and culture, the relationship between employees and their respective employer, type of tasks, and the relationship between employees and managers. When it comes to cultural aspects, we know that whenever formal processes compete against culture, culture always wins. The general benefit/purpose is ultimately the issue, or attempts are made to retroactively correct this, and somehow express it tangibly and convincingly for employees and managers.

The benefit as the starting point

This section describes a process which differs fundamentally from the approach previously outlined. Figure 6 shows a graphic representation of the four steps. The content of each step is the same as for the previous approach; only the sequence is different. We will briefly examine these four stages below.

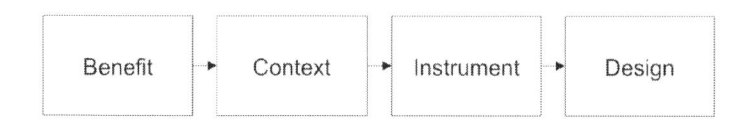

```
Benefit → Context → Instrument → Design
```

Figure 6:
The desired benefit as the starting point.

Before a company starts thinking about introducing performance appraisals, it needs to be clear about what it wants to achieve, and for whom. What is the professed *benefit*? Figure 4 showed an overview of known intentions: For example, to promote talent, and offer incentives for top performers. To identify underperforming employees so as to initiate suitable measures. To systematically plan constructive development measures with the employees. Or to manage the company using targets and sub-targets. In the end, it's about how relevant the actions are. Anything that is irrelevant, and which, at best, appears interesting only, should perhaps not be incorporated into an institutionalised approach. Another question which constantly arises is that of *who* benefits.

Once it has been established what is to be achieved and for whom, the company's *framework conditions* then need to be examined. What is the nature of tasks like? Is work carried out in complex, sometimes unforeseeable projects, or do the employees perform recurring tasks based on clearly defined routines? Do they do this individually or in teams? How do managers and employees interact? What is the prevailing understanding of leadership in this context? How much responsibility do employees have, and how dependent are they on their employer? These are all questions which must be answered. Chapter 4 will explore them in detail. The responses to these questions will directly influence the manner in which attempts are ultimately made to achieve the set targets. In light of this, it is clear to see that a standard textbook approach is not a good idea. In many cases, a traditional annual performance appraisal is in fact completely the wrong thing to do. While this notion will make sense to most readers – one-size-fits-all has rarely been successful -, recent years have demonstrated the vast extent to which relevant framework conditions are virtually ignored in practice. Even the numerous books on the topic give the impression that there is a right way of conducting performance appraisals. This impression is deceptive and dangerous.

Only once the framework conditions have been understood should the focus shift to selecting *instruments*. Following this logic, the conclusion reached may well be that the annual performance appraisal is the wrong instrument for achieving the ultimate goal. Many HR professionals love the performance appraisal instrument. For some, it will be like the case of those who love their hammers and thus see every problem as a nail which needs to be driven in. Later on, various alternative, agile instruments will be presented based on targets and framework conditions. These include peer ratings, team reviews, and modern forms of project management, just to name a few.

Finally, the *design* of the respective instrument must of course be considered. How do you want to do what you have ultimately decided to do? There are many possible options here, depending on instrument. At this point, it will suffice to address a number of aspects using the example of the performance evaluation – assuming this instrument is deemed suitable:

- Who is being evaluated?
- Who is evaluating? Who are the relevant players? The direct manager, colleagues or more senior managers? Or perhaps even customers?
- What are the performance evaluation criteria? Are there universally accepted criteria?
- Is the performance evaluation conducted uniformly throughout the entire company or does it differ according to functions, divisions, management levels or countries?
- Is there a set distribution plan for the evaluation?
- Is it possible to make qualitative judgements?
- Can or must a performance evaluation be conducted? Who decides this? The company? The manager? The employee?
- Who needs the result? Who is informed of the evaluation? Just the employee themselves? HR? The management?
- Is the evaluation documented? If so: How? In a system or on paper?
- How often should employees be evaluated? What prompts a performance evaluation?

This list is not exhaustive. It should once again be explicitly stated that we cannot assume such an instrument (in this case, the performance evaluation) will be appropriate. Design elements as listed above only apply if the instrument is deemed constructive and suitable.

The complexity of the issue at hand should by now have become clear. That's why the next few chapters will attempt to gradually explain the finer details of the four abovementioned steps: Benefit, Framework conditions, Instrument and Design. We'll start with the conventional benefit categories.

In summary

- When developing and implementing annual performance appraisals, the instrument is usually focused on in terms of design – the *whether* and *how*.
- Before any decisions are made, there needs to be a clear idea of what is to be achieved, and who the customer is. The framework conditions should then be properly understood. Only thereafter does the issue of a suitable instrument and its design become important.

The usual intended Benefits

If, as recommended above, HR managers are asked why they have introduced performance appraisals at their company, they often respond as follows: "It is vital for managers to take time out to discuss fundamental issues at length with their employees at least once a year – because there is no chance of doing so during hectic everyday operations. This is in turn important so as to ensure a relationship of trust is promoted between the manager and his/her staff". I've seen a company's policy stating: "One-on-one reviews should contribute to making open exchanges of opinions and trustworthy dealings between supervisors and staff a matter of course in future". And that is indeed nice, albeit somewhat bold. I ask myself how HR figures here. The usual reply: "Managers unfortunately don't do this of their own accord often enough", is then commonly followed by a reference to the "gentle nudge" which is supposed to come from HR. Since when is the HR department responsible for trustworthy dealings between employees and managers? But if the purpose of an annual performance appraisal seems rather bold, then the "gentle nudge" will prove to be just as futile. At the end of this chapter, I will examine this aspect of building trust and relationships in greater detail. The benefit categories addressed in this chapter, on the other hand, are very objective in nature. In actual fact, most annual performance appraisals seek to generate tough, process-related decisions and judgements. So let's take a closer look at the different benefit categories, and what they specifically mean.

Judgements and decisions

HR professionals should not get involved with this aforementioned approach. They should particularly not take the stance of forcing grown adults, colleagues, into a one-on-one conversation just because it seems to be somehow important. Business relevance tends to be missing here. One-on-one talks always serve to build trust, so it is logical to believe that performance appraisals will be no different. However, if we examine modern-day annual performance appraisals in more detail, we notice that the results generated by this instrument have/are designed to have often very specific consequences for managers, employees and companies. Trust may be a pleasant bi-product, but, ultimately, it's about judgements and decisions. These are the actual outcomes of annual performance appraisals. Looking now at relevance, the focus is on the following questions: Which *judgements* are required? Which *decisions* need to be made? Who needs these? What for? Relevance arises from concrete targets designed to be achieved through an activity. That's why this chapter highlights the conventional targets and benefit of annual performance appraisals. To do this, the most important purposes from the overview in Figure 4 above are selected and summarised, and the individual points addressed in Figure 7 below (cf. Eichel & Bender, 1984).

Figure 7:
The usual benefit categories of performance appraisals.

The term "performance appraisal" will, for now, only be used sporadically, as this section is about the potential benefits achieved by companies, rather than the special system itself. So let's shift our thoughts away from the instrument for a moment. Later on, we will come back to it in relation to intended benefits and framework conditions, and critically reflect on its possible application.

Rewarding the best

One of the oldest and most widespread principles of pay management is undoubtedly that any form of work or service deserves remuneration (cf. McCoy, 1992). The underlying assumption is as simple as it is problematic: if employees are given the prospect of a particular incentive for extra work, they do more.

But things are much more complex than they initially appear. It is worth mentioning two key findings here.

Children love painting pictures. If we start giving them a lolly or something similar for each picture, they will continue to paint. But they will stop doing so if no more lollies are offered. There are now all kinds of variations for these sorts of experiments (cf. Lepper, Greene & Nisbett, 1973). They demonstrate that material incentives reduce intrinsic motivation, which becomes a problem given that intrinsic motivation usually leads to better output. This phenomenon was known as the "Overjustification effect" in psychology (Deci, Koestner & Ryan, 1999), and particularly applies to tasks requiring creativity. For routine tasks, on the other hand, extrinsic incentives may significantly improve performance.

The effect that injustice has on employees' performances is just as scientifically based as the effect of material incentives on intrinsic motivation. Money has huge potential to reduce the motivation of high-performing employees. If three employees, an A, B and C-player, receive the same salary, this has been proven not to motivate the C-player. It similarly demotivates the A-player. And that's something a company really cannot afford to let happen. It's why many successful companies follow the motto of: It's better to pay fewer employees a lot, than a lot of employees too little. The focus is on not restricting outstanding performances through unfair salary distribution.

As indicated above, it's not about identifying talent here, but rather avoiding demotivation among strong performers. These are two completely different aims. The former takes into account both the performance and the potential of the employees. Performance-based payment, on the other hand, solely involves evaluating performance. Depending on task environment and organisational structure, two differing approaches may be suitable here, as will be detailed throughout this book.

Addressing the weak

It could be intuitively assumed that weak performance is the opposite of strong performance. In essence, however, these are simply two extremes of the same continuum. Understanding how success is achieved is a far cry from understanding the reasons for failure. After all, health is not necessarily the opposite of illness. So it's very difficult to compare the manners in which both cases are handled. That's why the identification of underperforming employees, coupled with the formulation of suitable solution strategies, is viewed as a separate category of possible intentions.

The reasons for systematically addressing underperforming employees are obvious. In addition to business management considerations, according to which an employee's performance is not worth the money he/she costs, sociopsychological effects also play a major role. Not reacting to weak performance demonstrates to the colleagues of the employee in question that it's not worth their while to put in good performances. Word gets around that "nothing happens" even if performance is not optimum. High-performing employees in turn might question their position within the team or indeed the company as a whole. After all, such employees define their value based on the performance of their immediate environment.

In this respect, performance evaluations, being the core component of annual performance appraisals, have always aimed to declare underperforming employees as such. As will be illustrated later on in this book, there are short-term and long-term measures for these contexts. Short-term measures involve promptly tackling an employee's inefficiency or performance slump. The employee is given a yellow card, and, if things go well, the matter is addressed directly. Red cards, on the other hand, are more of a long-term nature. They can involve segregation, involuntary termination or internal relocation – either horizontal or vertical. This is where we see many companies wanting to have a list of all underperforming employees constantly at the ready, regardless of what is to be done with said employees there and then. Cynics would call this a "black list". As will be explained further on, the annual performance appraisal is more about long-term prospects than short-term. The so-called case-based performance appraisal is commonly used for the latter, but its logic and interlinking with other HR instruments are a completely different story.

Identifying talent

In his autobiography "Jack: Straight From The Gut", the legendary former CEO of General Electric (GE), Jack Welch, tells how he would visit business units as a young CEO, and how the managers there would have eagerly prepared KPIs on profitability, quality or sales. In the initial months, Jack Welch would regularly surprise the managers with what was for him one of the most important questions: "Who are the most talented people here, and what are you doing with them?". This aspect is still an essential component of GE's successful business model even today.

This idea of systematically identifying and encouraging talent has now gone around the world, and has undoubtedly become *the* key element of structured talent management. It essentially consists of classifying employees based on two dimensions, namely in terms of their current performance level and their potential. Nowadays, it is rare to find a talent management system which does not adopt this approach (Silzer & Church, 2009), hence employees are classified according to the well known Performance Potential Grid (see Figure 8), often also called the "9-box" due to its layout. This classification usually takes place during so-called talent reviews, in which high-level managers jointly assess their employees.

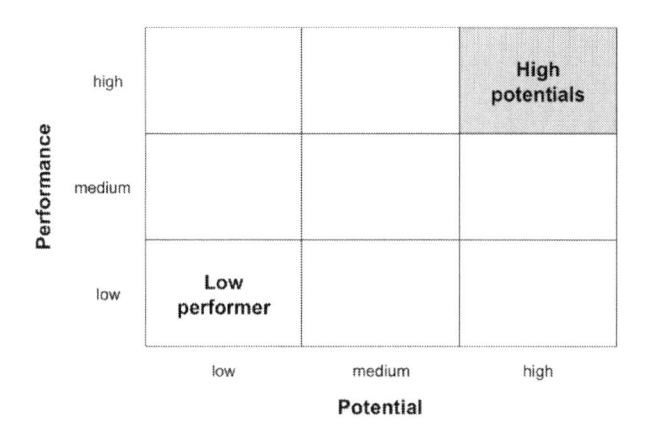

Figure 8:
The Performance Potential Grid.

Many different names are used to denote talent; a common example is "high potentials". They are sometimes also referred to as "stars" or even "heroes". They ultimately all mean the same thing. High potentials are those employees who not only constantly exceed expectations (performance), but who are also deemed to have considerable, long-term possibilities for development (potential). Some companies have quantitative rules to classify employees, e.g. that 10% must be identified as high potentials, and 10% as low performers (low performance and low potential). The rest can be distributed over the remaining fields.

At most companies following this logic, this identification of talent or high potentials is the starting point for long-term and sometimes intensive development programmes. The judgements made here are initially relevant to HR, since HR is usually responsible for providing or co-ordinating possible development measures. The management should particularly also be interested in the high potentials group. After all, they are the ones being treated as the future colleagues and successors for key positions at the company.

In practice, high potentials are rarely identified as part of the annual performance appraisal, though the appraisal still plays an important role in this context. For instance, it is commonplace for direct supervisors to be able to nominate employees from their team for a talent review. At a practical level, the respective manager appears to simply tick the relevant box under the "possible high potential" category on the appraisal form. The chosen employee is then examined in more detail in a separate stage. In other words, his/her direct superior triggers the process.

Determining internal suitability

Many businesses dream of a company-wide skills database for employees using suitability profiles, with a view to appointing staff according to their abilities. Through a list of requirements, geared around the respective job descriptions, profile comparisons (matchings) are then performed, and the relevant employee's suitability for specific jobs and tasks determined. In actual fact, it has always been a key notion in HR to compare requirements with suitability profiles in order to ensure employees are appointed in keeping with their skills and knowledge. In his textbook, my colleague Bröckermann (2007) hits the nail on the head with regards to HR placement planning: "the criteria must be specified in a requirements profile in order for them to be compared with the employee's suitability later on" (p. 169). In relation to HR placement planning, he previously writes that people want to "determine which employee should be when, where and how". There are two main processes for establishing suitability profiles: employee selection and employee assessment. The latter is today considered a key component of annual performance appraisals.

Structured competence appraisal form the methodological bases for this. Judgements are made subjectively by the respective manager, whereby the employees are often asked to give their own rating. Discussions then essentially address the skills for which the employee's and manager's views differ. There have been decades of academic discourse regarding the validity of these judgements (cf. Murphy & Cleveland, 1995), and this aspect will be explored in greater detail later on. At this point, experienced HR professionals will note that this process is not about validity, but rather a comparison between self-assessment and external perceptions. The employee and manager exchange their thoughts on the employee's skills, which is valuable in itself. Agreed. But as soon as this aspect becomes the focus, it is no longer (just) about determining internal suitability, but rather about the direct supervisor providing feedback – an aspect addressed as a separate benefit further down.

Developing employees

Development used to be a relatively easy process: Employees underwent training and then "graduated", having been lastingly prepared for the task ahead. In an age of rapid technological changes, the half-life of relevant knowledge is becoming shorter and shorter, hence the need for lifelong learning continues to grow. In view of this, an increasing number of employees are nowadays finding it virtually impossible to tell what they will have to be able to do in two or three years' time. Any employee who stops learning now may no longer be employable in a few years to come, given the emergence of new challenges.

Ensuring this employability is a complex task requiring constant examination of various factors. Put simply, it involves each employee regularly answering the following questions, in light of current and future developments: What should I learn? What do I want to learn? What can I learn? An individual employee will rarely be able to answer these alone, as they demand a high degree of self-reflection and examination of their professional future (see Figure 9). The direct supervisor commonly comes into play here.

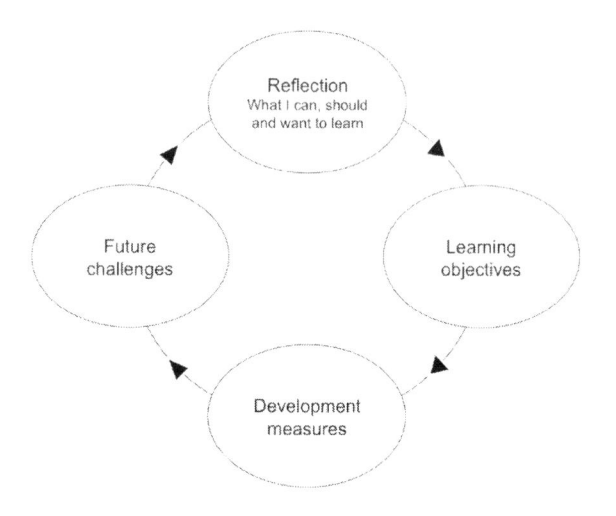

Figure 9:
Ensuring employability.

On the whole, the classic understanding of employee development is to formulate answers to these questions, define learning targets, and initiate suitable development measures. And the annual performance appraisal typically acts as the institutional framework for this discussion.

Offering prospects

In recent decades, we have seen a shift towards a greater focus on employees during annual performance appraisals. It's no longer just about the company's or manager's expectations of the employee, but also, conversely, the employee's expectations of his/her employer. Target objectives have become the target agreements, which implicitly enable the employee to reject objectives "from above". Notification of pre-made judgements has instead become a dialogue. In this respect, it was logical to start addressing the employee's long-term expectations of his/her personal development, particularly in view of the rising talent shortage and associated problem of employee retention. Employees stay at a company if they feel the company can offer them personal prospects. This is at least an implicit assumption, which may play a role here.

Prospects are less about short or medium-term learning, and more about long-term careers. The term "careers" is associated with a number of different stereotypes. Perhaps the two most common notions are 1) that careers mean management careers, and 2) that higher-ranking managers determine the careers of subordinate employees. Both views are extremely outdated. In addition to management careers, companies are now increasingly also facilitating expert or project careers (Trost, 2014). Although this distinction is largely more theoretical than practical, we can at least observe a trend towards a wider range of options. What is more important than this aspect, however, is the growing decision-making power of talented and motivated people. Previously, promotions would be simply advised to a hopeful employee: "Mr Johnson, in our executive committee we have been talking about you. You'll now be taking charge of the purchases department. Congratulations and all the best!". At more modern companies, which cater to the preferences of their best employees, career options are discussed jointly, and possible prospects agreed on. In this respect, offering prospects means creating mutual transparency about employee expectations on the one hand, and about his/her options within the company on the other. This in turn requires assessments, evaluations and often also decisions from all parties involved.

Learning through feedback

Learning without feedback is inconceivable. All functioning systems are based on feedback. Without feedback, we wouldn't even be able to hold a coffee cup. Life itself requires control loops with feedback. So the need for feedback is always justified. In real-life HR operations, however, the issue of feedback is primarily understood as meaning feedback given to employees about their performance and behaviour. And they never receive enough of it. For years, the media have constantly been referring to the long-term study carried out by the Gallup opinion research institute on the so-called "Engagement Index" (Gallup, 2013). So year after year, it is "confirmed" that employees are apparently not given enough feedback or shown enough recognition. No matter which study on feedback or feedback culture you consult, it is rare to find one stating the contrary. And this aspect probably won't change even in years to come, due to the needs of young, upcoming generations. Anyone who has grown accustomed to the Internet, Web 2.0 and social media in recent years is no longer willing to wait more than 24 hours for an answer. Anyone who posts something on Facebook, tweets something on Twitter, or sends a message on Whatsapp expects likes, comments, retweets or responses within minutes.

In the end, it simply boils down to the fact that employees need more feedback! And anyone with a traditional, hierarchical way of thinking will immediately know who should be giving an employee feedback – his/her manager. Because giving feedback is seen as a managerial task. Hardly anyone can conceive that *obtaining feedback* can also be the employee's responsibility. Combining the need for feedback from the manager with the desire for order and structure leads us directly to the annual performance appraisal. Whether or not feedback through an annual performance appraisal actually encourages or even enables learning, however, remains to be seen. We'll come back to this idea later on in the book.

Managing by objectives

How do you get 100, 1,000, 10,000 or even several 100,000 employees to contribute to achieving one single company objective – in their own way, playing their own role? Materials flow into an automotive company from all different sides, with modern, functioning cars coming out the other end. In between, hosts of people perform various tasks to achieve this amazing added value. Among other things, the solution to this problem lies in task sharing or an operational and organisational structure. Objectives and KPIs help with management, and there are many different approaches to handling these. One key example is cascading. Overarching goals, which are defined in a rather general manner here, are gradually "broken down" over all hierarchical levels. This approach is based on the well known idea of "Management by Objectives" (Odiorne, 1965), in which subordinate goals and KPIs are derived from overarching agreements and arrangements. Many companies believe the goals are actually passed down from one level to another as part of the annual performance appraisal. For the employees and managers acting within an organisation, this means they are committed to certain objectives at various times. And where there are goals and KPIs, there are also checks to make sure they have been reached. Objectives and the monitoring thereof thus always appear to go hand in hand.

Motivation through objectives

At many companies, however, objectives not only serve as tools for co-ordination and management, but also to motivate employees. In the late 1960s, psychologists Locke and Latham (1984) established a theory on the motivational effect of goals, based on a simple experimental paradigm. When assigning someone a task, there are two different possibilities. In possibility A, the subjects are asked to "do their best". In possibility B, a specific, challenging objective is set. Numerous experiments incorporating this paradigm show that the presence of goals tends to lead to higher performances. This theory is known under the self-explanatory name of the "goal-setting theory", and has been used in industrial and organisational psychology to examine the question of what motivates employees. The practical relevance is clear. But I will later demonstrate that setting goals for motivation purposes follows different rules to setting goals to manage processes and companies.

Retaining employees

One aspect tying in closely with that of prospects is the retention of high-performing employees. Keeping these at the company involves a different set of rules to those applied when simply offering them career options. Good employees don't just leave companies of their own volition because the company didn't provide career prospects. A number of other factors within or outside the company frequently come into play here. Although voluntary resignations do start to emerge over longer periods of time, an employee's tendency to look further afield only becomes apparent once the matter has reached an acute stage (Phillips & Edwards, 2009). In actual fact, many managers only notice it when it's "too late". For this reason, more and more companies are now shifting towards the idea of assessing the turnover tendencies of their high-performing employees, particularly in key functions or positions, early on, so as to be prepared for any turnover risks, or to utilise options to actively counter these.

At a practical level, this means that managers at many companies are urged to tick the relevant box on the annual performance appraisal form if there is a turnover risk. Other companies in turn discuss desired work conditions with their employees once a year, e.g. in relation to flexi hours or defining weekly working time.

The last few pages have briefly outlined the various benefit generally intended with the annual performance appraisal. And there should be no doubts as to the value of these goals. Feedback is certainly important. Goals are important. Prospects are important. Identifying potential is important. There is little reason to question these intentions. But we are still left with the burning question of whether performance appraisal is a suitable instrument and a suitable institutional framework for successfully filling all these benefit.

In summary

- The annual performance appraisal always results in judgements and decisions – nothing more, nothing less. Trust-building may be a positive bi-product.
- People often use annual performance appraisals to try and reward the best, address the weak, identify talent, determine internal suitability, offer prospects, develop employees, learn through feedback, manage companies, motivate through objectives, and retain employees.

Performance appraisal customers

We have so far spoken about the benefit which companies usually want to associate with performance appraisal. But one key question has not been addressed: *Whom* should the performance appraisal primarily benefit? It would generally be assumed that all participants and their interrelations would benefit from such a procedure. After all, it is very often said that, first and foremost, performance appraisals create clarity between a manager and his/her employee, for instance in terms of mutual expectations or assessments of behavior and performance. In view of the previously discussed benefits and objectives, however, it becomes evident that it is not just the employee or the employee *and* his/her manager who benefit from an annual performance appraisal; in many cases, it is also the HR department or executive level. If, for example, performance appraisals are conducted in relation to company management, the senior management would obviously be the primary beneficiary.

Whenever I ask HR managers who benefits from the annual performance appraisal, they usually answer by saying that everyone benefits in their own way – managers, employees, the management board etc. To some extent, given there are usually many different objectives, this response is justified, though possibly also naive. If we look a little closer, we note that every company has authorities which excel in certain areas as dominant drivers. If we then examine the manner in which an HR instrument is used, we can see that it reflects the interests of specific authorities. And whenever differing authorities have differing interests, needs and problems, we can expect conflicting objectives. Compromises or solutions focused on one particular direction are the natural consequence.

The situation escalates when an HR instrument is introduced to benefit a specific authority (e.g. the employees or managers), without them expecting it. An example of such a case is when attempts are made to explain to managers that the annual performance appraisal will make their lives easier, when the managers in fact consider it a chore. Anyone with experience will know that this is quite a common occurrence.

At the start of this book, I said that the performance appraisal is a *system*. This doesn't mean managers occasionally discussing something with their staff. It is instead about systematics, uniformity and comprehensive application. It has also become clear that performance appraisals rarely operate on their own, but are rather connected with other affiliated instruments and processes through relevant interfaces. The crucial point here is that systems always require someone in charge, an authority which attends to content, implementation and operation. This role is usually played by the HR department, which leads to the burning and highly relevant question: on whose behalf, and from which standpoint, is HR acting by introducing the performance appraisal into the organisation structure and maintaining it there? The answer to this question has significant implications for the possibilities, limitations and types of annual performance appraisals, as will be discussed in subsequent chapters.

Four scenarios

Four typical company scenarios will be illustrated below. Firstly, two real-life sample situations:

An HR manager took on this role at a company a few months ago. He had previously been an HR manager at another company, an international corporate group. Performance appraisals are his hobbyhorse, not least because he had successfully helped introduce one with his former employer. He now also wants to please his new employer with this instrument. He particularly sees an opportunity in the fact that his new company offers him a "green pasture" of sorts – the perfect platform for many new HR ideas. A few weeks later, he convinces the management of his plan. They give him the reins with a generous budget and some words of encouragement. After all, dialogue can never go astray, nor can goals or feedback. And recording results can't do any harm; it will instead promote professional, sustainable interaction.

While this brief account is bound to evoke memories for many HR professionals, the following example may be less familiar:

A company's management responds to the increasingly drastic talent shortage, and decides to do more for employee development. This company embraces autonomy, and it is clear from the start that, even in future, employees will be responsible for their own development and goals. The idea is for managers to act more as coaches or mentors. A performance appraisal method is established, and the HR manager is commissioned to devise a suitable scheme.

The starting points couldn't be more different. Both cases involve introducing an annual performance appraisal. In the first example, the HR manager takes the task on himself. He may well be the customer of his own instrument. He wants to professionalise *his* HR work. In the second example, the employees are the dominant customers, even though the order comes from the management. In the end, the idea is for the managers to also enable the employees to better fulfil their responsibilities.

Due to their systemic nature, performance appraisals must always be ordered by the management. But the dynamics and HR's role can still vary greatly, as demonstrated by the two examples above. In order to apply this notion at a more systematic level, Figure 10 illustrates four typical setups, each of which will be explained in detail below.

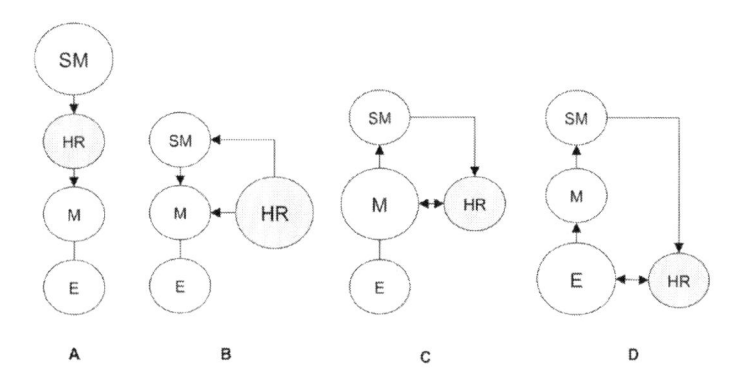

Figure 10:
The customers of the annual performance appraisal, and the role of HR.

Each of these setups features four authorities: Senior management (SM), HR, managers (M) and employees (E). They also each have one circle which is larger than the others. This indicates which authority is the driving force, and who is ultimately the primary customer of the annual performance appraisal – the latter factor being what distinguishes the setups from one another. We will now briefly examine the various scenarios.

The senior management as the customer (A)

Let's assume a company regularly conducts 360-degree evaluations for its middle management. This approach does bear a certain resemblance to performance appraisals, since it also involves evaluations. The burning question is who receives the results at the end. The manager involved? HR? Or senior management? The answer provides a reliable indication of who the customer of the 360-degree evaluations is, based on this company's understanding. If the senior management primarily receives the results, then it is clearly also the customer. It may have an interest in seeing which managers are evaluated well, and which not so well. And it is also conceivable for the senior management to use the results in relation to promotions or succession planning.

The senior management may focus on similar interests when it comes to performance appraisals. It considers it relevant to know how the employees' performance at the company is viewed by the respective managers. Where do the employees stand in relation to specific skills critical to the company? Which areas display the highest turnover risk? All these questions may affect the management's strategic priorities and interests. Managing directors often have a particular interest in cascading their strategic targets, which are gradually "broken" down from top to bottom as per the Balanced Scorecard (Kaplan & Norton, 1996). In this scenario, the company's management expresses a natural need to reliably and systematically transport the ideas devised at the top down to the bottom.

By introducing an annual performance appraisal, the senior management generally seeks to secure its *own* goals. It assumes it needs this system in order to be successful. Driven by this notion, it usually orders the HR department to develop a suitable system to then roll this out at the organisation, with the strong support and commitment of the upper management. We're essentially talking about measures of communication and qualification here, e.g. through relevant training. The managers are often the first targets here.

HR as the customer (B)

Very few HR professionals will see themselves as being the primary customers of a performance appraisal. After all, the whole idea of this instrument is to try and benefit the company and its employees and managers. Performance appraisals increase management quality and employee satisfaction. At least that is their intended, oft-cited aim. If we look a little closer, however, we see that things are frequently very different.

As already outlined in the example above, many HR departments seek to use the performance appraisal to professionalise *their* HR work. In this respect, performance appraisals are often there to maintain or even facilitate the HR department's HR management system (Culberts, 2010). HR needs the skills assessments from the performance appraisals in order to initiate the right development measures. It needs performance and skills assessments in order to make or prepare relevant HR decisions regarding the employees. The degree to which the employee achieves targets serves as the basis for determining variable salary components. Target agreements and goal achievement could become relevant (in terms of labour law) if an employee needs to be given a warning or if layoffs need to be triggered.

There's nothing wrong with any of this. What we do generally have to remember here is that HR obviously takes responsibility. The question is simply whether the company wants it like that, and whether this is good for the company in every respect. The moment the HR department, as the customer, takes responsibility for numerous HR issues and challenges, it adopts a certain attitude. It then assumes that it knows what's good for the employees and managers better than they do themselves. By collecting results from several performance appraisals, HR forms the basis for key decisions and measures. Many HR departments have extensive HR information systems which are often designed to make things easier for the HR professionals rather than the managers and employees.

As indicated in Figure 10, HR is the driving force here. Interactions with the senior management and lower-level managers are usually based on the idea of HR receiving orders and support from the senior management to introduce performance appraisal. When it comes to implementation, however, it is the managers who are then primarily seen as the relevant target group. They are the ones who are required to deliver the completed performance appraisal forms. And to enable them to do so, they are comprehensively trained by HR during implementation, and given the appropriate guidelines and handbooks.

Managers as the customer (C)

An HR manager recently told me, with great pride, that he had also "introduced performance appraisals" at his company. I now instantly respond to situations like this by asking "Why?". Visibly surprised, he continued: "Our managers aren't actually real managers. They're mostly technically educated specialists who have slipped into managerial roles, but who can't be bothered [his words] to talk with their people. We now want to use performance appraisals to give them a gentle nudge so that they finally take the time to speak with their employees about performance and prospects in a structured manner". The HR-centric approach is clear to see here. It is reminiscent of the aforementioned scenario in which HR wants something. But what do the managers want?

To a certain degree, I felt sorry for this HR manager. Because he would no doubt actually want a different setup to work with. Something along the lines of: "Most of our managers have a technical background. They have never learned how to properly manage staff. But they want to. They want to be good managers, and know that structured feedback is at least one possible approach. That's why we in the HR department have worked with some managers to develop a framework to help them meet their own requirements". The managers are the customers of the performance appraisal system here, with HR adopting a facilitating role. The managers are clearly the ones calling the shots here.

This type of approach can be driven by an accompanying manager evaluation – with the senior management as the customer. Employees rate their managers' performance and behaviour as part of regular evaluations, the results of which are then presented to the senior management. Faced with this pressure, managers try to optimise their leadership, potentially identifying suitable sources of leverage at performance appraisals. In these sorts of situations, performance appraisals may appear less as a (tiresome) compulsory exercise (imposed by HR) and more as a solution in the eyes of the managers.

The employees as the customer (D)

When companies introduce an annual performance appraisal, all managers typically undergo relevant training at some point. They learn how to evaluate performance, how to interpret pre-defined criteria, how to remain objective, how to start off and finish positively, how to define goals in a "SMART" way (specific, measurable, appealing, realistic time-bound), etc. Has anyone noticed that the employees themselves are rarely trained? Why is it almost exclusively the *managers* that are trained? The reason is pretty simple. It is assumed that the managers will conduct the performance appraisal. And if, during the course of a year, HR sees that several managers haven't fulfilled their duties, it deems the managers to have the problem, not the employees, which in turn prompts it to give the managers – not the employees – the oft cited "gentle nudge".

It's worth now momentarily looking at this from a different perspective. Because employees are increasingly taking responsibility for their goals and personal development, either individually or in teams – particularly at modern, autonomy-focused companies which treat employees as adults. Companies need to decide the path they wish to take here, especially when it comes to HR development, and namely the development of talent or potential management successors. Based on my observations, very few companies have grasped this notion. At this point, it's helpful to see the range of possible varieties (see Figure 11).

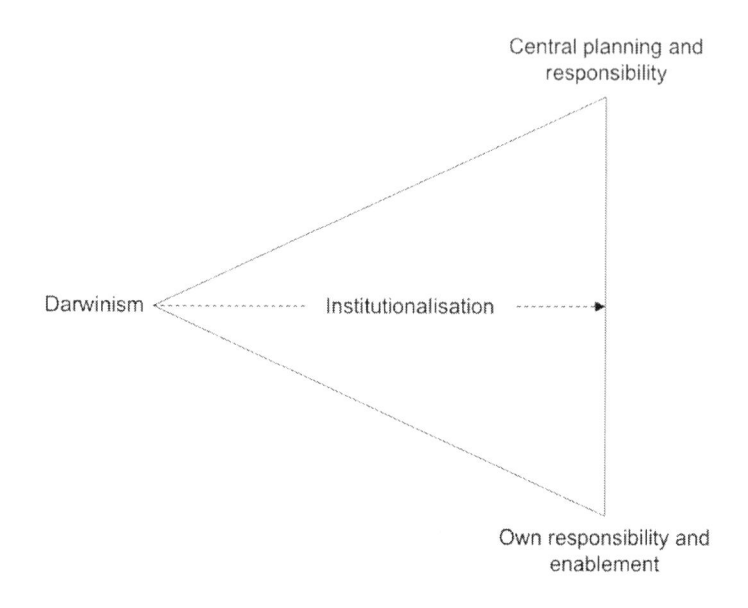

Figure 11:
Various methods of talent management.

When it comes to developing their staff, one option is for companies to do nothing at all. We could call this approach Darwinism - "The cream always rises to the top". While it is courageous to consciously choose this path, it is but one possible alternative. Increasing professionalisation, including of HR processes, is seeing fewer and fewer companies leave their staff development to chance or the natural course of things. This has resulted in HR development becoming institutionalised, along with processes, instruments, rules and methods. Companies can take one of two roads here. One leads towards central planning, where HR takes responsibility as described in scenario B (HR as the customer). Based on extensive information, e.g. on competence and employee profiles, career paths etc., the most rational possible decisions about employees are made, or at least prepared. HR takes it upon itself to know what is good for the employees and company. It's a different story in cases of individual responsibility, in which the employees are personally responsible for their own development. Unlike the Darwinist version, this variant doesn't involve doing *nothing*. The measures taken here pursue the sole aim of qualifying and enabling employees. Later in this book, we will also examine the question of whether and how the annual performance appraisal can contribute to this, and how this version should be approached.

There are currently no empirical findings on the prevalence of the various methods, presumably due to the fact that word has not got around about it – neither in practice nor (even less so) in the academic community. Based on my own experiences over many years, I would, however, dare to hypothesise that the planned, HR-centric variant is seen as the ideal, especially at larger companies. Conventional textbooks underline this view: a professional HR department takes responsibility, and acts as rationally as possible from a central position, based on comprehensive information. The fully integrated HR or talent management dream.

In summary

- When implementing an HR instrument, it is important to think about both *why* this is needed, and *whom* it will benefit.

- The annual performance appraisal can address the needs of various internal customers: Senior management, HR, lower-level managers, or employees.
- The instrument's design and application can vary greatly, depending on who is the customer.

Internal positioning

Whenever a company seeks to implement an HR instrument, it is recommended to clearly communicate this instrument's purpose to the employees and managers. This means explicitly answering two key questions: Why are we doing this? And: For whom are we doing this? As is generally known, it is often the easy questions which prove to be so hard to address in practice, hence the prevalence of vague responses.

Everyone somehow benefits

This problem first really became apparent to me in connection with employee *surveys* in the late '90s. At that time, I worked with a number of companies which were in the process of planning and conducting employee surveys. The logic was relatively clear: All employees would be asked to answer around 80 questions on a wide range of topics. All managers at every level would then receive the results for all questions, and all employees and managers would have to workshop them. It was an elaborate process carried out across the entire organisation every one or two years. Anyone wanting to annoy the HR manager responsible could ask them: "Why are you doing this, and for whom?". The reply would be something along the lines of: "We want to be able to evaluate the conditions for high job satisfaction, productivity and employer attractiveness, and gradually optimise these with everyone's involvement. Everyone benefits in the end –

employees, managers, senior management, the entire company and, last but not least, our customers". In other words: "Everything is improved for everyone". This again sounds like an attempt to allay world hunger. Experience has shown that employee surveys based on this classic model don't get anywhere near achieving their aim. The problem is that HR instruments are often overloaded with benefits for too many people right from the start, which is a recipe for conflict. There are too many customers and too many intentions packed into one single instrument. One of the key philosophies appears to be that if you're going to make the effort, you may as well try and benefit as many people as possible.

This risk is even greater when it comes to annual performance appraisals. The benefits described in the previous section illustrate the wide range of possible objectives. In actual fact, when the question of why performance appraisals have been introduced is raised, the same old endless lists of aims are churned out. In doing so, it is implicitly assumed that all objectives are compatible with one another, and that one single instrument is capable of satisfying all these aims and beneficiaries. I dare say this assumption is usually incorrect.

Intrinsic conflict of objectives

Annual performance appraisals frequently involve giving the employee feedback on his/her behaviour, skills and performance. As already described, the aim is for the employee to learn from this feedback. Many companies now agree that this sort of feedback requires open, respectful and trustworthy dealings, due to the fact that it entails highly sensitive and personal aspects. The risk of an employee feeling misunderstood, even hurt, in such a situation is far from low. Tact is needed – and not just from the manager's side. Everyone is familiar with this from their own personal lives. Discussions between life partners which start with "We have to talk" are not always the easiest. Which is why the phrase "The performance appraisal must be considered a sensitive matter at all times" (Hinrichs, 2009) can be found in many companies' works agreements, even if worded slightly differently. It's somewhat more detailed in an IT company's policy:

> We expect managers of all levels to conduct performance appraisals with the necessary care, respect and consideration for the employee as part of their managerial responsibility. [...] We expect employees to approach the performance appraisal positively, be receptive to criticism, and be willing to improve as per the evaluation, and speak openly about all problems (cited in Hinrichs, 2009, p. 22, translated by the author).

Seen in isolation, there is no reason to question this objective of learning through feedback and complying with the requirements of sensitivity, respect and openness. It's great if an employee and his/her manager are willing and able to assess matters as described. The customer of this dialogue should always be the employee themselves. They are the ones who should benefit from the manager's feedback. If the appraisal revolves around the cooperation between manager and employee, both participating persons are the beneficiaries of this discussion.

But many companies pursue another objective when it comes to annual performance appraisals, namely dealing with underperforming employees or rewarding their particularly high-performing colleagues. The managers conduct the same talks with their employees as detailed above. They discuss performance, behaviour, skills etc. However, the customer for this part of the appraisal is not the employee or the manager, but rather the senior management, often represented by HR. They need this information in order to substantiate decisions about the respective employee's future.

The conflict in this performance appraisal should by now have become apparent. Everything seems logical at first glance. After all, this scenario more or less reflects the desired reality at many companies. If we look closer, however, it immediately becomes clear that it is impossible to conduct a confidential and open appraisal to encourage employee learning through feedback on the one hand, and to simultaneously also forward the appraisal content to a central, superior authority, which then makes (possibly negative) decisions on this basis. The employee won't speak openly, but will instead negotiate. He/she won't admit to weaknesses, but will instead excuse them – even if the coporate policy states otherwise.

Similar conflicts are evident in many other aspects of performance appraisals, depending on how this system is designed at a company. The target agreement is another great example. Seemingly possessed by a certain naivety, many HR professionals assume objectives will motivate. The reference to this in the performance appraisal's internal communication (marketing) is also classic. Even assuming objectives will serve as motivation in most cases, it still raises the question of who the customer of this motivation technique is. In this case, the answer is clear: It should primarily be the employees themselves. They are the ones being motivated, even if the entire team and company ultimately also benefit from this motivation. In reality, many companies no longer set targets to motivate employees. They instead use the management approach described in an earlier section and later serving as the basis for a performance evaluation – which in turn determines an employee's future. This has nothing to do with motivation, leave alone intrinsic motivation. In this case, it is usually the management and HR who are the customers of the process, not the employees. The management primarily needs employee goals to control and monitor the performances of the business units and employees in cascade-fashion.

Mixed messages

Loading an HR instrument with too many objectives for too many beneficiaries inevitably leads to so-called "mixed messages", for which a company is soon punished by its employees. I recently held a typical conversation with the HR manager of a medium-sized automotive supplier:

Him:	I urgently need an IT system we can use to support our annual performance appraisals.
Me:	Why are you conducting performance appraisals?
Him:	So our employees can receive feedback on their skills from their managers, among other things.
Me:	Why?
Him:	Feedback is important for further development.
Me:	And why do you need a system for this?
Him:	So we can compile reports in the HR department.
Me:	What do you need these reports for?
Him:	So we can forward them to the senior management.
Me:	What does the senior management need these reports for?
Him:	It wants these reports.
Me:	Why?
Him:	That's just how it is.

At that moment, I thought to myself: "There they are again, the mixed messages". Feedback for learning is a wise idea. Supplying the senior management with reports on skills distribution may also be advisable for corporate management purposes. Can both be done at once with the same instrument? Is it possible to service two customers – employees and the senior management – in equal measure? I dare say not, at least not in this case. As already mentioned, the employees should be sent a clear message as to why something is being used in an HR capacity. Saying one thing and doing another is rarely viewed positively by employees. They are not dumb. And they often develop a high degree of curiosity and sensitivity when it comes to annual performance appraisals.

In summary

- Every HR instrument needs to be clearly positioned: why are we doing what and for whom?
- Overloading annual performance appraisals with various benefit expectations for all kinds of levels tends to render clear positioning impossible.
- Annual performance appraisals are often loaded with the interests of various authority levels, which can lead to mixed messages, conflicts, and mistrust.

Objective relevance

The previous considerations regarding the benefit of annual performance appraisals were very objective on the whole. They illustrated, rather prosaically, that thoughts about annual performance appraisals should always focus on the desired benefit. The benefits subsequently presented were, admittedly, very routine: Which decisions and judgements need to be made to enable certain measures? Which information is relevant for whom and why? What is documented how, and who receives this documentation? These are all very formal aspects.

Having time for one another once a year

But many companies believe performance appraisals are much more than just these objective aspects. The annual performance appraisal very often focuses on the employee-manager relationship. And this relationship naturally has an interpersonal level extending well beyond purely factual matters. It's not just about performance targets, skills expectations or potential assessment. For many employees, the manager is a very central person in their life. They sometimes spend more time with their manager than with their spouse or partner. The manager can thus play a key role in their own professional and personal future. For this reason, it is desirable for there to be a good, trustworthy relationship between an employee and his/her manager. It doesn't have to be this way in every scenario. It is certainly possible to have situations where an employee-manager relationship has a purely objective, formal basis, though these tend to be the exception.

For some companies, this is precisely where the annual performance appraisal comes in. It is rightly argued here that a functioning, trustworthy relationship requires communication and time, which are often lost in the hectic pace of everyday working life. At least once a year, the manager should take time out for his/her employees – to not only talk about business matters, but also about things affecting the interpersonal relationship. So it's no surprise that a number of companies particularly highlight this aspect in their internal benefits reasoning.

Some companies do this in a highly unilateral manner, by arguing that the performance appraisal is important so that the *employee* can build trust in the *manager*. This is presumably based on the implicit assumption that this unilateral trust relationship is primarily what ensures the employee does what the manager wants – a blatantly hierarchical approach. The horse must trust the rider, which is why a rider should talk to its horse a lot. Conversely, other companies focus more on the mutual trust relationship. The understanding here is that the employee should not only trust the manager, but the manager should also trust the employee.

Performance appraisals can have a toxic effect

If an HR manager argues that annual performance appraisals help build trust between employees and managers, he/she will rarely receive any objections from within his/her own ranks. The notion is too obvious: Firstly, you can't object to trust. And secondly, talks are a good way to promote trust. So far, so good. But what very few HR managers and managing directors realise is that well intended, prescribed talks on trust-building within the company can have a toxic effect. This idea is illustrated in the following *story of the man who gives his wife flowers*:

> *There is a man who has been giving his wife flowers every weekend for many years. He does this because he loves his wife with all his heart. His wife not only appreciates this gesture, but is particularly proud of it. He doesn't have to do it, and she knows he knows this. That's what makes this weekly display of affection so special and valuable.*
>
> *Meanwhile, in the capital, the federal government is growing increasingly concerned about the rising divorce rates in the country. Divorces are a social and sociopolitical problem. Following intensive discussions about what happily married spouses do differently to partners in failed marriages, the government has enacted a law ordering all the nation's husbands to give their wives a bunch of flowers once a week.*

How does the loving husband who has already been doing this for years without a law react? It will no longer be how it was before.

This man will not be welcoming the law, even though it now officially reinforces his natural behaviour. It would be better for him to immediately stop buying flowers and instead start taking his wife out to dinner once a week.

You can't institutionally order trust-building talks. If you do, you'll achieve precisely the opposite of what you actually want. This is simply because such talks can only be successful if both parties want this *intrinsically,* i.e. of their own volition. We are familiar with the concept of attribution from psychology. It revolves around the question of which causes a person can attribute to their own behaviour and which to the behaviour of others. The latter is of particular importance here: why does the other do what they do? Once extrinsic motivators, such as material incentives, the threat of sanctions, or institutional constraints, come into play, a person will always attribute the other's behaviour to these: they're doing it because they have to. In many cases, this may not play a role. When it comes to annual performance appraisals, however, this effect is striking, and can cause significant damage, especially if trust-building is the goal. Trust can only be built in dialogue if both participants are convinced they are each conducting it based on an inner, intrinsic drive. But this notion is thwarted when compulsory talks are introduced. Managers end up being serially manoeuvred into situations they find odd. Good management can be harmed by well intended management instruments, and poor management is not improved by them, as the following analogy seeks to illustrate.

Imagine the ministry for family affairs rightly assumes that talks between parents and children are important for the child's future. Let's further imagine that this ministry is motivated by this (correct) assumption to enact a law under which parents only receive child allowances if they conduct an annual upbringing appraisal. The parents would be required to document the appraisal in a specially designated form so that a trained official, sitting in his/her office, can check whether the parents are fulfilling their duty. I can't begin to think how parents would react to such an order. In any case, we can assume that this law would hardly boost the quality of child-raising in a given country.

But things are not too different at many companies, where HR managers ask their company managers, in a formal and documented manner, to conduct trust-building talks. This then results in scenes desired neither by the HR department nor by the senior management: "Peter, you know it's January and the annual performance appraisal is coming up. That's how HR wants it. We need to talk about our relationship. Firstly (looking at the form), they want to know how we see our co-operation. Peter, do you perhaps want to comment on that first?". We can understand how this sort of situation is – rightly – difficult for many employees and managers. What's particularly tragic is that it's precisely the managers who would conduct, or have always conducted, these talks of their own intrinsic volition, without any orders from the HR department and without any official form, who are punished.

A focus on objective relevance

Coming back to the benefits described in this chapter, where we talked about performance differentiation, identifying potential, feedback, and goals. All the benefits detailed here are of a primarily objective nature. Their relevance is based on what is to be achieved through necessary judgements and decisions. As already stressed, these objective ideas should serve as the starting point. By the '90s, the prevailing thought was that performance evaluations or skills assessments should be combined with talks with the employees in question. And this is largely true for the other benefits described here. Relevant judgements and decisions often cannot be made without such talks. But to argue that these required talks seek to build trust is clearly the wrong line of action.

In an institutionalised approach, the relationship level should never be separate from the objective level. Trust can only play a role insofar as the aim is for both employees and managers to agree on the respective judgements and decisions.

It is of course understandable if an HR department wants to take responsibility for the quality of management at the company. For instance, some companies have been told in employee surveys that their leadership quality is suffering, and that action needs to be taken as a result. People want managers to speak more with their employees, reflect on their relationships, clarify mutual expectations, and clear up frustrations or conflicts. But claiming to be able to influence the interpersonal relations between managers and employees through a compulsory, institutional approach is naive. The best case scenario here is that recommendations and assistance simply help the managers wanting them. A bossy manager with dictatorial traits will still display his/her "seasoned" behavioural patterns in a mandatory performance appraisal. Things don't change just because you're in private. If a marriage is rocky and filled with mutual mistrust, no guidelines or forms are going to help resolve the situation. These aids would instead be adopted into the existing behavioural patterns. There's no need to worry about the functional marriages.

For the reasons outlined in this section, this book will not be addressing aims such as creating trust, clarifying mutual expectations between managers and employees at a relationship level, or similar aspects any further. Its focus will exclusively and deliberately be on all things objectively relevant. HR managers would be advised to follow this approach, otherwise there is a risk of companies dismissing annual performance appraisals as some kind of psychotic routine.

In summary

- You cannot formally "order" and force adult managers and employees to conduct trustful talks.
- If people are extrinsically obliged to do something they intrinsically don't want to do, they tend to do the opposite of what's expected of them.
- An annual performance appraisal must focus on the objective relevance of the judgements and decisions it generates.

4. Framework conditions

Anyone who examines annual performance appraisals more intensively, reads books about it, attends seminars, or consults various advisors will quickly get the impression that there's just *one* right approach. Critical literature, on the other hand, often questions the fundamental benefit of this instrument in a rather polarising manner. But there's no "one best way", nor should annual performance appraisals be viewed as cure-alls or be flatly demonised across the board. We need to look into an organisation more closely, and understand relevant framework conditions.

Two extremely different working environments

Martin is a painter at the only paint shop in his small home town. He has clear work rules. His boss, who owns the company, makes clear orders and issues the jobs, and Martin and his colleagues perform them: This week at 21 Brooklyn Street you'll be double-coating 220 sq m of the façade with white silicon resin. Bumps need to be smoothed out, and edges need to be masked. Before that, the walls need to undergo careful high-pressure cleaning. The job is described explicitly in writing. At the end of the week, the boss checks the work as part of an official acceptance test.

In his spare time, Martin is involved in a project in his local church community. Together, they collect clothes and toys for underprivileged children and families in Africa. The project is run by the local priest. The work is of course voluntary. The project group regularly meets with their priest to discuss the next measures to be taken, and carries these out to the best of their abilities.

In just a few sentences, I have described two very different working worlds at two organisations involving the same person. Martin contributes to both, although the results differ greatly. But the main difference lies in the framework conditions. Martin's relationships with the respective organisations are polar opposites. At one organisation, he is a dependent staff member, doing what he's told. At the other, he contributes voluntarily. The task types also vary in terms of their dynamics and clarity. One is about specific jobs, while the other is about projects with an uncertain outcome. We can also assume that the roles of the respective managers will differ. We can at least expect the church project to be run in a less authoritarian manner than the paint shop. Aspects such as these will be examined in more detail below. For the moment, let's imagine what annual performance appraisals in both environments could look like from Martin's perspective – one with the master painter and one with the priest. In which environment would a traditional annual performance appraisal work? How would this instrument have to be adapted in each case? What would be the benefits of interest to both organisations?

Three dimensions

These two very simple examples already implicitly highlight the relevance of environment and framework conditions. Over the last 20 years, I have gained extensive experience in annual performance appraisals, both as an employee and as a manager. I have also studied numerous publications on this topic. Above all, however, I have spent recent years conducting many talks with general managers, HR managers and MBA students with professional experience – from a variety of industries and countries. The views on this issue couldn't be more diverse. Even if an annual performance appraisal is performed the same way at companies A and B, it is well possible for it to work perfectly at one company, and be dismissed as ridiculous and pointless at another. The framework conditions clearly play a critical role. Below we will look more closely at three relevant dimensions relating to framework conditions, and discuss their importance for annual performance appraisals (see Figure 12).

The employee's relationship with the organisation

The relationship between the employee and his/her manager

The relationship between the employee and his/her task environment

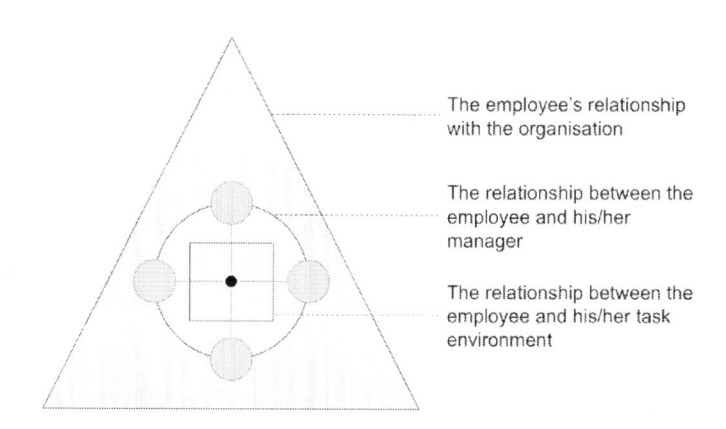

Figure 12:
The three dimensions of relevant framework conditions.

- The relationship between the employee and his/her *task environment*. Do the employees work on projects or on clearly defined tasks with specific results and processes? How complex and predictable are the tasks or projects? Who are the mutual dependents between tasks, and what are the resulting dynamics?
- The relationship between the employee and his/her *manager*. How do employees and managers interact? What is their relationship to one another? What is the managers' vision of themselves? What is the manager's dominant role? Is he/she more a boss, coach, partner or enabler?
- The employee's relationship with the *organisation*. Do the employees tend to work individually or together in teams? Is the organisation more of a hierarchy or network? How localised is the decision-making process? How much autonomy do employees enjoy? Are the employees dependent on the organisation or is the organisation dependent on the employees?

Whether or not a classic annual performance appraisal works at an organisation depends on how the organisation's framework conditions are achieved. Individual target agreements can operate well when there is strict division of labour. But when team work is involved, they don't, and can even have a negative effect on team performance. Managers who lead as partners or coaches will never conduct unilateral, formal evaluations of their staff. If it's the employer who is dependent on the employee, rather than the other way around – which will increasingly be the case in times of talent shortages -, employees are assessed in a more moderate fashion. This list of ideas could go on and on, and is purely designed to give you a taste of what is to come.

Readers whose work involves annual performance appraisals, either because they participate in them, are thinking about implementing such a system, or are testing the system at their company, may first like to reflect on the above questions. I will discuss the relevance of the answers in greater detail below.

Task environment

Are there jobs for which a traditional annual performance appraisal is hard to imagine? For which tasks would it be virtually impossible to implement a target agreement or performance evaluation? What about jobs like a prime minister, rock musician, author or stockman? Or how about extremely simple jobs with a clear routine and basic tasks: A ticket collector at a cinema, assembly line jobs with maximum labour division etc. Do target agreements, performance evaluations, potential assessments, skills assessments and HR development planning work the same way for all tasks – well or not so well? I dare say not. And we can certainly assume that this could have something to do with the nature of the job. But when differences arise, we are faced with the question of which task environment works well for all the elements of classic annual performance appraisals, and which less so. There may even be extreme conditions in which this system does not work at all.

The organisation as a machine

Many people have a traditional, textbook idea of what employees do at work: Tasks are described and structured into small, plannable units as part of labour division, resulting in jobs, positions and associated job descriptions, coupled with relevant KPIs and targets. These plannable units all form an overall entity designed to fulfil the company's overarching purpose. It is based on the notion of an organisation as a static, mechanistic whole – the machine metaphor (cf. Morgan, 1997). A clockwork company created by a genius, where every position corresponds to a separate cog. If the machine malfunctions, it is used as an opportunity to plan and structure things even more precisely, according to the "more of the same" principle.

In my seminars for HR managers or part-time MBA students, I like asking the question: "When was the last time you consulted the system for KPIs and targets relevant to your job?". The answer is usually: "At the last performance appraisal", which has often been conducted some six months before. "Are you familiar with your job description?". To this, a clear, unanimous answer: "I last looked at it at the time of my employment". "Thinking back to your job description, to what extent does your current role match the description?" The most common answers range from "I don't know" to "Has little to do with my current role" to "It's irrelevant".

How can that be? Wouldn't all companies have sunk into chaos long ago if employees aren't interested in their targets, KPIs or job descriptions on a daily basis? Yet most participants appear relaxed after this brief question-and-answer game. There's an easy explanation for this problem: Most employees' tasks don't go by the book – a trend which will continue and intensify in future.

From manual to mental work

We're seeing a massive shift from manual to mental work. The dynamics and uncertainty of the task environment are constantly increasing, forcing employees and managers to think about what they're going to do next, virtually every day. But just because medium to long-term goals and job descriptions tend to be irrelevant in daily operations, that doesn't mean employees work themselves into their day haphazardly and without control. They would no longer have the time these days. Mega trends like demographic change, globalisation and the rise in disruptive technologies have sufficiently penetrated many people's consciousness. We're familiar with the changing age pyramids. We have seen entire industries and technologies disappear – virtually overnight – in our lifetime. We worry at home when something dramatic happens somewhere in the world. All these mega trends are changing our working world. That's how it was in previous decades, and will continue to be in future. But the most significant mega trend is probably the shift from manual to mental work. It's not a trend which has set off a tsunami; there hasn't been a specific radical event which has suddenly made us aware of it. It's a trend which creeps up slowly. There are two things employees will do above all else in future: Think and communicate. What they think in future, and what they communicate, will be subject to increasingly dramatic uncertainty and dynamics. But mental or knowledge work doesn't just mean needing to use your head more than your hands for daily work. Clerks entrusted with very simple, repetitive tasks indeed do this to a certain extent. But we're talking here about continuously solving new problems, reflecting on one's own actions, changing perspectives, repeatedly dealing with new people, building and nurturing relationships, and much more.

The common knee-jerk objection here is that, even in future, there will still be people building houses, picking vegetables, transporting things from A to B, cutting hair, assembling parts etc. Of course that will be the case. "Someone will have to do the *real work*", as they rightly say in my local region of Germany. But there are two things going on here. Firstly, even though it will never totally disappear, repetitive manual work is constantly decreasing. This is partly due to increased automation. Coupled with this is the fact that more and more routine physical, manual work, particularly in Western industrialised nations, is being outsourced to low-wage countries. We don't need to assess this development at this point. We simply need to acknowledge that this development is happening. Secondly, there will be a central competitive factor, especially in places which enjoy modern technology. It's about product and process innovation: developing new, innovative products, and intelligently optimising the manufacturing thereof. Although these products and the associated process automation need to be physically created and implemented for manufacturing, their success is determined by two activities: thinking and communicating.

Task uncertainty

But what does task uncertainty mean in the working world? Different types of tasks will be examined in detail below. Three dimensions are relevant here:

- *Result certainty*. Are the results of a task clear right from the start, or do they only become apparent with time?
- *Process certainty*. Is it clear how a result is achieved?
- *Scope*. Is it a straightforward task or an extensive project?

If we put these three dimensions together, we get the diagram shown below in Figure 13.

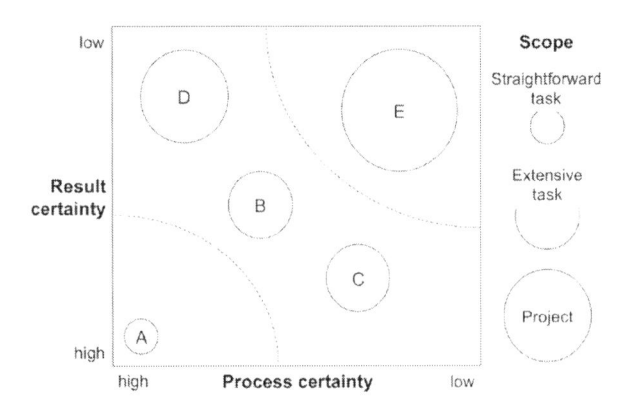

Figure 13:
Uncertainty of tasks and projects.

Hotels have the so-called housekeeping job, where employees ("maids") tidy the rooms every day. There are clearly defined routines and processes for this. The results are detailed explicitly, and follow clear, high standards – depending on the hotel. The time needed to perform the work is also unequivocally established. And because these times are relatively short – just a few minutes –, the task is very straightforward.

In the software development area of some development projects, it is not initially clear what the end result will be. While some software companies partly prioritise requirements beforehand using a simple schema – generating "must", "need" and "nice to have" requirements -, the developers don't have a clear picture of what the end product will look like right from the start. Instead of defining the requirements in detail from the outset and then adapting the resources, they often operate based on reverse logic, according to which the resources are there from the beginning, to then see how far they can be taken. The road to the end product is equally unclear. In the best-case scenario, there are set milestones.

Decisions regarding the appropriate next steps are made in short iterative loops. These sorts of development projects can be very complex in terms of the time and effort required.

If we classify these two tasks according to the diagram in Figure 13, we soon see that housekeeping is perfectly represented by task A in the bottom left corner (high results certainty, high process certainty, small scope). Software development tends to be reflected by task E. These types of tasks involve a high degree of uncertainty in terms of results and processes, and are extensive. Figure 13 shows them as a large circle in the top right-hand corner. Between the two extremes cited as examples here is a wide range of tasks involving varying scopes and degrees of uncertainty.

Performance appraisals in cases of high task uncertainty

Let's now imagine there's an employee who performs highly repetitive tasks with correspondingly small scope the same way every day (high process certainty) to consistently achieve the same, clearly defined result. This is obviously the most extreme potential case with the smallest possible degree of uncertainty. This employee's task would match a small circle in the bottom left corner of the matrix above. How would an annual performance appraisal go with this employee? The manager could simply set aside an hour to discuss "all kinds of things" with this employee, away from hectic daily operations. For example, how the employee is going in general. Whether he/she gets on with his/her colleagues. How he/she could improve overall. That would all be very nice, and no doubt a special form of acknowledgement and appreciation for the employee.

At this point, however, we need to focus on the goals and benefits mentioned in chapter 3, particularly the aim of managing companies and processes through target agreements. Because, as will be demonstrated, the task uncertainty significantly influences the question of the extent to which an annual target agreement is a suitable management instrument. In this extreme case, it is hard to imagine that individual, annually agreed targets are an appropriate way to manage processes. On the one hand, the targets here are clear by definition. On the other hand, the employee's work is not geared around medium to long-term goals, but rather around correctly performing minimal task sets in accordance with stipulated standards. If the company deems it necessary to change these standards, it is highly unlikely to announce this at a performance appraisal, but rather at the time the change appears important. In most cases, these standards also impact on more than just one single employee. I can still hear the words of a discount chain store's sales manager, who said to me: "Why should I have to agree on targets with my staff every year? All I want is for them to do their damn job [his words], and it's all good". While I do consider this view to be extreme, I understood what he meant, and he certainly wasn't totally wrong.

Let's now imagine another extreme case. A group of employees is working on a very extensive project with an unclear outcome (low results certainty) – a journey into the unknown, so to speak. The approach adopted by the team during the course of their work is equally unknown, because they are entering completely unchartered waters. But there is a vision, an idea of what the ultimate purpose could be, otherwise no sensibly run company would be willing to provide resources for it. These sorts of tasks are commonly found in scientific fields or in relation to developing highly innovative solutions. Working on such projects means living with uncertainties on a daily basis. Employees experience both moments of happiness and bitter disappointment – and they can fluctuate quickly. Projects focused on developing innovative solutions often also have tight deadlines. How do performance appraisals work in this sort of task environment? What's the situation, particularly in terms of the individual target agreement aspect? HR professionals who have already tried to introduce this instrument for these sorts of colleagues will no doubt have heard the phrase: "How can I think about targets for the next twelve months when I don't even know what will happen the day after tomorrow?". In the context of maximum uncertainty, targets are, by definition, not certain. Nor do they become certain by trying to force out targets during a performance appraisal. But if targets are defined, they are rarely real goals; they are, at best, acts of wishful thinking. Once a few weeks have passed, they will no longer be taken seriously. For employees with uncertain tasks, the oft cited and popular rule stating that targets must be defined *smartly* (in a *s*pecific, *m*easurable, *a*ccepted, *r*ealistic, *t*imed manner) seems extremely unrealistic.

An annual, individual target agreement is thus not advisable in cases of high certainty either, because the goals are clear from the outset, and relate to shorter, faster tasks. And while it may be desirable in uncertain environments, the nature of the tasks renders this impossible. But I don't want to suggest here that working out targets with employees is either pointless or infeasible. It is merely important to understand the simple notion (of key importance to annual performance appraisals) that an individual, annual target agreement is only advisable and possible for tasks involving a *medium* degree of certainty.

Non-motivating goals

When it comes to performance appraisals, people often assume that goals will motivate employees. Academic justification of this idea is usually based on Locke und Latham's so-called Goal-Setting Theory (1984): if two people try to complete a task to the best of their ability, the person who set themselves a challenging target beforehand will be the more successful. There are all kinds of supporting psychological experiments on this topic, most of which have been conducted in artificial laboratory settings, under controlled conditions. But what happens if an employee is forced to set goals when it is not possible to actually do so? The goals will end up being conservative and extremely vague (anything but "smart"). Hardly a "motivating effect". In practice, we can see that such situations are frequently avoided. And if not, then it's more about visions than goals. While the former are highly motivating, they are usually not bound to individuals, and achieving them involves variable salary components. What's more, visions tend to be of a longer-term nature, and are not part of operational short and medium-term company and process management.

Dynamics

Apart from the uncertainty aspect, the *dynamics* of the task environment also play a key role. As already indicated, there is a naive notion that a company's performance is the sum of its employees' individual performances. The assumption here is one of sequential performances along a linear value chain. Each employee makes his/her contribution to the company independently from the other employees. Collectively, the individual performances form the company's entire added-value contribution. In some company divisions, this is indeed how things work – more or less. In others, however, reality is very different. Some teams operate like a rowing eight. The overall performance is the sum of the individual performances. We know from social psychology, and particularly group dynamics, that this can certainly result in lost motivation and co-ordination (Latané, Williams & Harkins, 1979). But in this field, this assumption largely stands – even though a professional rower would assess the situation more specifically. Other teams function more like a football team. The success of a football team is not based on the sum of individual contributions, but rather on how all participants interact and co-operate. If one player performs poorly, it doesn't make the team 10% worse; the team is weakened *as a whole*.

Modern, complex organisations tend to follow the football team model rather than the rowing eight. The company's success results from the dynamic interplay of all or many tasks, functions and employees. The success of individual employees and teams also depends on co-operation with other employees and organisational units. This concept of an organisation no longer follows the machine metaphor, but rather that of an organism, where a company is regarded as a dynamic, cybernetic system, which in turn consists of elements which influence each other to varying degrees. Figure 14 shows part of a system of interdependent tasks. The circles represent tasks, and the arrows the respective impact each task has on another.

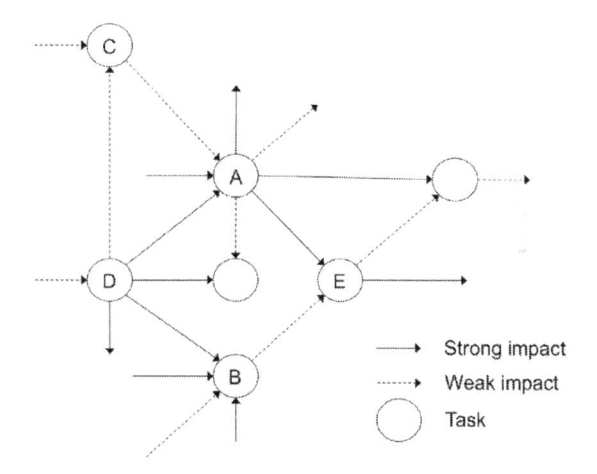

Figure 14:
The dynamics of interdependent tasks.

This idea is illustrated below using tasks. Some tasks are highly dependent on other tasks. At some companies, this may include sales activities. The sales department is only successful if the product quality is right, the marketing department does a good job, and the product management promotes competitive products. There are also tasks which have a significant influence on other tasks at the company, which may be the case for internal service functions, such as HR or IT. So there are tasks which have a strong impact on others, and there are functions which react strongly to the performances of other functions. In some instances, both cases apply, and in others, neither does.

Figure 15 shows a graphic representation of both dimensions: reaction and impact. It uses five tasks (A to E) as an example, based on the diagram in Figure 14.

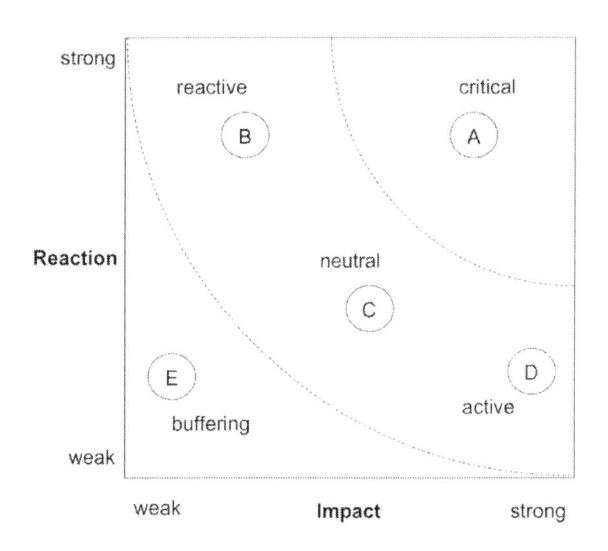

Figure 15:
Dynamics in a cybernetic sensitivity model.

This graph is geared around an idea coined by systems theorist Frederic Vester (1988), according to which the figure above is the product of a so-called sensitivity analysis. The resulting sensitivity model demonstrates the dynamic embedding of various elements within a system of mutual impact and reaction. In practice, this sort of model can be developed with few resources. We now need to address the implications of different task dynamics for performance appraisals.

The sales department is an example commonly used to illustrate how target agreements, and the associated variable remuneration, operate. This is presumably due to the fact that hardly any other area has such clear, often individual performance indicators. A sales team member's performance is measured on the revenue he/she generates. Period. But as easy as this seems for some situations, it is equally problematic in others. For a sales-force member who goes from house to house selling potatoes, it may well be this simple – and not just because of the high degree of process and results certainty associated with his/her task. If two sales-force members go around selling products on doorsteps in a comparable region, the one achieving the greater revenue is the more successful. It is, however, a completely different story for a sales team member operating in a B2B environment. If production plants (capital goods) are sold to key accounts, a responsible sales-force employee is highly dependent on the performance of others, even internally. Coupled with this is the fact that his/her performance also depends on external, macroeconomic conditions. The potato seller is not subject to intense dynamics. This task would be classified in the bottom left-hand corner (buffering) of Figure 15. The task of the sales-force member selling production plants would correspond to the top left-hand corner (reactive), while in a B2B environment, the sales employees are dependent on the delivery reliability, flexibility and quality of the production division, persuasive marketing, and the networks of some top decision-makers, just to name a few factors

The last example shows how difficult it is to evaluate an individual employee's performance when his/her task is embedded in a complex system of dependent tasks and conditions. If he/she is successful, it is only because the system *as a whole* is successful. In this type of scenario, target agreements are always tied in with conditions, making matters significantly more complicated. A manager who dares to rate a sales employee's performance poorly based on revenue will always trigger an avalanche of apologies alluding to the corresponding framework conditions: "How am I supposed to successfully sell this production plant on the international market if our marketing team is not able to provide English product descriptions without spelling errors?". These are the sorts of things commonly heard in practice.

In addition to reactive tasks (top left in Figure 15), there are also active tasks (bottom right). Active tasks influence downstream tasks, and are often found at the start of the value chain. A designer's task is a good example. The design of a product or component often has a considerable impact on production, marketing, finances and sales. One wrong decision here can cause lasting, far-reaching problems for other tasks. One error in active tasks has a similar effect to pulling one strand of a spider's web: it affects the entire system.

Finally, there are critical tasks (Task A in Figure 14 and Figure 15), where notions relating to reactive and active tasks must be viewed collectively. Everything that has been said about the aforementioned task types brings to bear in equal measure here. It is worth noting at this point that the 'key position' concept commonly found in HR management can be understood based on these ideas. In this context, a key position is a position associated with highly active tasks, and which is ultimately largely responsible for the success of the system as a whole (cf. Trost, 2014, Huselid, Beatty & Becker, 2005).

Goals create a focus, but also a blind spot

In real-life scenarios, hardly anyone will set "not diddling customers" as a goal. Hardly anyone will specifically pledge to go the extra mile in the case of short-staffing, or to be there for each other in the team. Hardly anyone will set the goal of sharing information with colleagues, or being helpful, empathetic and honest. Is there a bank advisor anywhere who has arranged a "smart" target of explaining the risks of the "product of the month" to customers if they know this will likely turn the customer away from the product?

The effect (activity) of tasks has fewer consequences for the performance evaluation than it does for goal setting. Employees who have set goals will focus on achieving them. After all, that's what goals are there for. They not only provide a point of orientation, but also a point of focus: what's important and what's *not*. The latter will hardly be mentioned in a target agreement. But by certain goals *not* being set, they are implicitly and automatically given a lower priority. This may mean that employees lose sight of relevant aspects, though these may be of major relevance to downstream tasks. For example, a designer who only worries about external aesthetics can generate considerable costs in production, and even affect the quality of an entire product. In this respect, conflicts of objectives are inevitable when it comes to active tasks. And as designers usually discuss their goals with their direct manager (design boss), these are often focused inwardly, ignoring the long-term and downstream impacts on the entire system. In the case of active tasks, it would thus be more logical for employees to set goals with those responsible for downstream tasks, rather than with their direct manager. But here, too, the complexity of the matter can escalate into an incomprehensible mess relatively quickly. And this is just *one* example. In practice, you'll find an entire cosmos of similar scenarios. In this context, an annual target agreement appears completely unsuitable as an instrument for managing companies and processes. Due to their high cybernetic importance, active tasks also require much faster control loops.

In summary

- We're seeing a trend shifting from manual to mental work. The work of the future essentially involves thinking and communicating, and is characterised by uncertainty and dynamism.
- A task's uncertainty is high if it has a large scope, and neither the outcome nor the method is clear and definable from the outset.
- Target agreements are only advisable for tasks involving a medium degree of certainty.
- Intense networking and interdependence between tasks results in a high degree of dynamism. It's no longer the individual who is successful, but rather the system.
- In a highly dynamic environment, particularly among active tasks, annual target agreements and individual performance evaluations can have a detrimental effect on the system as a whole.

Leadership role

Let's start with a small, simple exercise, where you take a blank sheet of paper and write down five tips for managers when it comes to conducting performance appraisals. Those who can't think of anything spontaneously can consult the Internet, where hordes of behaviour coaches and advisors describe how to do it right. The result could be something like this:

- Start the appraisal with a casual, innocuous question like "How are you?".
- Structure the appraisal and explain the process to the other person right at the start.
- Give the other person enough opportunity to comment on the individual points.
- Articulate critical points slowly and calmly. Keep your head upright, and look the other person in the eye.
- Take notes during the conversation, and explain important and relevant content to the other person.

So far, so good. Now let's give these points the heading of "Tips for having a conversation with your partner or spouse". Suddenly, these tips appear in a different light. They look domineering, at times odd and unrealistic. For some people, these tips even have contemptuous connotations. What sort of miserable relationship would you have to have with your life partner to hold a conversation in this manner? Most well intended advice on conducting annual performance appraisals is implicitly based on a traditional understanding of leadership. Here is the boss and here is the employee. There's a top and a bottom. And that's fine. Thousands of companies operate this way. In practice, we are, however, increasingly observing different relationships between employees and their managers.

As a professor, my university also urges me to conduct a performance appraisal every year. We call it an "employee dialogue", and it is very similar to the traditional approach of an annual performance appraisal in terms of content. When I'm asked to do it and consequently sit down to speak with an employee, it sounds something like: "Paula [I have changed the name], it's time for another staff dialogue. You know the deal. We spend the whole year talking about everything that's important to you and me, all the time, just as adults do. If something comes up or you need anything, come and see me. Are you able to fill out the form, or shall I do it? Then I'll sign it". This type of approach works because we co-operate as partners, and simply don't need this instrument. We agree on that. I of course cannot speak for other managers at our organisation. But I don't have any problem with objective evaluations or forms. As a professor who awards grades to students, it's part of my basic tasks. As a professor and teacher, I am the boss to a certain extent (which is usually a good thing). As a colleague and manager, I am a partner on equal footing. And since I have to take the blame for some things as an official manager, I am also allowed to make some decisions.

At annual performance appraisals, employees are assessed by their managers on various aspects, such as performance, competence and potential. Although it is common knowledge that this is no easy task for the managers, it is expected of them. "A good manager must be able to do that". If performance appraisals are not conducted as required, it is often attributed to the manager's incompetence; a notion which is unrealistic and dangerous. Because, depending on the leadership role, the annual performance appraisal can have a professionalising or toxic effect, and managers, especially the good ones, know or can sense this. This is essentially due to the social nature of evaluations.

The social judgement process

When a manager evaluates an employee, it's different to this same manager rating a book, for example, or a house, or a car, or a pizza. Interpersonal judgements always affect the relationship between the evaluator and the evaluatee. It is impossible to understand the dynamics emerging during the evaluation without understanding this relationship. In some situations, the relationship between a manager and an employee may not even permit unilateral judgements. The possible relationships between employees and managers will therefore be addressed in greater detail below.

We can work on the simplified assumption that a manager knows how to rate his/her employee, and simply articulates and documents this judgement at the performance appraisal. In reality, however, things are a lot more complex, and have little to do with this rather naive notion. At this point, it is worth taking a closer look at the cognitive process of social judgement (see also Fiske & Taylor, 1991). For the sake of simplicity, we will imagine a practical situation in which a manager (let's call him Steven) evaluates an employee (Mary) on her team-working skills. What happens? It may well be that Steven has already made a judgement of Mary, since he has known her for many years, already assessed her a year ago, and has hardly noticed any changes since. But if he doesn't have a pre-judgement during the performance appraisal or when preparing for it, he needs to form one (see Figure 16). This is then followed by a series of characteristic steps – conscious or subconscious (cf. Illgen & Feldman, 1983).

```
                    ┌─────────────────┐
                    │ Interpretation  │
              ┌────▶│  of criteria    │
              │     └────────┬────────┘
              │              ▼
     no       │     ┌─────────────────┐
       ╱╲     │     │   Retrieval of  │
      ╱  ╲    │     │     relevant    │◀─────┐
     ╱ Pre-╲  │     │    memories     │      │
    ╱existing╲│     └────────┬────────┘      │
    ╲judgement╱              ▼               │
     ╲  ?   ╱      ┌─────────────────┐  ┌─────────────┐
      ╲    ╱       │     Initial     │  │  Editing/   │
       ╲  ╱        │    judgement    │  │ adjustment of│
        ╲╱         └────────┬────────┘  │  judgement  │
     yes │                  ▼           └─────────────┘
         │         ┌─────────────────┐        ▲
         └────────▶│  Assessment of  │        │
                   │    judgement    │────────┘
                   │  consequences   │
                   └────────┬────────┘
                            ▼
                   ┌─────────────────┐
                   │  Articulation of│
                   │    judgement    │
                   └─────────────────┘
```

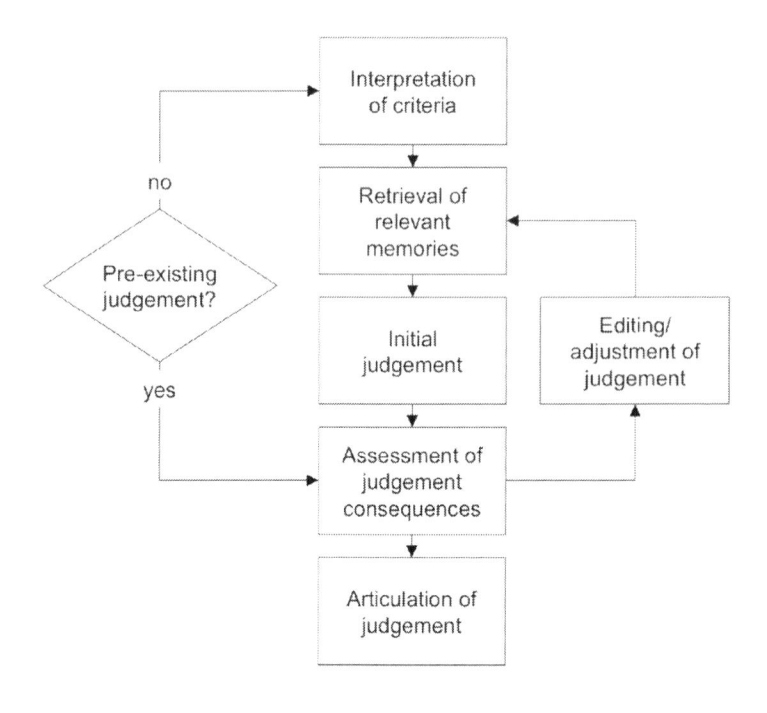

Figure 16:
The social judgement process during a performance appraisal.

Steven first needs to interpret the criterion of team-working skills. Team-working skills for a call-centre employee are different to those associated with a project manager. In this case, behavioural anchors with clearly defined behavioural patterns can only help to a limited extent. Once Steven has an idea of what he considers team-working skills to be, he will try to recall relevant observations and experiences involving Mary. He must rely on his memory, particularly since he – like almost every manager – has not kept a diary throughout the year. Many psychological effects come into play here, and we won't be going into these in further detail (see Fiske & Taylor, 1991). In any case, this step alone entails a degree of uncertainty for most managers. What comes to mind when I think of my employee? Have I forgotten something? What was it again?

At some point, Steven will make an initial judgement. He may come to the conclusion that, on a scale of 1 (Basic) to 4 (Expert), Mary is a Level 2 in terms of her team-working skills. Steven will now assess the consequences of his judgement. What will happen when I tell Mary? Will she see it the same way I do, or is there potential here for additional explanation or even a conflict? How relevant is the judgement to Mary's future or salary (she has just bought a house and needs the money)? Am I fulfilling my responsibility? Am I jeopardising my good relationship with Mary by articulating my judgement in a manner I consider appropriate?

Based on this assessment of possible consequences, a manager may adjust or correct the judgement by trying to recall further memories of the employee. As seen in psychological research, there is a risk here of a manager systematically searching for content to confirm the initial judgement. This will become more intensive the more negatively the consequences of the initial judgement are viewed. It is a cycle of forming judgements, remembering additional content, and assessing the consequences, and it continues until the manager feels somewhat confident. It's not about validity, but rather initially about the manager's soundness of judgement. One has nothing to do with the other. Ultimately, however, the focus is on the relationship between the evaluator and the evaluatee.

This process illustrates that forming judgements as part of a performance appraisal is always a social process. If person A evaluates another person B, it's different to person A evaluating an object. The subjective assessment of the judgement consequences is of key importance, particularly when a judgement needs to be communicated directly, as is commonly required in performance appraisals. These anticipated consequences in turn depend on the type and quality of the interpersonal relationship on the one hand, and on the appropriateness of the judgement on the other. There is a difference between a manager making a judgement of an employee deemed replaceable and dependent, and an employee considered a close, imperatively required confidant. There is also a difference between a judgement only being communicated verbally, and it being documented and forwarded to the HR department for further processing. If the relationship between an employee and his/her manager is based on trust, this process will lead to different results compared to a relationship built on power and subordination.

Evaluator or judge?

When people interact, mutual judgements are made. It's impossible for humans *not* to judge. My students frequently appear intimidated when I tell them, during a lecture, that every time I look a student in the eye, I simultaneously form a judgement. Conversely, for example, I, too, was judged by more than 100 students within the first few seconds of walking into the classroom for the first lecture. It's human nature. Man wouldn't be able to survive in his social environment if he didn't constantly make social judgements.

Managers also make judgements of their employees – daily, hourly, and really in every social situation. These judgements are also always action-guiding – more or less. They determine what a manger says or decides. Herein lies a key argument, which is often raised in relation to formal staff evaluations. It is argued, for example, that it's a matter of fairness that an employee know what his/her manager thinks of him/her. After all, it affects him/her directly. This argument certainly carries weight. And an open exchange does indeed potentially create opportunities through mutual perception and evaluation, as long as it is conducted appropriately, empathetically and, if necessary, diplomatically.

The great management thinker Douglas McGregor (1960), whom I highly regard, calls managers who evaluate employees formally "judges". So are managers evaluators or judges? They're evaluators because they're human. So judgements are ok. Sharing personal judgements with employees can be very productive. We can't categorically say this for judges. There's one simple difference between judging and evaluating. When managers make judgments of employees (which they do by nature), but simultaneously also document these judgements and forward then to a central, relevant authority, they go from being evaluators to judges. This is a significant difference for the employees affected. Hardly any professionally-minded employee will be opposed to personal feedback. But many will have a problem with the feedback being quantified along set scales and irrevocably forwarded to the HR department or even the senior management. Employees tend to want to be evaluated, but not always judged.

This fine difference plays a key role in the thoughts expressed below. It will become clear that certain leadership roles will allow evaluation, but not judgement. The classic boss, who essentially wants employees to do what he/she wants, does not see judgement as in any way conflicting with his/her own understanding of leadership, but instead identifies it as part of his/her tasks. A manager acting as a coach, however, will never do this. And rightly so. The various roles a manager can adopt will now be examined.

The relationship between employee and manager

What do employees do when they have a problem? There are generally five behavioural patterns. Firstly, they'll go to their manager and say, "Boss, I've got a problem. What should I do?".

The boss will then tell them what they need to do. Secondly, they will go to their manager and say: "Brad, we've got a problem, let's talk about it". Brad: "What do you suggest?" They will then work together to find a solution, for which the manager ultimately bears responsibility. Thirdly, the employees go to their manager and say: "I have a problem. Let's talk". The manager will ask "What's the problem? What's your solution? Have you thought about the risks, alternatives etc.? How sure are you that your solution will work?". The employee retains responsibility. Fourthly, the employees go to their manager and say: "I have a problem and a solution. But I need your help". Fifthly, the employees themselves try to fix the problem, alone or with colleagues. The manager does not get involved here, so only the first four behavioural patterns are relevant in this respect.

These four, simple situations illustrate four different leadership roles: Boss, Partner, Coach and Enabler, which are each described in further detail below (see Figure 17).

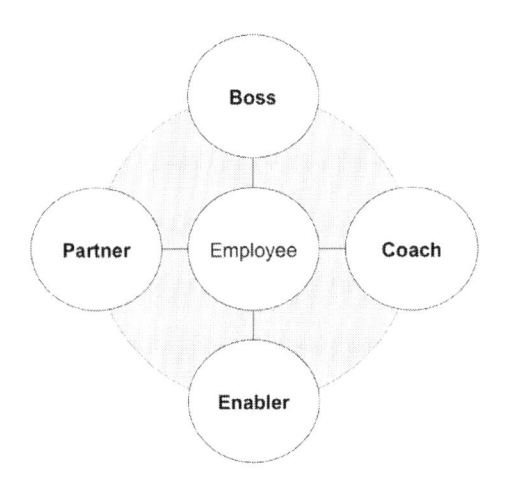

Figure 17:
Four possible manager roles.

As will be shown, the role of the manager is a key factor in determining whether or not a traditional annual performance appraisal works and is appropriate.

The manager as the boss

The manager can adopt the role of *"Boss"*. This rather forceful term is purposely used because it best describes what is meant here. If the boss manages a large number of employees, he/she can also be called a "ruler". This is based on the stereotypical notion of what makes a "boss". The boss is above the employees, whom he/she has "under him/her". He/she tells the employees what they have to do, and controls them accordingly. There is an implicit assumption here that the boss not only has a power advantage over his/her staff, but also better knowledge. He/she knows how to do things right. A boss' concept of leadership revolves around one central question: How can I get the staff to do what I want?

Conversely, employees live with the awareness that they have done a good job if their boss – not the customer – is satisfied. The relationship between bosses and "their" staff is characterised by hierarchical superordination and power. Since the boss knows everything, the employees "under him/her" are comparatively replaceable and dependent on him/her. We tend to see a classic division here between thoughts and actions. The boss thinks and the employees act. In extreme cases, the employees don't have to think at all. Henry Ford aptly expressed this with his famous quote: "Why is it every time I ask for a pair of hands, they come with a brain attached?". As will be illustrated below, many companies use this role when devising their annual performance appraisal. In practice, however, another role is slowly gaining ground – that of a partner.

The manager as a partner

Knowledge-intensive sectors and industries in particular are seeing managers increasingly adopt the role of a *partner*. Partners act on the same level as their employees, and consider themselves a key element of the team they are managing. They only differ from other employees in that they bear specific responsibility for the overall result achieved by their team or department. One typical example is the role of a dean at a university faculty. A dean runs the faculty, and bears a high degree of responsibility for it achieving its targets. But a dean is not a boss. He/she is elected by the other faculty members, whom he/she represents to the university management. A dean will never issue instructions to professors in his/her faculty, or copy a book for them, just to cite an extreme example. While he/she can instruct professors to hold certain lectures, this is always done with mutual consent. The manager as a partner is usually found in knowledge-intensive areas where the success of a team or department depends on the creativity of the employees. Creativity cannot be ordered. It can only be enabled. Mick Jagger was and is the bandleader of the Rolling Stones. In the early years, he adopted a partner role, an equal-ranking band member with particular responsibilities. When Mick Jagger later took on the role of boss, the band broke up for an extended period – according to an undoubtedly subjective account by Keith Richards.

The need for a partner role frequently results from the relevant knowledge possessed by the employee and manager, which has seen a shift in weighting in today's modern working world. Figure 18 shows a simple comparison between a traditional hierarchical workplace and a modern, knowledge-intensive working environment.

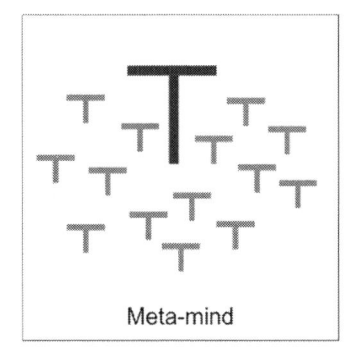

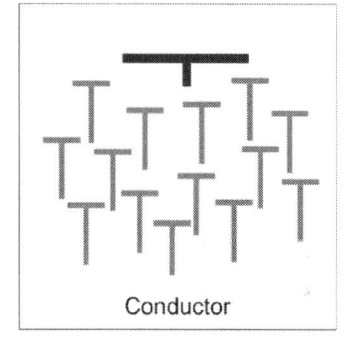

Meta-mind | Conductor

Figure 18:
General knowledge, expert knowledge, and the role of the manager.

The Ts in Figure 18 represent people with general knowledge (cross bar) and expert knowledge (vertical line). The large, black T is the respective manager. In the traditional environment, the boss has extensive general and expert knowledge. He/she acts as a meta-mind, to a certain extent. The employees are the same, just a bit smaller in every respect. If someone has a question, the boss will know the answer; or the employees are at least urged to ask – even if someone else has a better response. In a knowledge-intensive, complex, creativity-dominated world, the manager has a lot of general knowledge. He/she has an overall idea, and knows a bit of everything through experience. He/she also has basic expert knowledge, usually from an earlier stage in his/her career. Every employee has better knowledge than their direct manager in their field of expertise. A manager in a partner role is equivalent to the conductor of an orchestra, in which each of the musicians can play their instrument better than the conductor. Complex projects operate in such a way that a group is orchestrated by various experts. Anything else would be inconceivable here. The half-life of relevant knowledge is growing shorter and shorter, meaning no employee can properly keep up with new findings. They need to find a point of focus. It is for this very reason that, particularly in technical fields, employees without a specific focus area cannot be permanently considered an expert. This already gives rise to implications regarding the evaluation of performance and skills as part of performance appraisals. But the partner role is of course also possible in non-knowledge-intensive fields.

Managers acting in a partner role gear themselves more around trust than power. They do so out of an awareness that they depend more on their employees than the other way around. Large and uncertain projects see teams and their managers faced with considerable complexity. This is traditionally countered with extensive planning and highly detailed mutual agreements.

Since the times of the great sociologist and systems theorist, Niklas Luhman, we have known that trust is the most powerful way to reduce social complexity. Humanity has always been aware of this, at least implicitly. But it seems that this realisation has shifted out of focus with the development of increasingly intricate planning and control instruments from management studies and a rise in elaborate legal regulation systems (cf. Luhmann, 2000).

The manager as a coach

A manager acting as a *coach* leaves the employees to take responsibility wherever possible, which is why questions are a coach's most important leadership instrument. He/she won't tell an employee "Try going from left to right; that'll help", but will rather ask "Have you thought about any alternative approaches?". This will rightly remind trained occupational and organisational psychologists of what is known as "non-directive communication". A coach implicitly assumes that the employee knows how to solve the problem, or is at least able to devise a solution independently. As soon as a coach gets the impression that his/her employee doesn't know how to proceed further, he/she will discuss with them, in a non-directive manner, how to find a way of devising a functional solution: "What could help you proceed further with this matter? Have you tried looking at it from a different perspective? Who should you speak to? How sure are you of your plan?".

This role is very difficult to maintain in practice – due less to the managers themselves and more to employee expectations and their socialisation in professional life. Managers who try to adopt a non-directive approach will regularly hear phrases like: "Boss, just tell me what I should do. Then I'll do it and it'll all be good". This places demands on the boss. For the employee, it's a suitable strategy, usually learned over several years, to evade responsibility. And is it any wonder? Many have learned, over decades, to do what their boss tells them. There are of course situations requiring a boss to take control. I myself am a sailor, and am all too familiar with such situations. When a storm develops, putting the boat and crew at risk, the skipper must perform his role as boss, even when his prevailing notion of leadership is one of coaching. Clear, rapid decisions and announcements, coupled with purposeful actions, are always better than discussion and joint reflection here, despite the fact that some decisions won't always be optimum. Good managers who lead non-directively know how to distinguish between such situations, and act accordingly.

The manager as an enabler

Finally, a manager can also be an *enabler*. Managers who identify with this role essentially consider their task to be that of creating an environment for their employees in which these are motivated and able to put in top performances. Here, too, the focus is on the employee. Extreme forms of this role can be found in sport or art. For instance, Sir George Martin was the manager of the Beatles. In this capacity, he was neither boss, nor partner, nor coach. Ultimately, his job was to ensure the four band members were able to do what they did best: write songs, record songs, and perform in public. The Rolling Stones' manager, Prince Rupert Loewenstein, held this role for over 40 years. It is significant to note that he had no idea about music in general, nor did he like that of the Rolling Stones.

In this employee-manager relationship, the employee is like the manager's customer, even though it would hardly be expressed as such in practice. The manager is considered successful if the employees are happy and productive. Conversely, the manager is held to account if the employees complain about unfavourable, restrictive framework conditions, whether it be in terms of organisation, procedures or infrastructure.

Role conflicts

These potential manager roles have considerable implications for the implementation and success of an annual performance appraisal. The aforementioned, influential management theorist,

Douglas McGregor, examined the role of managers and its importance on performance appraisals in his groundbreaking book, "The Human Side of Enterprise", as early as 1960. He summarised his thoughts with the phrase "The role of judge and the role of counsellor are incompatible" (McGregor, 1960, p. 117). The role he describes as "counsellor" is more or less identical to that of "coach" detailed here. But we can define this idea further. A partner can give an employee feedback on an employee's performance. But as soon as this judgement is documented, forwarded to the HR department, and used to derive positive or negative consequences for the employee, the manager becomes what McGregor calls a "judge". A partner or coach will find this role extremely difficult, since their relationship with their employee is based on trust, and maintaining mutual trust takes top priority, particularly in this partnership-like setup. Sticking with the Stones example: As the undisputed bandleader, Mick Jagger will have given Keith Richards feedback on thousands of occasions throughout the band's history. Mutual judgements are a key element of rehearsals. But can you imagine Mick Jagger asking his fellow band member to undergo a strictly scheduled annual performance appraisal? "Keith, it's January; time for our performance appraisal". It's not what partners do.

A boss, on the other hand, has absolutely no problem formally evaluating an employee. His/her position and relationship with the employee is based on power and hierarchical superiority. Instructions and control are normal. In these framework conditions, an employee evaluation and corresponding report to the HR department is part of everyday logic. A coach will never formally evaluate an employee; this would be completely inconsistent with his/her relationship with the employee. While a coach can encourage an employee to critically reflect on their own performance and skills, he/she will never be the one to make a definitive judgement, leave alone document it and inform HR, unless the employee requests this. A manager in an enabler role will similarly only make judgements of an employee to a limited degree – much to the same extent as a professional supplier would do of its customer.

Partners evaluate differently

I occasionally conduct a simple experiment with my students during my lectures. I form random groups of four, whose task is to use a prepared floorplan to design the perfect three-bedroom apartment, marking the walls and doors accordingly. The plan only shows the exterior walls. I in turn randomly divide these groups into two sides: A and B. In side A, I appoint the group leader, who has to explain the task to the group, but should keep out of the work itself. He/she is allowed to check on things from time to time. In side B, the group appoints their own leader, who is in turn allowed to actively participate in solving the problem. Both leaders are responsible for the outcome. As is clear to see, I have artificially created differing managerial roles. In side A, I have created a boss, and in side B, a partner (see Figure 19).

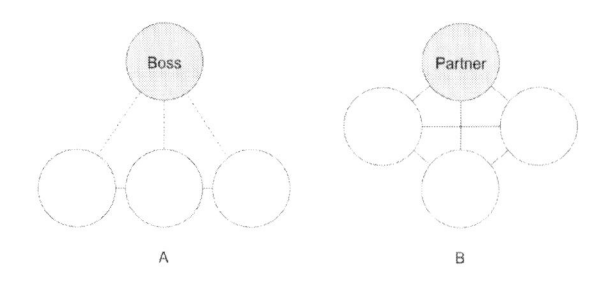

Figure 19:
Boss and partner in a simple simulation.

After about 20 minutes, I stop the exercise and call the leaders over to me to evaluate the result. Partners evaluate their group results significantly better than bosses overall. Subsequent, independent assessments show, however, that, from a more objective point of view, group B's results (partner) are really no better.

This simple experiment impressively illustrates the dynamics involved when evaluating performance in different manager roles. Depending on the role adopted, performance, skills and potential will be evaluated based on completely different principles, regardless of the HR department's idea of a performance evaluation. This will be demonstrated below using the roles of boss and partner.

Boss and partner in performance appraisals

If the senior management or HR department asks its managers to evaluate their employees, a judgement will ultimately be received for each employee – provided HR insists on it. But what actually happens between this request and the final outcome couldn't be more different, depending on the role. Figure 20 shows a simple comparison of two scenarios, described below.

	Boss	**Partner**
Relationship basis	Power	Trust
Employee reaction	Negotiation	Reflection
Subject of evaluation	Employee's performance and skills	Joint performance, co-operation
Handling of duties	Fulfilment	Defence, Tactics
Judgement documentation	Report to HR	Confidentiality

Figure 20:
Performance evaluation comparison for the roles of Boss and Partner.

Let's start with the boss. As the relationship with the employee is based on power, the boss will more or less dominate the performance appraisal. He/she does this because he/she can. Anyone in a position of power will maximise this – an effect of social psychology which has been known for decades, and which can potentially even lead to drastic behaviour (Zimbardo, 2007). The subjects of the evaluation are the employee's performance and skills. The manager's main question is: "Has the employee put in the performance I, as a manager, expect of him/her?" and "Does the employee demonstrate abilities consistent with the requirements I have placed on him/her?". The employee is evaluated based on the aforementioned process of social judgement. The manager is acutely aware of the consequences of his/her judgement, but also approves any negative consequences for the employee. He/she accepts this as part of the system. In view of this, the manager sees the employee evaluation as a duty and managerial task. The employees, in turn, are equally aware of the judgement consequences, which is why they try to incorporate and discuss their personal interests rather than openly and honestly reflecting on weaknesses. Since the manager accepts the system, he/she will duly document his/her final judgement and forward it to the HR department. The whole affair seems clear, logical and unambiguous to the boss. His/her actions are part of a system assigning him/her the position of manager. He/she may consider dutiful completion and documentation of the performance appraisal further proof of his/her high leadership quality. After all, he/she also earns recognition from the HR department.

It's a completely different story for the partner and his/her employees. As the relationship is characterised by trust, a formal evaluation constitutes a potential threat. Partner judgements aren't unilateral, and this perception particularly originates from the fact that the evaluation entails consequences and is designed to be forwarded to the HR department. The partner doesn't have any problem giving the employee feedback on his/her performance over the last twelve months. Giving feedback is certainly compatible with this role – as McGregor puts it. Unlike bosses, however, partners consider themselves partly responsible for employee performances. It's a joint effort. The employee's skills are just one side of the coin. It's about co-operation and mutually complementing different (varied) strengths. In this respect, the partner cannot evaluate his/her employees without also evaluating himself/herself. Another reason why the evaluation is perceived as a threat is because it involves the risk of negotiation, which would conflict with the notion of mutual openness and confidentiality. Because the aim of a performance evaluation in this sort of relationship is to jointly reflect on a collective performance rather than engage in unilateral negotiations. Anything else here would be inconceivable, since the focus is on preserving mutual trust. In the end, the system is skilfully, even strategically, bypassed as far as possible. One is verbal, the other is documented for the records or HR. The manager and employee also know that a performance appraisal adopting the usual hierarchy is only wise if both parties want this. An official request for a formal performance appraisal can actually harm a person's natural willingness to communicate, particularly from the manager's side, as illustrated in the aforementioned story of the man who gave his wife flowers. Managers who conduct regular talks with their staff of their own volition (intrinsically motivated) may be corrupted by the introduction of a performance appraisal (extrinsic motivation): "Is my manager conducting these talks because he wants to or because he *has* to?". In this scenario, the natural progression is for the performance appraisal to be defended by the intrinsically exemplary manager.

Good and bad managers

Here we see a management dilemma which may accompany performance appraisals. Many companies associate "good management" with the dutiful implementation of annual performance appraisals, precisely as per the official guidelines, including relevant forms. A manager who doesn't conduct regular talks of this kind can't be a good manager. This notion is based on a traditional, hierarchical understanding of management. There are perpetuated ideas of how performance appraisals should be carried out. Chapter 2 already addressed the common approaches: a manager evaluates every employee's performance, competencies and potential at least once a year. Goals are set for the future. Personal development measures are discussed. The list goes on. Judgements and decisions are ultimately documented and provided to the HR department. Managers who follow this process are officially "good managers".

This approach is certainly well intended, and primarily works when the manager performs the role of a boss. In all other roles (enabler, coach, partner), however, it harbours considerable potential for conflict, and is only compatible to a limited extent.

Managers who see themselves in a capacity other than that of boss will avoid this approach or intelligently adapt it to their role. They won't end up doing what the HR department asks of them – usually without the HR department even realising it. Because it is difficult to tell from the completed form how the judgements and decisions were actually made. In an official, HR sense, managers who tend to avoid this process are not fulfilling their managerial responsibility. And this is recognised by the time the next employee survey comes around, when statistics show they do not give clear instructions or set "smart" targets. The fact that the good managers do not give "clear instructions" or "set smart targets" is conveniently ignored when interpreting these survey results.

In summary

- Conversations and social judgements always reflect the interpersonal relationship between the participants. The implementation of formal communication rules is adapted to this existing relationship.
- The dominant role of a manager determines the relationship between him/her and his/her employee. These roles can be distinguished as Boss, Partner, Coach and Enabler.
- An evaluator becomes a judge if their judgement is documented, forwarded, and used to draw specific conclusions.
- Certain stipulations for annual performance appraisals cannot be compatible with certain manager roles. A coach or partner will never act as a judge.

- Good management doesn't necessarily have to mean the annual performance appraisal is conducted in the exact manner desired by this instrument's creators.

Organisation

A former student from my faculty recently called me, desperately seeking advice. After successfully completing his studies, he took on a job at a large German automotive supplier. He told me he felt chronically "underchallenged" at work; for weeks he had found himself with nothing to do from the early afternoon onwards. He had obviously spoken to his boss several times and made himself available for additional tasks, but his efforts had appeared to be in vain. I know this student, and personally regard his motivation and skills highly. While there are no concrete, empirical figures to prove it, I would expect the number of employees with similar fates to be quite considerable.

At around the same time, I bumped into another former student at the airport. I asked him how he was going, and he told me, enthusiastically, about his work. The comment which struck me most was: "We've got so many interesting projects I could work on, with great colleagues. It's just a shame time is so limited".

Instruction and control versus autonomy

These two examples show the extreme poles of a wide spectrum of organisations. In the broadest sense, it's about an employee's relationship with his/her organisation. In the first case, the employee "belongs" to the company. He makes himself available to this company, which can employ staff at its own discretion and according to its own rules. I dare say this notion of an employee-organisation relationship is more prevalent than first feared. It's obvious just from common language use. For example, staff members are "employed", "assigned", "transferred" and "seconded" abroad. The company "does" something with the employee. The implicit thought here is that the employer is fully entitled to do this, since it's the one paying the employee's monthly salary. These types of companies are run based on the principle that the organisation knows best what is good for its employees, and uses them accordingly. The organisation guides the individual employee's actions, determining not only his/her tasks, but also his/her professional development.

These companies are contrasted with their other, usually more modern counterparts, where employees are not "victims" or mere servants of superior structures, rules and decisions, but rather active authors. They bear responsibility. Employees don't just get involved in projects; they initiate them, often autonomously. At many innovative businesses, employees even follow the unwritten rule that new ideas should be developed and promoted "underground" for as long as possible before they are potentially shaken down, halted, or even blocked by strategic decision-making committees – the company as a living cosmos of social and content-related possibilities.

An eternal conflict of dogmas

These two worlds are based on two opposing management approaches. On the one hand, there is the classic approach of Frederick Taylor's scientific management (Taylor, 1911). They lead into a system characterised by direction and control. On the other hand, we have more humanistic approaches, which focus on self-actualisation and personal responsibility. I refer here to masterminds like Douglas McGregor (1960), who devised the contrasting notion of Theory X and Y, but who ended up clearly arguing in favour of Theory Y. According to this theory, employees naturally strive for responsibility and self-regulation. Other thinkers, like Chris Argyris (1960), in turn emphasise the difference between formal and informal behaviour at organisations, highlighting the conflict between "official" organisational structures and informal (independent) actions (cf. Katzenbach & Khan, 2008). Simply speaking, it's about the dilemma between direction and control on the one hand, and autonomy combined with self-regulation on the other (see Figure 21).

Direction and control	Self-regulation/ Autonomy
Theory X	Theory Y
Formal organisation	Informal behaviour
Top-down	Bottom-up
External influences	Self-determination
External responsibility	Personal responsibility

Figure 21:
Contrasting management approaches.

Ever since both these views became common knowledge, there has been an often dogmatic conflict over which is correct. In recent years, many (self-proclaimed) management gurus have earned a lot of money defending one approach over another as consultants, speakers and authors. And these discussions will continue, as there will never be a definitive solution.

It is frequently said that creative people, who play a particularly pivotal role in an age of a knowledge economy and innovation, prefer to take responsibility and have self-regulation. Today, we know that this is only true to a limited extent. Many others will plead that the younger generation seeks responsibility. Based on my own observations, this notion doesn't seem to stick either. In my lectures, I usually show my students the two management cultures in Figure 22, coupled with the question of which style they prefer. Management culture B obviously represents direction and control, while management culture A reflects autonomy and self-regulation. The responses are evenly balanced, even though just a few years ago I would have expected a preference for model A.

Management culture A	Management culture B
We want our employees to act like mature adults, so that's how we treat them. Every employee bears responsibility for his/her actions. Our aim is for all employees to ultimately get involved of their own volition for the good of the entire company, and make their own individual contribution. There are no rigid structures or control from a higher authority here, nor are these necessary.	Employees want to be managed and need structure. That's why we see it as a central management task to clearly tell employees what is expected of each individual. Trust is good but control is better. Organisations need clear rules and someone to make sure these are followed. Anything else would result in chaos, and the whole company would ultimately suffer.

Figure 22:
Two management cultures.

For this same reason, I will not be commenting on which approach is best. All that's important is to know that companies adopt one or the other. At one company, employees elect their boss, while at another, the boss is "presented" to them. At one company, all employees will have their own budgets, while at another, even a pen purchase needs to be approved by the CEO. At one company, employees set their own goals, while at another, these are set for them. But there are of course grey areas. As will be explained throughout the course of this book, this dimension of *autonomy* has a considerable influence over whether and how performance appraisals function in practice.

More autonomy – less direction and control

I was recently once again invited to a company, where I was told a story I felt I had heard many times before over the last few years. The company has been running for 60 years, and today employs 1,200 staff. It has been shaped by its sole founder, whose name also happens to be the trade name – a true patriarch and father of the company. In its long history, there has only ever been one person making the decisions. The patriarch has always been present, in person, any time, including on weekends and until late into the night. His business was his life. When he wasn't nearby, his presence would be felt in an almost metaphysical manner. The psychological contract between him and his employees was easy: You work for me, do what I say, and I'll take care of you. This worked out well for the employees. They didn't have much say, but they had security and, above all, they always knew where they stood. A few months ago, this original founder passed the company onto his son. Open-minded, eloquent, smart, and armed with an MBA, the son has now set about revamping the business. His motto is: "Allow responsibility". He wants the employees and managers to make decisions, take responsibility, and not do what they're told, but rather, what makes most sense. They should question things and challenge the allegedly "tried and tested". Threatened by global competition and intense pressure to innovate, he knows he has no other choice. Product complexity and market dynamics have become too vast for him to independently make the call as to what must be decided on where and how. You don't need me to tell you that this project – a cultural shift in the company – is hugely difficult. What matters to me is the fact that I am faced with such stories on almost a weekly basis. I know of lots of companies seeking to make the switch from direction and control to autonomy and self-regulation. But I don't know of a single one going the other way. Although I don't want to make any conclusive statement as to which approach is better, there is currently a clear trend towards more autonomy. This development has many faces, and appears in all kinds of forms. The example mentioned here is just one of countless others.

Three relevant dimensions

In addition to autonomy, however, there are two other relevant dimensions associated with the employee's relationship with the organisation, namely professional independence and the extent of lateral collaboration (see Figure 23). These two dimensions will be examined in detail below.

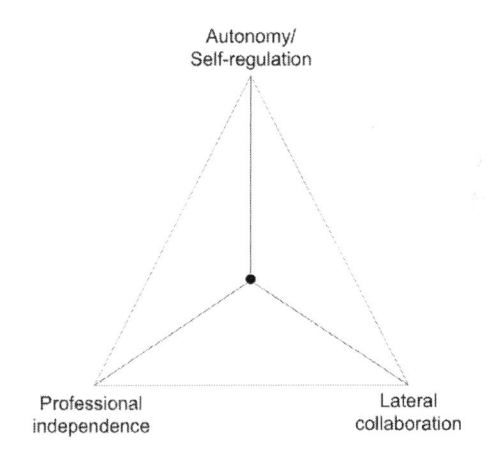

Figure 23:
An employee's relationship with his/her organisation.

Professional independence

The dimension of professional independence relates to this existential relationship between the individual and the employer. It describes the extent to which an employee is dependent on the organisation, his/her employer. Some labour market visionaries assume employee independence will increase significantly in future, which will also be reflected in new employment contracts. Professional independence is an extreme variant of autonomy. Companies are demonstrating a growing trend towards hiring self-employed people like freelancers (cf. Malone, 2004).

Professional independence has gained considerable prominence as part of the rising talent shortage. Organisations will become more and more dependent on employees rather than the other way around. This is simply due to the freedom of choice enjoyed by well educated, mobile employees. When it comes to recruitment, the word is that businesses are applying to candidates and not vice versa, which is why platforms like LinkedIn are gaining in relevance compared to classic careers platforms like Monster. The former platforms contain talent, the latter, jobs. Companies are increasingly adopting modern recruitment methods for certain divisions. They develop an employer brand, actively approach candidates, maintain loyalty ties with promising talent, and convey a positive applicant experience during the selection process[2].

Talent management teaches employers that they don't own high potentials. These high potentials are increasingly following their own personal life plans rather than a career path defined by the company. It is becoming more and more common for talent to consider themselves independent from their employer. Either their employer offers them prospects according to their personal career

---

[2]I described these approaches in detail in my book "Talent Relationship Management" (Trost, 2014).

and life plans, or they change employers. That's why it is no longer that easy to surprise a talented colleague with a promotion or otherwise have control over an employee's career as if he/she is the company's property. Employee loyalty is also becoming a serious challenge (Phillips & Edwards, 2009).

This is not the case in all divisions of a company, however. There are areas in which a company could at least theoretically allow itself to treat its employees as if they "belong" to it. These are areas in which staff replacements are quick and easy. But it's a different story in areas where an employer has problems covering often large-scale staffing requirements. These areas are also known as "bottleneck functions". And it is here that intensified conditions on the external labour market are becoming increasingly relevant.

This book operates on the assumption that the annual performance appraisal works differently in bottleneck functions compared to other functions. As detailed further on, the employees' professional independence creates particular dynamics, especially when it comes to evaluating performances and competencies. This topic has become a major issue in recent years, namely in relation to handling rare experts and establishing high-ranking careers. Take George, for example. George is an undisputed expert in database development. The company, his colleagues and his managers all know that if George were to leave, they'd be faced with a crisis. People like him are a rare commodity on the labour market – or at least they don't go around looking for jobs. And George knows this. After all, other companies often try to headhunt him. George is what could rightly be called a "nerd": technically brilliant, interpersonal relations don't interest him. He prefers to avoid people, meetings and informal encounters. He loves complex problems, and trying to solve them in peace. He doesn't need or want anything more. This is what he's good at; his social skills border on acute autism. And now comes the crucial question: How is the annual performance appraisal conducted with

George? Apart from the fact that George has considerable control over his goals due to his technical superiority over his manager, he also knows that not much can happen to him if not all his goals are achieved; his manager will still give him a relatively favourable evaluation. In an extreme case, his manager will adjust the competence or performance evaluation so that George receives the result he expects. Angering him with honest feedback, or even risking the employment relationship, appears to be the least appropriate option. Keeping George takes top priority.

Lateral collaboration

The classic line worker (if there is such a thing) works alone at his/her station. Many journalists and writers work alone. Teachers, taxi drivers and insurance brokers are usually also on their own. Some athletes practise individual sports, such as golfers. The same is true for soloists, sculptors, cabaret artists and the like. These people's performances are individual performances, and the results can be attributed to their own, individual work.

Conversely, there are people who operate in teams or as part of large networks. For example, semi-autonomous work groups have long found their way into modern production processes. Employees organise themselves, and are jointly responsible for more comprehensive components, or even for an entire product. Employees in knowledge-intensive areas work almost exclusively in projects and corresponding project groups. A team is now not simply a collection of employees doing similar things at the same location. Several teachers can hardly be called a team just because they work at the same school and in the same classes. A group of people only becomes a team if they pursue common aims, and achieve these through direct co-operation and communication with one another (Forsyth, 2014). A team is thus a closed unit with inter-dependent team members. In semi-autonomous work groups, for instance, teams are formed for the long term. Staff changes only occur in exceptional cases, e.g. if an employee moves to a different position internally or leaves the company. But some companies, like consultancy firms, also have changing teams, where a new project team is usually formed for each customer project. Even if some colleagues consistently work with one another due to their professional focus, the teams as a whole are variable and temporary. In an extreme case, temporary teams are constantly being re-formed using employees from many different company divisions, depending on availability and task, or the teams form themselves. In practice, these are known as "fluid teams". Organisations operating based on this principle are also called "network organisations". Even though there are hierarchical structures, the employees co-operate as needed, temporarily, and laterally across multiple disciplines and divisions.

In addition to autonomy and professional independence, this aforementioned *lateral collaboration* plays a key role as a third dimension in annual performance appraisals. The term "lateral collaboration" denotes the horizontal, often self-regulated co-operation between teams and employees of the same hierarchical level.

Is an individual target agreement advisable when employees render their services as teams? Should team members be evaluated based on standard competence criteria if the focus is simultaneously, and rightly, on diversity? Should managers at a network organisation be the ones evaluating employees if the internal customers are actually the better authorities? How do you plan individual personnel development measures in an arena of social learning? Questions like these raise initial doubts about the compatibility between a traditional annual performance appraisal and an environment of distinct, lateral co-operation.

The annual performance appraisal may be an instrument primarily suited to a company setup characterised by hierarchical separation, on any scale. We created *divisions*, thereby *dividing* up various sections of the company. Rarely is the meaning of a word illustrated so dramatically. We then split the work, and therefore the people responsible for the resulting tasks. The notion of sections in ever-diminishing units was the central principle in business management and organisation studies, designed to reduce complexity and control complex structures. And to ensure that every employee ultimately knew what he/she had to do in his/her role in order to contribute to the entity as a whole, the annual performance appraisal was born. The performance appraisal enabled organisations to break goals and tasks down, from top to bottom, into individual, bite-size chunks. Today, we can see that this hierarchical division has fulfilled its purpose: people and units which ideally work better together have been split from one another. Throughout the course of this book, we will further examine the issue of how the objectives of a performance appraisal comply with lateral co-operation, and whether there are any better alternatives.

Two opposing scenarios

The previous sections addressed three dimensions which describe the relationship between employees and their organisation, and which appear relevant in the context of the annual performance appraisal. Theoretically, we could now rearrange the possible characteristics of these three dimensions and identify a number of different scenarios. But we are deliberately refraining from doing so. It instead appears wiser to compare and contrast two extreme scenarios, and discuss the implications for the annual performance based on these. Figure 24 shows two different scenarios, A and B. The manner in which these two scenarios affect performance appraisals is examined below. To make things clearer, we'll look at the two alternatives for fictitious employees Adam (A) and Bianca (B).

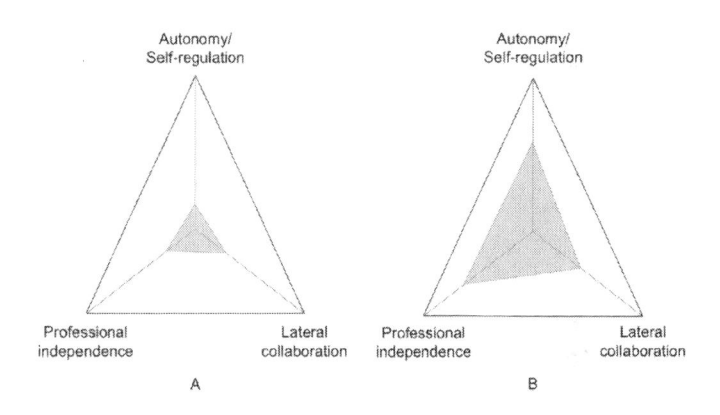

Figure 24:
Two sample scenarios of an employee's relationship with his/her organisation.

Adam (scenario A) is a financial planner for private clients at a bank with very little decision-making scope. The financial products he offers his customers are stipulated by a central authority, which also urges him to sell certain products ("product of the month"). Every offer and every contract over a specific financial threshold must be reviewed by his boss before anything is signed. His working hours are clearly regulated; his day begins at 8.15am and usually ends at 5.30pm. Friday afternoons from 3pm onwards are flexible. Adam is happy to have found employment at the bank. He doesn't see many other alternatives in the rural region he currently lives in with his family (Adam is 48 years old). Adam has very limited professional independence in this respect. Collaborations with others are just as scant. Although he has a lot to do with people as part of his job, he essentially works for himself. At best, he co-operates informally with colleagues when a difficult question about a new financial product, for example, needs to be quickly clarified.

Bianca (scenario B) is an automotive process engineer. Together with her colleagues, she works almost exclusively on development projects for customers – predominantly from the automotive supplier industry. She has huge decision-making scope. Apart from stipulated standards, defined customer expectations and cost frameworks, her team is responsible for deciding how solutions are developed, and what most technical solutions ultimately involve. Fixed working hours and timekeeping are rarities at her company. The team arranges things independently. In the end, solutions need to be delivered. How and when Bianca and her team complete this task is up to them. Most of the time, however, they are under deadline pressure, which is why almost all of them tend to work more than the hours stated in their employment contracts. Bianca is highly sought after on the labour market due to her expertise and experience. Competitors often approach her – in person or through social networks on the Internet. She could move to another company at any time, in some cases for a higher salary. Bianca not only works in a team, but is also very well networked within the company. She maintains functional, largely informal contact with colleagues in other relevant areas, such as sales. They come to agreements when this is deemed necessary for the parties involves.

When examining these two cases, readers will no doubt be thinking of their own personal examples. Let's now imagine how the annual performance appraisal is carried out in these two contexts. You don't need to be super smart to realise that Adam's will play out differently to Bianca's. I dare say this would still be true if the same instrument were used for both of them, or indeed even if both of them worked at the same company. There are many differences here. Firstly, the target agreement.

Self-set goals serve as motivation

Target agreement is often justified at a scientific level using the Locke and Latham goal-setting theory (1984), which essentially states that people with goals are more motivated than those without. The theory has long been researched, with a constant focus on the question of which conditions best reflect this basic assumption. The moderator variable of Commitment has emerged as one of the favourites. A goal only and primarily serves as motivation if the person gets behind this goal, feels intrinsically committed to the goal, and "embraces the goal". While this finding may seem banal, it has taken many years of research for this view to be backed up by science. Furthermore, one psychological finding with a similarly scientific base states that an intrinsic commitment to goals particularly exists if the affected persons have been actively involved in defining the goals, or were even largely responsible for this. If we additionally bear in mind that active, responsible goal-setting is only conceivable with a certain degree of decision-making scope, we reach the simple but important conclusion that motivation through objectives requires such scope. In our example, Bianca ("We will increase the efficiency of component X by 8%") will display greater motivation than Adam ("You will achieve a sales target of X thousand Euros over the coming year with this life insurance") through self-set goals.

It is worth noting here that goals are particularly relevant when there is a high degree of decision-making scope. At many companies, this scope is associated with flexible work structures, similar to that described in our practical example. Employees have no fixed working hours, and often no fixed places of work. In view of this, companies rightly place emphasis on employees committing to specific goals. How, when and where the relevant persons ultimately achieve these goals is up to them. In this sense, goals can constitute a basis for trust and business security.

Autonomous goals – autonomous learning

Performance appraisals now tend to discuss development goals as well as performance goals, addressing issues such as employability and the continuous adaptation of employee competencies to cater to the goal-related challenges. Here, too, the employees' decision-making scope is of great importance. It revolves around the central question of whether it is the company or the employees themselves who take responsibility for employee development.

If it is the employees who are responsible for their own development, this doesn't mean they are "abandoned" or left to their own devices here. It instead works on the assumption that employees know best when it comes to their needs and how these can be met. There are companies at which employees have their own continued education budgets. For example, they independently organise themselves into so-called "Communities of Practices", informal work groups designed to encourage members to learn from one another, among other things (cf. McDermott, Snyder & Wenger, 2002). So independent learning doesn't mean the company does nothing. It is instead about operating as an enabler to create a framework within which employees can independently fulfil this personal responsibility. We can assume that employees who set their own goals, or who at least have a considerable influence over these, are also responsible for their own development. It is difficult to imagine employees acting independently in relation to their future performance, but then being "imposed" with specific development measures top-down. This assumption also applies in a converse manner: an employee whose goals are set for him/her will rarely be consciously given responsibility to take care of his/her own relevant development measures – "In future, you will formulate quotes in English. Now see that you improve your language skills accordingly". However, we cannot discount the fact that this scenario does still exist, particularly at poorly managed companies.

Target agreement and performance evaluation in teams

The classic performance-appraisal approach of individually agreeing on development targets with dominant influence by the manager completely breaks down when employees not only have a high degree of decision-making scope (Bianca), but also operate in socially-networked teams. In these sorts of scenarios, modern companies in particular are increasingly adopting an approach based on the ideas of Peter Senge and the learning organisation (Senge, 1990). Employees learn – they cannot *not* learn – by working together every day on challenges important to them individually and the organisation as a whole. Learning together and optimising things at the company are inextricably linked. Individual, annual performance appraisals between employees and managers play virtually no role here. What counts is the continued, often independent exchange between colleagues in and between teams, based on challenges they deem relevant for themselves and in terms of the company.

Let's now come back to the two scenarios A (Adam) and B (Bianca) above. While an individual target agreement may certainly be suitable for Adam, Bianca would find it very odd. Bianca works in socially-networked project groups. Individually agreeing on performance targets would conflict with the collective aim of achieving project targets in co-operation with colleagues. In this sort of setting, individual target agreements may even lead to considerable disadvantages for the respective project group, as teamwork can only function successfully if the respective team members subordinate themselves to the overarching group targets, and put their individual goals second.

Individual, in-group performance evaluation is similarly problematic. As will be explained in detail in chapter 5, bosses need to think about alternatives to the top-down evaluation. Teams of course also have both stars (high-performing colleagues) and underperformers. Stars tend to want to be identified as such, and recognised accordingly. The question, however, is whether this evaluation should come from the direct manager (as is the case with the classic performance appraisal) or from colleagues within the respective team – a star is only a star if the others think so too.

Standardised requirements which prevent diversity

The majority of companies conducting performance appraisals apply standardised, quantitative processes. The idea in itself is quite simple. Employees are classified on multi-tiered scales by their direct managers using predefined criteria. Typical criteria include: Comprehension, co-operation with others, ability to work under pressure, punctuality, expertise etc. Particularly technocratic approaches compare these ratings with a target profile, identifying specific areas requiring development, coupled with suitable development measures. The dispute over the meaningfulness of these approaches goes back a long way, both in practice and science (cf. Murphy & Cleveland, 1995). And there's no end in sight. What matters here is to think about the extent to which individual, standardised skills and traits can play a role in a team setting. Teams are often successful because the mix of team-member skills is varied. It's about diversity. Four John Lennons would certainly not make the Beatles. It is common to find HR departments both championing standardised rating processes, and demanding diversity, without even noticing the conflict in their actions. In many cases, it is thanks to the proven lack of objectivity and validity associated with these rating processes that, despite being applied (incorrectly), a certain degree of diversity still manages to slip into work groups, ultimately contributing to their success.

In scenario A, it could well be wise to rate Adam's skills. He works in relative isolation. His successes are essentially of his own making. In this respect, it would be conceivable, at least theoretically, to define relevant competencies for him, and reflect on these in terms of his character. In Bianca's case, however, rating skills using standardised competence models makes much less sense.

Rare talents should receive better praise

Let's for a moment hypothesise that both Adam and Bianca put in comparable performances, each in their own role. Who will their respective managers rate better in the performance evaluation? Probably Bianca. Why? Because the organisation needs her. The organisation is more dependent on Bianca than Bianca is on her organisation. That doesn't mean Adam isn't needed. But, unlike Bianca, he has fewer options on the labour market, and thus has a lower degree of professional independence. Adam is dependent on his organisation, and his manager presumably knows this. The dynamics emerging here relate to simple, human needs for safety and esteem (middle levels of Maslow's hierarchy of needs). A manager will instinctively show greater recognition to an employee he/she urgently needs. In any case, he/she will find it harder to give a rare talent an evaluation perceived as negative by the employee concerned. On the other hand, a manager will be less hesitant to give negative feedback to an employee who seeks safety and is dependent on his/her organisation. We saw an example of this phenomenon earlier in this chapter with the latently autistic nerd, George.

Of particular importance here are employees in so-called bottleneck functions. Bottleneck functions are areas in which the company has great difficulty finding sufficient, qualified staff (Trost, 2014). In this respect, bottleneck functions are the direct consequence of the oft noticed and increasingly cited talent shortage. This talent shortage has a direct impact on how performance appraisals can or do operate. At this point, it is first necessary to highlight the perspectives on which classic performance appraisals and the associated evaluation process are based. In essence, the company – represented by the manager – is concerned with the extent to which the employee fits its ideal. Does the performance match expectations? Does he/she demonstrate the skills relevant to his/her job? Does his/her behaviour meet company-specific standards? This implicitly involves a power divide in which the manager and company adopt the stronger position. In times of talent shortages and employees who are difficult to secure and retain, this perspective is an illusion with (in some cases) disastrous consequences. It has, in fact, long been the sought-after employees who propose their own special requirements to their employers.

In summary

- We can distinguish between two extreme management philosophies – one based on power, instruction and control, and the other on trust, *autonomy and self-regulation*.
- Organisations are becoming increasingly dependent on their employees, rather than the other way around. Experienced employees are particularly *professionally independent* at expert organisations affected by talent shortages.
- Modern, knowledge-intensive companies are increasingly dominated by network organisations, team work and informal structures (*lateral collaboration*), while classic, hierarchical and work-sharing organisations are gradually being phased out.

- An employee's relationship with his/her organisation based on lateral collaboration, professional independence, autonomy and self-regulation has a huge impact on the manner in which the annual performance appraisal is/can be applied.

Hierarchical world – agile world

In order to be able to evaluate the practical possibilities of the annual performance appraisal, and discuss alternatives, we need to take into account relevant framework conditions as described in this chapter – task environment, and the employees' relationships with their managers and their organisation. We looked at aspects like dynamics, task uncertainty, autonomy, professional independence, manager roles etc. In theory, the various possible framework conditions result in a number of potential combinations. We could now discuss the annual performance appraisal at a theoretical level based on each combination, but this approach is inefficient and rather confusing. For this reason, I will only be outlining two extreme scenarios, each with contrary framework conditions for all dimensions addressed. We'll call these two extremes the *hierarchical* world and the *agile* world. This simplified distinction also appears appropriate, given that the dimensions examined here are not independent from one another. For example, autonomy is usually associated with a high degree of lateral collaboration. Partner-like management tends to be found more in an uncertain, dynamic task environment, while the classic boss implies less autonomy and less professional independence for employees.

The hierarchical world

The hierarchical world is reflected by highly conservative, traditional organisations and working environments. The employees' work is based heavily on the division of labour. The employees don't need to worry about how the individual tasks dovetail into one another; they just concentrate on their specific cog in the overarching mechanism. The dynamics between the various sections and tasks are consequently low. Task certainty is high, as the employees know, at all times, what they need to achieve, and how they are to go about it. There are binding job descriptions, procedural instructions, rules and standards in place for this. The dominant role of the managers in the hierarchical model is that of the boss. He/she makes decisions, and is on a different level to "his/her" employees. There is an authoritarian distance between the manager and the employees "below". The relationship is characterised by power. The employees are dependent on their organisation, and have very few other options on the labour market. In this respect, they are happy to have found work as employ*ees* of their employ*er*. They are urged to do what the organisation tells them. Decisions are made at the top and executed at the bottom. In this model, there is a degree of separation between thoughts and actions – the former are generated at the top, and the latter are performed down below. If the employee comes up with his/her own ideas, official channels must be followed, or hierarchical, centrally co-ordinated approaches such as in-house suggestions schemes are applied. The company takes full responsibility for employee development, and determines which development measures are relevant and necessary for the respective employees and employee groups. The working environment is also dominated by all kinds of controlling instruments. For instance, there are centrally designated working hours, coupled with corresponding timekeeping systems and fixed places of work. Working from home is only permitted when approved, and in compliance with strictly formulated conditions. The employees essentially work alone. Although they are structured into teams and departments, each employee is individually responsible for his/her own work. Real team work with joint targets, independent collaboration or communication, or a lateral co-operation across multiple departments hardly exists at an employee level.

The agile world

The agile world describes the other extreme. The task environment is highly uncertain. Employees work on projects whose results can only be estimated very vaguely. At best, there are priorities and limited time and financial resources. Right from the outset, the approach is never clear. The employees also work in a highly dynamic environment with distinct mutual dependences between tasks and departments, which is why it is difficult to evaluate the results of individuals or entire teams in isolation. Whatever is achieved is a joint effort. The employees are not only included in decision-making processes, but also enjoy a high degree of personal responsibility and autonomy in general. They are more familiar with what they do than their respective managers are. There are flexible working hours, and no central timekeeping. While the company does provide work premises, the employees are free to choose where they work (when possible). The employees are usually very highly qualified experts who are largely personally responsible for their development. They know best what they need in order to complete their tasks optimally. Self-controlled and informal in-team learning also plays a key role. Work is only performed in teams; any other approach would make it impossible to do justice to the projects' high degree of complexity and scope. Where necessary, the employees work proactively and in close consultation with adjacent departments – in some cases informally as a lateral collaboration. Managers usually adopt the role of coach or partner, and work on the same level as their employees (their colleagues). The employees know they are sought after on the labour market, and could join another company any time – and the managers are aware of this too.

Companies will tend to identify with one of these two extreme models, or perhaps slot in somewhere in between. Hybrid forms of course also exist. It is equally possible for these two different worlds to co-exist at the same company. While the Production division may adopt one model, Research & Development may follow the other. Figure 25 shows both the hierarchical and agile worlds, based on the framework conditions described in Chapter 4.

Framework condition	Hierarchical world	Agile world
Task certainty	High	Low
Task dynamism	Low	High
Dominant manager role	Boss	Partner/Coach
Autonomy/ Self-regulation	Low	High
Lateral collaboration	Low (Division of labour)	High (Teams, networks)
Professional independence	Low	High

Figure 25:
An overview of the hierarchical and agile worlds.

While the characteristics of an agile world are described here, they should not be misconstrued as a definition of agility. This section is not about defining agility in itself, nor is this book about agility. But glancing at the aforementioned characteristics, they will indeed reflect aspects associated with agility both in literature and practice (cf. Bernardes & Hanna, 2008; Kettunen, 2009).

Agile HR for added innovation and resilience

This comparison of the two worlds should not only be seen as a purely academic exercise, but also as an appeal or indeed a wake-up call to managing directors and HR professionals. For many years, I have considered it one of my main tasks to address and understand developments in company environments, and the associated implications for HR management. This has seen me increasingly confronted with the issue of "agile HR" in recent months. I am constantly asked in interviews about what I believe to be the most important HR development trends, and I have been ranking agility in number one spot for some time. This is no accident, because the challenge for greater innovation and adaptability is something of concern to a growing number of companies. It is usually labelled as resilience (cf. Gunderson & Pritchard, 2002; Conner, 1992). Resilience is understood here as being a system's ability to react to changes or problems, so as to return to a stable condition. In an increasingly dynamic world, I dare say this requirement has rarely been as important to organisations as it is today, and responsible decision-makers know this. Agility in turn addresses this ability. In other words, most resilient systems are agile systems. One of the most resilient systems we are familiar with nowadays is the human nervous system and brain. This is more comparable with a network organisation than a hierarchy of superordinate and subordinate nerve cells. For example, the brain doesn't contain one specific super nerve cell which, like a CEO, makes all ultimate decisions.

Given the above, it is no surprise that, even in an HR context, more and more people are raising the question of how flexibility and resilience can be boosted. We soon realise that it's about time old, familiar HR approaches described in textbooks some 20, 30 years ago are scrutinised. Many HR approaches are highly technocratic, and revolve around a hierarchical understanding based on the assumption of a stable world. This view has already been addressed and critically examined at several points throughout this book.

The strategic priority of maximum creative innovation ties in closely with the resilience challenge. Innovation requires a company to be able to continuously anticipate, and indeed even shape, market developments. Technologies and products considered cash cows today could be out-of-date and superseded tomorrow. History is littered with examples of budding and dying technologies, for example in the fields of mobility, IT, energy and communication (cf. Christensen, 1997). For businesses, innovation means consistently reinventing themselves and their products, and making them marketable. This has comparatively little to do with structural and process stability. Here, too, we are faced with the question of what the right HR responses to this particular challenge are. While this is a very broad and exciting topic in general, we will now primarily focus on the central matter of whether the annual performance appraisal, as we know it, can withstand these developments and requirements, and whether this instrument is a suitable HR response to modern-day issues.

In summary

- We can distinguish between two extreme working worlds: the hierarchical and the agile world.

- The *hierarchical world* is dominated by a high degree of labour division with clearly defined tasks, and by a management style in which the employees do what the "boss" tells them. Employees are dependent on their organisation, work individually, and have hardly any scope for their own actions or decisions.
- In the *agile world*, the tasks are highly dynamic, and characterised by great uncertainty in processes and results. The dominant management role is that of a coach and/or partner. The employees have considerable professional independence, and work informally in teams and networks, enjoying a high degree of personal responsibility, and controlling their own actions.
- More companies are moving from a hierarchical to an agile world than the other way around.
- Classic HR management approaches are based on a hierarchical view, and are hardly compatible with an agile world. This largely also applies to annual performance appraisals.

5. Possibilities and limits

Does the annual performance appraisal help us understand each individual employee's and entire teams' needs for learning in an agile environment? Can managers in a hierarchical world identify their employees' potentials? Are managers in these systems even the right authorities? Do goals also serve as motivation when employee tasks involve a high degree of process and results certainty? These are the sorts of questions which will be addressed in this chapter. The collective, central issue revolves around the notion of: For which types of benefits can the annual performance appraisal act as a suitable instrument in its traditional form? We will be looking at different framework conditions here, as addressed in Chapter 3. This chapter will also suggest some alternatives which may help meet the conventional benefit requirements in agile and hierarchical worlds.

Chapter three of this book presented logic for tackling annual performance appraisals in four stages. Once the goals/intended benefits are clear, the framework conditions should be examined, and this was done in the previous chapter. The next steps involve finding a suitable instrument and assessing its design. This chapter primarily revolves around the third step – that of the suitable instrument. And since this book is about annual performance appraisals, it focuses on this instrument in its traditional form.

Chapter 3 already briefly outlined the various benefits of performance appraisals. These benefits will be re-examined now, and discussed in terms of their practical achievability through annual performance appraisals. In doing so, it becomes clear that some benefits can indeed be partly achieved or supported with performance appraisals, while for others, the appraisals play no role, or at least not the role usually associated with them. In some cases, it also becomes apparent that different benefit aims can conflict with one another. As already mentioned, this system is often overwhelmed with expectations regarding benefits, which is why Neuberger (1980) rightly mentions the oft cited "jack of all trades" so many companies strive for. We will now try to systematically iron out these issues from a neutral, undogmatic, but no less critical perspective.

Rewarding the best

High-performing employees want to be recognised as such and treated accordingly. Companies claiming to be performance-oriented rightly assume that this requires a differentiation in performance. In view of this argument, staff evaluations at many companies are seen as givens, to the extent that they are not questioned enough. Things all seem very simple and obvious at first. Employees are distinguished by their performance, and must therefore also be treated differently. Period.

Performance as a continuum

In practice, a distinction is often made between A, B and C-players, or there are at least rough evaluation categories under which the employees are classified. This is implicitly based on the assumption of a performance continuum (see Figure 26).

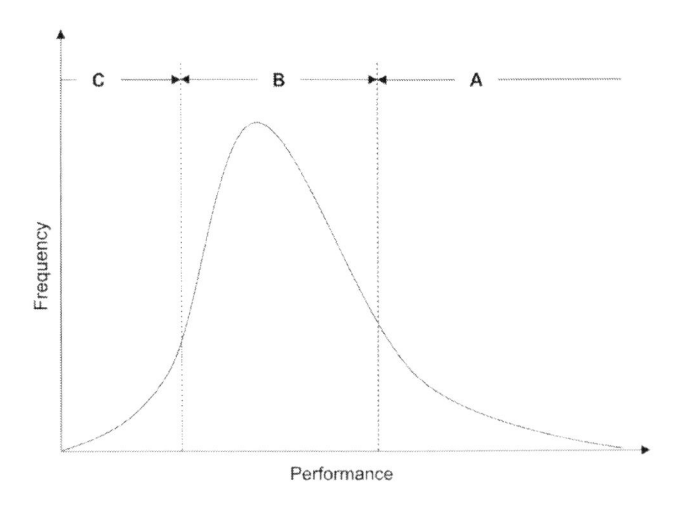

Figure 26:
An assumed performance distribution[3].

This assumption misleads us to look in both directions – negative (C) and positive (A) – at the same time and using the same instrument – an approach not without problems. In his

---

[3] If companies don't select the employees at random, but instead require a certain level of aptitude, the performance distribution should never be normal, but rather skewed to the left, as in this figure.

152

autobiography "Jack: Straight From The Gut", the former CEO of General Electric, Jack Welch, describes himself as a gardener who goes through his garden with a watering can and clippers. He waters the strong ones, and cuts off the weak. What sounds very romantic here often has brutal consequences in practice. What is helpful about this metaphor, however, is the idea that two different instruments are needed to deal with the high-performing and underperforming employees. This applies to the evaluation itself, but also to the resulting outcomes. A is no more the opposite of C, than health or physical fitness is the opposite of illness. Illness is not the negative end of a health scale, but rather an exceptional circumstance requiring special measures at a specific time. This section therefore only addresses how the best employees can be identified. Identifying underperforming employees is discussed separately in the next section.

Let's now assume a team includes two employees, A and B. Both officially have the same job, work in the same environment, and report to the same manager. The only difference between A and B is that A performs better than B (as indicated by the letter). B's performances are just average. Both employees are aware of their differences in performance. So why should a company officially distinguish between A and B? There are essentially two answers to this: (1) Because A needs to be specially rewarded for this and (2) because A could be a potential candidate for further development measures. We will now only be addressing point 1 – specially rewarding high-performing employees.

As already mentioned in chapter 3, performance-based payments are not totally beneficial. On the one hand, we know that variable remuneration can weaken employees' intrinsic motivation. This is known as the overjustification effect. On the other hand, however, we also know that not rewarding performance can demotivate high-performing employees.

In general, it is inevitable for companies to distinguish between performances, and there is no question that giving high-performing employees special treatment is a good idea. This attitude prompts companies to leave it to the direct managers to identify the high-performing employees, for it is argued that this is an inherently managerial task. Who else should be responsible for it?

"You're an A-player to me"

At the end of chapter 4, we distinguished between two extreme worlds – the hierarchical and the agile world (cf. Figure 25). A general assumption can be made here that a classic, annual evaluation of individual employees conducted by the direct manager only works in the hierarchical model. This approach is more problematic in the agile model. Many statements have already been made in this respect regarding the framework conditions in chapter 4:

- If the employees' tasks are highly dynamic, i.e. the individual performance is dependent on the performances of others, this cannot be assessed in isolation by one single manager. If an employee is a high-performer, this is primarily because the system as a whole is conducive to achieving certain, outstanding results.
- In an uncertain task environment, it is virtually impossible to articulate objective, long-term expectations in the form of binding targets – which significantly limits the possibilities for a performance evaluation later on.
- If a manager is acting in the role of a coach or partner, there is a risk of a conflict of roles. A coach or partner cannot simultaneously be a judge with his/her employees, making future-relevant judgements about an employee, and documenting and forwarding these to a central authority, such as the HR department. The natural

consequences are (largely invalid) inflationary evaluations skewed in a positive direction.
- In knowledge-intensive areas primarily employing experts, direct managers will rarely be able to conduct a valid evaluation of an individual expert's performance. They do not have enough technical knowledge to understand what the expert does, and what can be appropriately expected of him/her.
- Performances are increasingly becoming the work of teams. "Placing individual employees on a pedestal", so to speak, runs the risk of demotivating the rest of the team. This may result in rivalries and dysfunctional behavioural patterns, which ultimately reduce the performance of the team as a whole.
- When employees work together in teams, their individual performances can only be evaluated if this individual performance can be identified. But in a dynamic, uncertain task environment, this is rarely possible, or only possible to a limited extent.
- Managers will give more positive evaluations of employees they urgently need and on whom they are dependent. They naturally tend to indirectly use – and indeed abuse – a performance evaluation as an employee retention tool.

This list of arguments is overwhelming. It demonstrates that, while identifying high-performing employees is certainly one option, naivety in this respect is highly problematic, particularly in an agile world. In a hierarchical world, on the other hand, many of the aforementioned arguments lose their relevance. If tasks are clearly definable, the working conditions and requirements stable, labour divided and departments subdivided, if the manager acts as a boss, and the employees are more dependent on the organisation than vice versa, the classic form of individual performance evaluations conducted by the direct manager may still work, to a degree.

In recent years, I have come across a number of companies where the dominant approach is equivalent to what is described here as the agile world. At many of these companies, however, diligent HR professionals have tried to introduce a classic version of the performance appraisal. So what happens? The managers don't have anything against it, since differentiating between employees seems like a good idea. And the reasons for this were outlined earlier on. The headaches come when it's time to conduct the employee evaluations, e.g. at the start of a year, and advise the employees of the results before HR hear about it. And as these managers are rarely psychologists, it is difficult for them to articulate the critical points listed above. The silent suspicion that something is amiss with this system is also suppressed, because the company officially equates fulfilling the evaluation duty with "good management".

What now? Identifying A-players in an agile world

Ever since I have been more intensively focusing on the topic of performance appraisals, I utilise every opportunity to ask high-ranking managers in particular about their opinions on this. A former CEO of a leading global IT company recently gave me the curt response of "A company is really only performance-oriented if it conducts performance evaluations". Fine. But the question is how this performance focus, and the associated evaluation, is implemented. This CEO wanted to give the impression of looking at the bigger picture, which CEOs often do in order to convey consequences. I want to take things even further: A company is only performance-oriented if the employees speak openly about their performance within the team, instead of banishing the topic to the confidential silence of an annual performance appraisal.

While a top-down evaluation is common and indeed feasible in the hierarchical model, a mutual employee evaluation should be considered in agile settings. We talk about *peer ratings* in this context: Employees giving each other grades, points, badges or similar, and adding a few words to justify their decision. Evaluations by internal or even external customers are also conceivable in an agile world. The process may be conducted anonymously, openly, or even in groups. This alternative can sometimes of course also be considerably dynamic. Here, too, it is crucial to make the instrument clear and unambiguous to the employees, and clearly explain why it is being implemented. We see a major difference between whether a peer rating is carried out in order to learn from one another and clarify any conflicts/expectations or whether it serves to define variable salary components. It functions as one or the other – but not both simultaneously.

To avoid demotivation, an agile setting should focus on the principle that an A-player in a team is only an A-player if the others think so too. A second principle in an agile world involves the manager rejecting the role of sole judge. Peer rating may once again be a suitable solution here.

All these ideas give the impression that it would be unnecessary for a manager to conduct an employee evaluation in an agile model. The practical recommendation is a different story. A manager who fulfils his/her responsibility as a coach or partner will go through the peer ratings in a separate meeting with the employee. Possible questions asked by the manager could be:

- Do you feel the evaluations are an accurate reflection of you?
- What particularly surprised you and why?
- What does the feedback mean to you?
- What will you be working on in future?

In an agile setting, however, these reviews will only be held at the employee's request – a principle consistent with the notion of his/her personal responsibility. Neither the manager nor the HR department will be able to force him/her into this. While the employee's ultimate evaluation is forwarded to the HR department in order for the variable salary to be established, the results of these reviews will remain solely with the employee, who should be the primary customer thereof.

In summary

- An individual evaluation of employees working in teams, whose task environment is highly dynamic, does not appear advisable.
- Managers acting in the role of coach, partner or enabler avoid formally evaluating their employees.
- In an agile world, employees are only A-players if their colleagues and customers think so too.

Addressing the weak

Companies should not only be familiar with and recognise their high-performing employees; they should also keep an eye on their underperforming staff. This applies to both hierarchical and agile models.

Performance first, the person second

While they can be called anything from low-performers and underperformers to the more cynical "dead wood" or even "warm bodies", we'll stick with the term "underperforming employees". In order to examine this issue more closely, let's forget the annual performance appraisal for a moment, and look at the manner and frequency with which underperforming employees are/should be addressed. This will help explain what the annual performance appraisal focuses on in this context, and what it doesn't. Any specific case laws will be disregarded, since this issue knows no national borders. Figure 27 shows a graph of the typical trend.

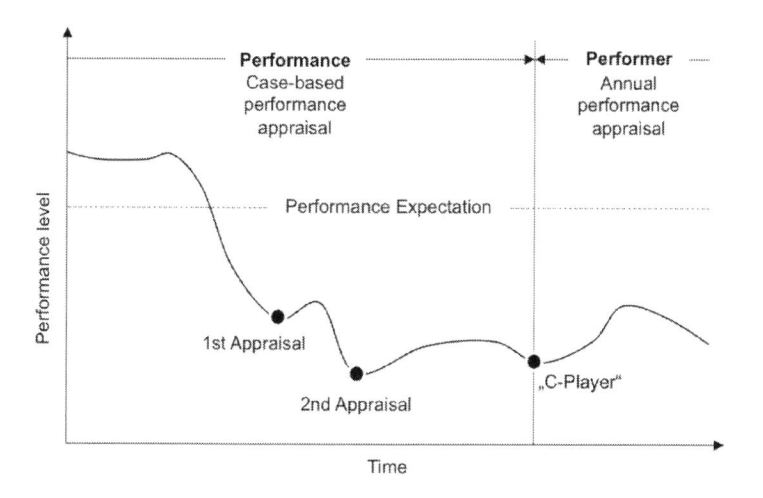

Figure 27:
Dealing with underperforming employees.

Figure 27 shows the performance trend of a fictitious employee over time, as well as the expected performance level. As illustrated by the curve, the employee visibly drops below the expected level, and remains there. If this sort of performance dip is noticed, it is generally a good idea, as a manager, to conduct an initial, case-based appraisal to discuss the situation with the employee, compare self-assessments and external assessments, and try to attain a joint understanding of the problem. It is usually at this point that the "Want to", "Can do" and "Allowed to" dimensions are examined, and relevant measures derived. As a result of this initial appraisal, the employee remains under "constant monitoring". Assuming the employee's performance does not improve, a second, third or fourth appraisal is held. At some point, the first warning may be issued. Up to this point, the actions taken with the underperforming employee have been focused on his/her *performance*. This is the subject of the discussions. After a certain stage, however, this changes, and the focus shifts from merely the performance to also include the employee himself/herself – the *performer*, who is labelled a "C-player". Possible solutions are considered before things get to this point. The environment, tasks, qualifications and motivation are all taken into account. But once an employee is "officially" branded a C-player, *he/she* becomes the problem, and it is more a question of what to do with the person themselves, rather than his/her performance issues.

Unlike case-based appraisals, the annual performance appraisal primarily addresses this final aspect, the identification of C-players. Once a year, all employees are classified under various performance categories, and many fall into that of "underperforming employees". This is not about feedback or an opportunity for the employee to learn something. That's not what this approach is designed for. Nor is it about management by objectives. That doesn't tend to work with this type of annual performance appraisal. And unlike case-based appraisals, the annual performance appraisal can be harmful when it comes to helping underperforming employees out of their slump. It is usually conducted too late for this, as demonstrated below.

Waiting 'til it's too late

Most managers who have had to conduct classic performance appraisals throughout their career will presumably be familiar with this typical situation: An employee is known to be one of the underperformers. The other employees in the team or department see it too. It's obvious. The employee regularly arrives too late, rarely takes the initiative, does not deliver on his/her promises, makes mistakes, etc. Anyone reading this will no doubt be reminded of a past or present colleague. It will soon be January, the time for performance appraisals. That's the official moment when people "lay (or have to lay) their cards on the table". In order for the manager to secure his/her own position, a list of all recent offences is compiled (since there had been no time to keep a daily diary). The employee will respond in an even more perplexed manner if he/she has put in a particular effort in the weeks prior to the imminent performance appraisal to ensure he/she obtains a positive evaluation. This is sometimes known as the "Santa Claus effect" – similar to when children behave extra well in the lead-up to Christmas to ensure they receive presents from Santa.

While we certainly must not have too much sympathy for the affected employee here, the situation does have a degrading element to it. Professional management means addressing performance weaknesses as soon as they become acute; not waiting for the annual performance appraisal. As already mentioned, health is not the opposite of illness, and poor performance is not the opposite of outstanding performance, even if it seems that way at first glance. It is important to ensure that poor performance is not misconstrued as an illness here – the analogy is simply used here as a means of clarification. We treat illnesses as soon as they arise; we don't wait until our next check-up. From this, we can conclude that the *annual* performance appraisal is not a suitable approach when it comes to dealing with specific employees' performance problems. The general rule of thumb is that a performance appraisal should never involve surprises. Anything that has not already been said beforehand should not be brought up at the annual review. It is a completely different story for the aforementioned *case-based* performance appraisals, which are conducted whenever appropriate. This rightly raises the question as to why companies ask all managers to identify underperforming employees during their annual performance appraisals.

Dismissal lists?

These thoughts lead us to an extremely critical point relating to conventional practice. As already mentioned on numerous occasions, one of the key components of the annual performance appraisal is to assign employees to performance categories. One of these is category C: Low-performers, or underperforming employees. Since the annual performance appraisal is conducted as a company-wide exercise, a list of all C-players emerges once a year. It is indirectly based on the performance evaluation, which of course also includes categories A and B. The former has already been discussed in the previous section. It's not the main point of focus here. What does require closer examination is the comprehensive identification of C-players at one common time during the year. Most HR professionals initially won't think twice about this approach. It is so prevalent that it hardly raises any eyebrows. Whenever performance is evaluated once a year – a line of action which is hardly questioned -, there will always be employees whose performances are rated poorly. So what is the problem? There are in fact some important reasons why these practices should be viewed with great scepticism. But first let's look at the common arguments put forward by HR and/or the management:

- "Once a year, we want to know who the underperforming employees are at the company, so necessary measures can be taken for those concerned."
- "We want to get our managers to name their underperforming employees at least once a year, otherwise the company as a whole runs the risk of ignoring the problem – something which we neither want, nor can afford."
- "We want our employees to know that poor performance is unacceptable. We encourage a performance-oriented culture, and do all possible to actively counter inadequate performances."
- "If we know who is putting in poor performances over a longer period of time, we will also know who at this company is not worthy of a pay increase or promotion."
- "We need to centrally record and document underperformances to ensure we can act in a legally sound manner if things get serious (which we of course hope does not happen)."

Anyone subscribing to these points has an extremely hierarchical way of thinking. In these cases, it is the senior management (flanked by HR), not the lower-level managers, teams or employees themselves, which bears responsibility for employee performances or non-performances. Higher authorities are the customers of the performance evaluation here, not the actual party concerned. This results in "dismissal lists", kept in the drawers of superior decision-makers. None of this has anything to do with feedback. It in fact tends to impede honest, eye-to-eye feedback. The most critical point, however, is the fact that neither underperforming employees nor their managers or teams are helped, because large-scale lists like these, created just *once* a year, are not sufficiently synchronised with individual needs. They usually arrive too late, as already discussed. In the end, the comprehensive, annual identification of underperforming employees can only involve terminating relations with said employees as part of an annual "clean-up", or lowering variable salaries. This approach would be inappropriate for anything else.

It's all about positioning

As a professor and university lecturer, I'm used to a similar approach: At the end of the semester, all students sit an examination, and anyone not meeting expectations fails. It's as simple as that. All participants know the rules. Not once have I ever received feedback from a student telling me this is somehow brutal or unfair. Conversely, we professors of course also strive to explain performance expectations as clearly as possible, and set appropriate standards when evaluating students. In this respect, the university, like the entire education system, is very hierarchical – the knowledgeable lecturers on the one side, and the learning students on the other. There are leaders and there are those being led – top and bottom. One group has the power, the other does not.

This approach is certainly also feasible for businesses. There are clear performance expectations and goals. Those who repeatedly fail to reach or fulfil these fail the annual appraisal, and can either leave the company or accept low, variable salaries. If all this is communicated cleanly and transparently, and all participants are aware of the rules, there is nothing initially wrong with this approach. The identification of C-players as part of annual performance appraisals is perfectly suited to this. And that is fine for the time being.

It is, however, important to critically examine matters when HR asks all managers to identify underperforming employees once a year, justifying this by saying it's about feedback, learning or even eliminating individual performance weaknesses. This is a romanticised notion of a method purely and essentially designed to get rid of C-players or penalise them financially. But if all this were not actually stipulated, identifying underperforming employees would be simply irrelevant. What we are left with is great uncertainty and a bitter taste in the mouth.

No babysitting in an agile world

In practice, formal performance evaluations are often justified by the fact that managers always make judgements of their employees, whether they want to or not. Because whenever people interact, they cannot *not* judge each other. And since social judgements always have consequences, it is implicitly or explicitly a matter of fairness and mutual openness to make judgements as objectively as possible, particularly when they are negative. This argument certainly has merit, and has already been discussed sufficiently elsewhere. We should, however, think about who makes judgements when, about whom, and which judgements are ultimately relevant to whom. While it is primarily the manager who is interested in, and who officially evaluates, the employee's performance in the hierarchical model, in team setups this is mostly the task of the team members, internal and external customers, and even the employees themselves. In an agile world, it is the employees who bear responsibility for the success of their co-operations.

Many years ago, social researchers at the University of St Gallen used victorious sports teams to examine what successful teams do differently to those less successful (Jenewein & Heidbrink, 2008). They also examined the Alinghi sailing team, winners of the America's Cup. One strategy which emerged from the research results was the "No baby-sitting strategy": if one or more team members are not happy with the performance of another team member, it is their job, not the team leader's, to resolve this problem or conflict. In hierarchical worlds, it's usually a different story. If an employee doesn't toe the line, the boss attends to this personally – who else?

This approach in an agile environment is a typical way of handling underperforming employees. Let's imagine a development team whose joint task is to develop a complex logistics solution for a customer. The team consists of seven members from different fields, including a team leader. So what happens if one employee's performance is consistently below average in an agile context? The first problem is the fact that, in an agile environment, expectations are difficult to define due to the low degree of process and results certainty associated with the tasks. Classic approaches in which targets are agreed on individually and regularly with employees, and are then used to evaluate an employee's performance/target achievement, reach their limits here. Tasks tend to be discussed in short cycles, and agreed on jointly. Overarching goals and milestones affect the team as a whole rather than just the individual. But this only really poses a problem when we tackle the situation using classic, textbook approaches. In real life, team members can quickly tell when an employee is falling below collective expectations. People can usually sense it. There is initially no need to worry about identifying weak performance here. If this scenario arises, it normally results in conflicts, frustration and bad vibes. In an agile world, it is the team's task to resolve this problem together, moderated by the team leader. If things go well, the team leader conducts what is known as a case-based appraisal with the employee concerned – even though this name is not always used in real life.

If none of this helps, and the affected employee's performance does not improve despite intensive efforts by the manager and the entire team, his/her social environment will react. While the problem of underperforming employees is gradually scaled upwards in a hierarchical world so that a central authority can reflect on the consequences, it is the system itself which is the problem in an agile environment. The employee is repelled, to a certain extent. In the example used here, the colleagues of the employee concerned will distance themselves from him/her. The employee may be met with mistrust. In any case, the degree of interpersonal acceptance is reduced. This is a normal sociopsychological process. It's how friendships end, couples break up, and groups disband. New relationships are built. The affected employee will take action himself/herself, perhaps voluntarily leaving the team or even the company, which may particularly be the case if he/she has alternative career options. This all happens without said employee officially being identified as a C-player at any point through a formal process such as the annual performance appraisal.

To trained HR professionals or workers' councils reasonably familiar with labour laws, the aforementioned scenario may sound very haphazard or even improper. The notion of leaving staff members and teams to handle underperforming employees seems strange. It raises the fear that employees may be left alone and potentially treated unfairly, and that anything that happens will be precarious and unstable in terms of ethics and labour law. However, those employees and managers familiar with agile framework conditions will be well versed in situations like those mentioned above, and will be able to recount numerous cases which, while painful, were still handled ethically.

In summary

- Case-based performance appraisals address performance. Annual performance appraisals address the performer.

- Case-based performance appraisals are often a good idea in the event of underperforming employees. Annual performance appraisals are not conducted in sync with the acute problem.
- Annual, formal identification of underperforming employees only makes sense if the company wishes to dismiss the identified employees, or reduce their variable salary.
- In an agile world, the employees, teams and managers are the ones responsible for dealing with underperforming employees.

Identifying talent

One of the best, most important ideas of HR management is to identify talented employees as early as possible in order to prepare them for key positions down the track. This is known as talent management. Employees identified as talent, high potentials, future managers, top talent, stars or heroes usually receive various forms of support and grooming over the years, ranging from coaching, mentoring and action learning, to part-time MBA courses (cf. Conger, 2010). Most importantly, however, they are trusted with particularly challenging tasks and projects, known as "stretch roles". This also includes secondments abroad, assisting the management board, and even acting as representatives at a higher level. Or else talent can be left to do whatever they enjoy doing. They are given trust, freedom and the necessary means. This is all preceded by the identification of talent.

Since the late '90s, driven by bestsellers like "The War for Talent" (Michaels, Handfield-Jones & Axelrod, 2001) or the example of Jack Welch at General Electric, high potentials have been determined based on a joint assessment of performance and potential (Bartlett & McLean, 2006). This involved nothing more specific than the direct manager evaluating both the performance and potential components. It is still common practice at many companies, even though the actual approaches vary. Below, we will therefore be examining the central question of the role which can be played here by the manager, and particularly the annual performance appraisal, and that which cannot.

Evaluating potential

There are many different views on what is known in practice as "potential". The consensus is that potential describes a person's tendency to develop well beyond his/her current skill level. If, for example, a young athlete is said to have "potential", it means he/she has the ability to improve greatly over the coming years (Joch, 1992). Potential is a hypothetical in this respect. At companies, there are two distinct views here. Absolute potential, for example, means that an employee is recognised as having the capacity to achieve a certain level within the company at some point (e.g. managing director, general manager), regardless of his/her current level. Relative potential, on the other hand, means that an employee's capacity is evaluated relative to his/her current position: does the employee have the potential to fulfil a role two levels above his/her current level over the next five years?

Nowadays, relatively reliable psychometric tests can be conducted to assess performance dimensions such as intelligence or lasting personal dispositions like personality. Performance can also be classified based on framework conditions and task type. But what about potential? As already mentioned, potential is a future-oriented, hypothetical factor. Estimating potential means predicting someone's possible development, which is difficult by nature. One way of broaching this issue is to examine seemingly successful approaches from the business or sporting world. The latter has, in recent decades, particularly witnessed great efforts to predict whether, for example, six-year-old children will turn into competitive swimmers at an international level more than ten years down the track (cf. Joch, 1992). If we now pool all positive and visibly successful approaches for identifying potential together, we end up with a very simple picture (cf. Silzer & Curch, 2009). There appear to be three quite obvious dimensions suitable for such predictions: performance to date, motivation, and personality:

- *Performance to date.* Has an employee's performance developed well above average in recent years? Has the employee demonstrated outstanding learning abilities in various areas?
- *Motivation.* Is the employee enthusiastic about what the company does? Does he/she love what he/she does so much that he/she would (theoretically) do it for nothing? Is the employee not only prepared, but also hungry, for new challenges?
- *Personality.* Does the employee behave in a mature, moral manner? Is he/she stable in terms of the principles underlying his/her decisions? Can the employee be trusted to act as a role model for others?

Anyone looking for a standardised process here will be disappointed. These criteria can only occasionally be applied in the employee's respective context. Outstanding employees indeed often stand out from the crowd, which, on the one hand, makes matters more manageable – including for untrained managers. On the other, however, identifying talent requires the employee to work in a task environment matching his/her talent. We see this in everyday life. If, for example, ambitious parents force their son Justin to take ballet classes, his true talent as a footballer may never be identified. There are probably more undiscovered child prodigies around the world than discovered, because they have never been given the opportunity to prove their talent. Similar scenarios exist at businesses too.

The manager as a talent scout

I know of companies where managers are urged to classify their employees directly using a Performance Potential Grid. At other companies, the managers indicate whether or not they consider an employee to have great potential by merely ticking the relevant box during the annual performance appraisal. This simple act of box-ticking results in the employee being examined more closely in a subsequent step. This usually takes place in so-called "talent reviews" or "talent conferences", where the managers from a larger unit decide who will be treated as a high potential in future and who won't (Dowell, 2010).

In practice, however, we are increasingly seeing that the direct manager alone is not the right authority to be deciding on an employee's or high potential's further progression. There are several reasons for this:

- A direct manager is hardly capable of assessing whether an employee has the potential to fulfil a position the manager himself/herself has never reached. The target positions of a high potential are above the level of the direct manager. In the same way, a coach in a lower league cannot assess or decide which of his players has the capacity to achieve long-term success in a higher league in which the coach himself has never played in.
- If talent management is to work properly, it must be clear, right from the time a high potential is identified, which possible forms of assistance will be offered to him/her, provided the employee himself/herself agrees to it. In any case, the company must be willing, at the time of identification, to significantly invest in the employee, e.g.

in the form of international secondments or by assigning him/her learning-intensive, challenging tasks and projects. This investment very rarely comes from the direct manager.
- A direct manager often lacks the motivation to put his/her "own" staff in the mix for higher positions for fear of losing them. While this motivation can be boosted – usually through a corresponding target agreement -, it frequently conflicts with the manager's quest to achieve his/her own business targets. And the manager's personal obligation is understandably higher than his/her obligation to the company.
- The last point ties in closely with the employee's dependence on his/her direct manager's assessment. The direct manager becomes a bottleneck for the employee. If a manager does not consider an employee to have any potential, the employee's chances of career progression may (wrongly) be halted.
- Evaluating performance is a highly challenging task for any manager. It becomes even more so when evaluating potential, not least due to its hypothetical nature. So there is a realistic risk of managers ultimately being out of their depth.
- Whether or not high potentials are elevated to top positions after receiving the relevant assistance is usually determined by executive managers. Practice has shown here that trust in the respective candidate is primarily what counts when filling a top position. In this respect, the focus when appointing a candidate should be on whether the decision-maker, not just the direct manager, has confidence in a high potential.

These points indicate that the direct manager cannot play a key role in identifying talent. The suitability of the annual performance appraisal as an instrument in this case is also highly questionable. Figure 28 once again illustrates selected, relevant scenarios. It shows the relationship between employee, manager, target position and decision-maker from a traditionally hierarchical view.

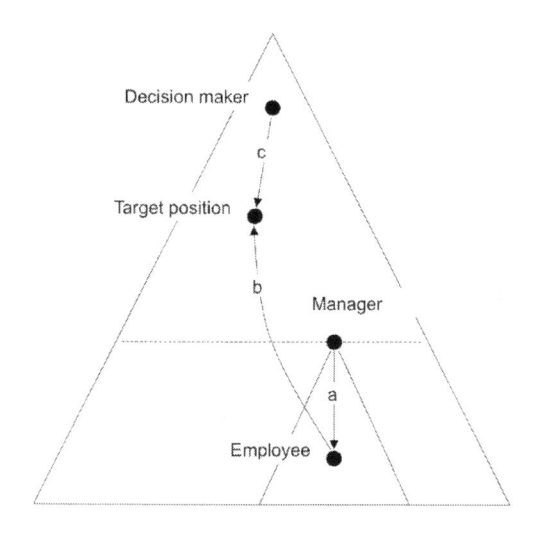

Figure 28:
The manager identifies talent.

We can see here that the direct manager can only take responsibility for a limited space (the small triangle). He/she cannot and should not identify an employee as a talent (a) because the employee's path to the target position (b) continues above the manager's area of influence, and it is ultimately the decision-maker situated above the target position (c) who fills the target position.

Talent managers

Hierarchical organisations have a way out of the aforementioned problem which, according to their own observations, is becoming increasingly popular. I recently came across one of many examples in the form of a global logistics company. This company has what is known as a talent manager, who reports directly to the CEO. He himself held a managerial position for many years, enjoys the full confidence of the executive board, and has excellent people skills, which he develops and applies with great enthusiasm. All high potentials at the company are selected with his input, as he adopts the role of coach and advisor. He further describes his job as follows:

> I spend the whole year travelling the world, speaking with high potentials and managing directors. I'm constantly trying to understand the internal needs, as well as the abilities, maturity level and preferences, of our most talented people. I arrange opportunities for internal development, because we believe our high potentials particularly learn through challenges faced in areas new to them. I'm the first port of call whenever a vacancy arises. So I'm not only an internal talent manager, mentor and coach, but also an internal executive search consultant of sorts.

This is based on the principle which states that talent should be identified at the same level where long-term decisions on high potentials are made, whether it be in relation to assistance measures or the filling of relevant target positions. More and more companies are introducing the aforementioned *talent managers*, who co-ordinate and often significantly influence the processes for identifying and supporting talent. As shown in the example above, these people have already been able to successfully gain experience in top positions, and enjoy maximum trust from the relevant decision-makers. Most of these talent managers report directly to the CEO.

So what would be a feasible scenario for identifying talent in a hierarchical context? The critical point is the fact that internal selection of high potentials is not a task performed by the direct manager, but rather always with the active involvement of a talent manager and higher ranking manager. As the direct manager is closest to the employee, he/she is the one who brings the employee into the mix, and discusses this employee's suitability with the aforementioned authorities. Only then is the employee informed of the outcome, provided it is positive. If the direct manager, talent manager and senior manager *don't* agree on the respective candidate's suitability as a high potential, the employee is not told the result.

If the employee is rated positively, he/she will most certainly be advised. The managers will also ask him/her whether he/she is willing to undertake an intensive development programme. The focus here is on both professional and private preferences and ambitions. This is where the performance appraisal comes in. It is important to note here that the performance appraisal does not involve assessing potential, for the reasons already mentioned above. Said assessment is done beforehand. In this instance, the performance appraisal purely serves to discuss the employee's views in the event of a positive rating. This in turn involves what would be classified as an individual, case-based performance appraisal. It's impractical to wait to discuss such content at an annual performance appraisal unless this sufficiently coincides with the annual talent identification process.

The scenario described above certainly works in a hierarchical world, and companies operating with this sort of structure will like this approach. Decisions are prepared top-down. A high potential's direct manager is actively involved, not bypassed. To a certain extent, the company still has the employee at its disposal even if he/she is "brought onboard" at the end of the process. It's a completely different story in an agile world, as we will see below.

The employee involves himself/herself

If you ask professionally successful people about the key to their success during their careers, you will rarely hear them say they had been identified as a talent or high potential at some point in their lives. For decades, people rightly or wrongly climbed the career ladder or achieved important life goals without ever being part of a talent management programme. I don't mean to undermine the significance of such structured programmes by saying this. We simply need to be aware that professional development is also possible without formal structures, processes and methods. If we take a closer look at the biographies of highly successful people, we notice a shared logic of success (cf. Robinson, 2009). It doesn't matter who you take, whether it be Barack Obama, Bill Gates, Arnold Schwarzenegger, Lewis Hamilton or Richard Branson. No matter who they are, successful people are never thrown in the deep end. They seek out ways to jump in themselves. They don't wait for opportunities; they seize them. They unconditionally love what they do, and want to be the best at it. And they never pass up a chance to prove this to the world. They don't mix with weaker performers in order to look even stronger, they mingle with the elite.

This is based on the idea that talent always find a way. All a company needs to do is make sure it doesn't obstruct this. Talent develop their own strengths. To a certain degree, this contradicts classic talent-management approaches, where strategic requirements are the driving force: A long-term need for talent in key positions is identified, and high potentials are trained based on pre-defined, clearly described criteria as part of a structured talent development programme (cf. Rothwell, 2005; Fulmer & Conger, 2004). These efforts centre around a static competence model stipulating the requirements for those holding key or managerial positions.

In an agile world, this approach will naturally cause problems. One main reason for this is the fact that people only have a rough idea of future requirements. Agile organisations in particular will oppose the notion that all employees in key positions must each fulfil a common set of skills. The focus here is more on team categories, and diversity within the teams.

Unlike the traditional, hierarchical approaches, an agile world tends to be driven by the talent. The employees themselves are responsible for their development, just as they are for setting and achieving their goals. They independently join networks within the company in order to learn about new career opportunities. An employee in this sort of world knows that the only way he/she will progress in his/her career is if he/she himself/herself takes the initiative. For employees who have internalised this culture, knocking on the door of the HR department and asking when they can expect their next promotion is an alien concept.

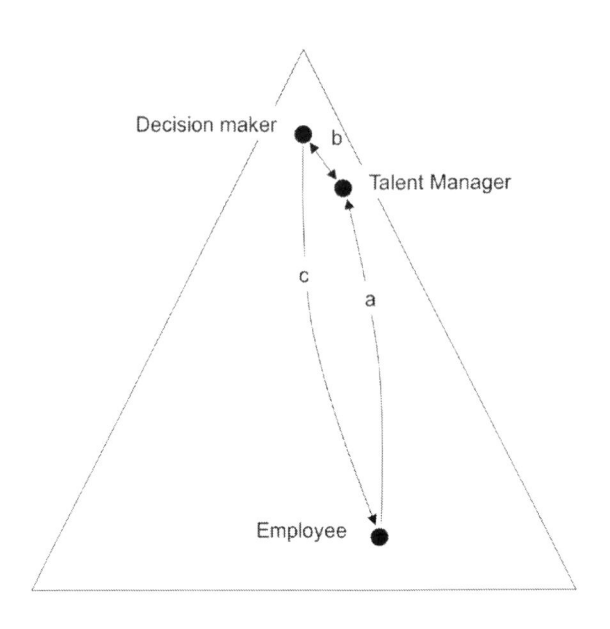

Figure 29:
The employee puts himself/herself in the mix as a talent.

The real-life scenario in this agile model is illustrated by Figure 29: An employee applies for a development programme directly with the talent manager (a), who is in close consultation with top decision-makers (b), who are in turn responsible for appointing internal candidates (c). This last step usually occurs as part of so-called talent reviews or talent conferences, where top managers jointly decide on candidates and further HR development measures. The direct manager clearly plays no active role here. If, after a successful talent nomination, there are talks between the employee and his/her direct manager, it tends to be the employee who speaks to his/her manager rather than the other way around.

Alternatively, it is expected that more and more companies will, in future, consider involving fellow staff and even customers in the talent nomination and identification process as part of their "agilisation". This will mean employees aren't deemed high potentials just because the manager thinks so, but because peers and customers also have confidence in their potential. While this is indeed a highly visionary approach, it cannot be discounted.

In summary

- The direct manager is not the suitable authority to be identifying talent. At best, he/she can assist with a nomination process. The annual performance appraisal plays a secondary role here.
- Decisions concerning the identification of high potentials must be made at the same level where decisions concerning the filling of key positions are made. A talent manager can intervene here.
- In an agile world, it is primarily the employees themselves who take the initiative when it comes to their careers. The company essentially acts as an enabler. The direct manager and annual performance appraisal do not play a key role here.

Establishing internal suitability

Certain jobs require certain abilities in order to be successful. The person best displaying these abilities is deemed the most suitable for the respective jobs. Who would seriously object to this statement? It is a basic principle of recruitment – both internally and externally – and is therefore one of the fundamental assumptions applied when assessing suitability. It is even part of what is widely understood as being the central aim of HR management: the right person at the right place at the right time. So let's run through it. In order to drive a forklift successfully, you need to actually be able to drive a forklift. Anyone who can do this is suitable, at least in this respect. A sales officer working with industrial goods must be able to negotiate. A chef must be able to cook. A customer service employee at a call centre must be friendly. None of that is a problem. But let's now look at some more challenging cases. On a scale of 1 (basic skills) to 4 (outstanding skills, expert), what degree of communication skills does an HR professional need? What level of competence is required for "creative thinking" when it comes to a retail outlet manager? How well does a member of a printer development team need to be able to think strategically? The more complex the task, and the more tasks are embedded in team structures, the more difficult the matter becomes. How can you properly assess both requirements and abilities? Who does that at a company? The more you think about this simple suitability principle in real life, the greater the gulf between textbook approach and functional reality.

In hierarchical worlds, this all seems to work well, to a certain extent. In an agile world, however, it quickly reaches its limits. On the one hand, this is due to the highly unstable requirements here, and on the other, to the dynamics governing how employees independently identify, seize and even form tasks. It seems almost a given here that, after just a few years, employees will have a different job to the one they were hired for. The recruitment process itself is less about specific positions and more about careers and relevant opportunities at the company as a whole, even if this does all start with one specific job. Although employees may spend years doing their job, their work will have little in common with the key requirements specified at the time of their employment. By nature, these companies allow employees to shape and organise their jobs themselves in a phenomenon known as de-jobbing. Careers develop naturally based on acute and future challenges within the company, individual preferences, talent, and the trust others place in an employee. In this respect, the employees are aware that the company provides a full spectrum of opportunities and challenges, where they must find their own way, driven by their own interests. The employees see their company as an internal job market of sorts, where they build networks, fight for opportunities, and constantly involve themselves internally. The classic concept of *personnel placement* is foreign to these companies, but is an accurate description of the approach adopted in a hierarchical world.

Personnel placement – A home depot for staff

The traditional concept of personnel placement unambiguously conveys the notion of employees being allocated roles at the company by a central authority. Decisions are made about them. The employees appear to "belong" to the company, and it is the management's responsibility to use the available resources in optimum fashion. Both the relevant literature and real life itself adopt often very technocratic approaches here: On the one hand, the specific requirements for each position are clearly outlined based on job descriptions, resulting in *job* profiles. On the other, all employees are assessed in terms of their competencies, resulting in *employee* profiles. These employee profiles are created as part of competence evaluations, considered to be a central component of the annual performance appraisal. An automatic comparison of job and employee profiles then determines which employee would fit best in which position. Checks are also conducted to ascertain whether another position would be better suited to an employee's strengths.

Peter Cappelli (2012), a leading professor in Human Resource Management at the Wharton School, refers to this, slightly cynically, as the "Home Depot Syndrome":

> [..] filling a job vacancy is seen as akin to replacing a part in a washing machine. We go down to the store to get the part, and once we find it, we put it in place and get the machine going again. Like a replacement part, job requirements have very precise specifications. Job candidates must fit them perfectly or the job won't be filled and the business can't operate (p. 19).

Cappelli is unmistakably referring to the machine metaphor – the company as a large, static mechanism developed and assembled by an overarching, mega-intelligent authority, where the individual cogs work and passively fit into one another precisely as the great creator intended. It is one, perhaps even the primary, notion of what management actually is. Components don't think, nor do they intuitively adapt to their environment. A practical HR example would be something like this:

> The tasks and authorisations are clearly defined in a job description for each position. This is then used to create a list of requirements which the employees must meet in order to be able to complete and fulfil the assigned tasks and authorisations. It is up to the employee review to determine how the respective employee meets the job-based requirements.

The above text will sound strange, threatening, even scary, to representatives of agile companies. "Authorisations", "assigned tasks", "job-based requirements" which "must be met" are not part of the vernacular or core values at agile companies. Representatives of hierarchical companies, on the hand, will not find it odd, since they consider this manner of thinking normal. They implicitly operate based on the following assumptions:

- The company is a combination of individual positions with specific, definable requirements.
- Job-based requirements are stable in time and content.

- Job-based requirements can be appropriately identified and clearly described.
- An employee is only considered successful if he/she meets set, job-specific requirements.
- An employee may be successful in his/her own individual position.
- Managers may appropriately assess relevant employee skills.
- An employee's evaluation in one particular position also applies to other positions, and is therefore transferable.

Even in a hierarchical context, the validity of these assumptions is highly questionable (cf. Breisig, 2005; Buckingham & Vosburgh, 2001), while representatives of the agile model will simply reject them all. As already described in relation to the framework conditions in chapter 4, an agile world operates based on completely different principles:

- The company is a network of co-operating, self-regulating teams.
- Employees define their own tasks, in accordance with acute challenges, their preferences, and talent.
- Requirements are ambiguous, constantly changing, and hard to foresee (tasks highly dynamic and uncertain)
- Employees cannot be successful alone – only in co-operation with others.
- Employees can successfully contribute very varied (diverse) skills to projects.

There are, of course, situations in which classic personnel placement works well, such as production factories, where various machines are used, and it is clear which employees can operate which machines. If an employee drops out, whether through illness, leave, or a terminated contract, it is quick and easy to see who fills his/her place. These sorts of situations are highly static, predictable and plannable – and are therefore very different to agile environments.

It is hard to find a benefit which better illustrates the difference between a hierarchical and agile world than the issue of establishing internal suitability. In the former, it is usually up to the managers to evaluate their employees according to clear criteria, often applying structured competence appraisals. This is considered a key fixture of annual performance appraisals. The results are passed onto the HR department, which in turn takes central responsibility for ensuring staff are employed appropriately, consistent with their strengths. The HR department is also the customer of this process, because it is dependent on an employee rating in order to ultimately be able to act professionally and (apparently) rationally.

In an agile context, this approach is totally irrelevant, as evidenced by the fact that job descriptions and requirements are dispensed with, not because these instruments are not wanted, but because they do not fit with everyday operations.

Internal talent markets

In an agile world, employees are responsible for their own careers. They follow their own career paths at the company – or even outside it. From a company perspective, this then raises the question as to how its HR requirements can be met at all times if employees are "doing whatever they want". How can an HR manager ensure he/she fulfils his/her basic responsibility, namely, always having the right employee in the right place?

The afore-quoted Peter Cappelli has an answer to this too, referring to what appears to be the flaw in the machine metaphor. If, for instance, one cog in a clockwork mechanism malfunctions, the entire mechanism stops working. If a company or a department is an employee down, life goes on. There of course needs to be a response. Other employees take on new or expanded tasks. New employees are hired. Colleagues are re-trained. Agile environments don't do *nothing*. The this-is-not-my-job phenomenon is similarly foreign to employees here. After all, there are no job descriptions preventing employees from doing something different to what is specified for them.

But instead of placing employees via external control, much like a chess player would do to its passive pieces, agile companies develop an internal platform for positions where there is an acute or anticipated demand. Qualified colleagues are sought internally, in setups akin to in-house talent markets. Managers headhunt employees, including internally. On the one hand, this can lead to conflicts, and on the other, to healthy competition which can be appropriately regulated with relevant rules.

We'd love to!

Two companies produce and sell metallic household items, such as pots, pans, cutlery, mincers, nutcrackers etc. Both companies A and B have their own online portal through which customers can purchase the products. Both portals are connected to the Amazon marketplace, and can be easily found via Google's Shopping function. But the stories behind each of these are very different. Company A is a traditional, hierarchical company, while company B reflects a more agile world.

Here's the history of company A: In 2010, the management decided to build a company-own online channel to market its products. A suitable budget was approved, and an aim formulated. By the end of 2015, 20% of sales were to be achieved through this channel. This goal was established in writing in the sales manager's target agreement. Armed with an adequate budget, this sales manager contacted the HR department to ask for help in building a suitable team of internal and external candidates. Corresponding skill sets were devised, the favourites being teamworking ability, communication skills, creativity, customer focus, problem-solving skills, and conceptual thinking. Since the company had already been conducting annual performance appraisals for years, the skill sets of all available employees could be viewed directly, allowing appropriate candidates to be selected and placed in the project accordingly. Once the team had been formed, it got started and developed the first pilot test.

And now for the history of company B, which, even today, has no annual performance appraisals. Two young employees who had grown up with the Internet wondered why, in 2010, the company and, in particular, its products could hardly be found online. One of these employees had been exposed to, and impressed by, the online-sales function at his previous employer. So the two of them got going and joined heads – informally and without any official orders – to consider the idea of an online channel. Having discussed it with numerous other colleagues, with a positive response overall, they developed a plan, which they then presented to the management in 2011. Several critical issues meant they had to further develop and adjust this, before presenting it for a second time soon after. The message was: "We'd love to". They were granted permission, and received an adequate budget for a pilot test. Beforehand, however, both employees were asked a central question: "What do you need to make the project a success?".

These two stories illustrate a number of differences between a hierarchical and agile world, although these will not be examined further here. What we need to focus on at this point is the issue of establishing internal suitability. Those in an agile world will, of course, also have to answer the question of whether the employees who independently come up with an idea in a team are ultimately the ones best suited to leading their promising proposal to success. But the dynamics of how employees acquire and go about their tasks are completely different. There is no centrally established, standardised skill criteria, e.g. as part of an annual performance appraisal. The employees find their own way into their positions. Suitability comes into focus in concrete cases, and in relation to specific challenges. Said challenges are not defined by a central authority, but are instead reflected on through coaching with the relevant persons.

In summary

- Requirements can only be set for tasks based on labour division, with a high degree of process and result certainty.
- In agile structures, the team and internal customers themselves decide who is suitable for a task. Centrally managed skill profiles are virtually unheard of.
- Employees in an agile world arrange their own tasks by independently getting into position and attempting to implement their own ideas.
- Overall, the annual performance appraisal can only potentially be used as an instrument for establishing internal suitability and personnel placement in hierarchical contexts.

Employee development

Companies often have competence models for managers. These are initially nothing more than a description of what a successful manager must be able to do at the respective company. Astonishingly, these models hardly differ from company to company. Some skills – such as customer focus, team-working abilities, strategic thinking and *employee development,* "developing others" – appear to be permanent fixtures in almost every model. What does employee development mean for a shift manager at a car manufacturer's plastics factory? What does the leader of a regional sales team have to do in order to meet this specific requirement? What does the head nurse do with the regular nurse? How can a school principal develop its teachers? And what does Mick Jagger do with Keith Richards?

Theoretically, we would assume that managers have more experience than their employees, thereby enabling them to generously share their knowledge. In practice, this is not always the case, and is in fact becoming increasingly rare. Managers provide feedback, which facilitates daily learning. They speak with their employees to discuss the employees' long-term development prospects, and initiate relevant measures. This section, on the other hand, focuses on identifying and meeting short-term development needs – a key component of annual performance appraisals when it comes to employee development. It is a component often also referred to as "employee development meeting" or "development dialogue". Again, the basic idea here is very simple: Once a year, the employee and his/her manager get together and discuss the employee's future development. They reflect on current and future requirements, and frame these in terms of the employee's existing abilities. Specific measures are planned, whether it be training, tasks or coaching, which are designed to help achieve the agreed development targets.

If annual performance appraisals solely focused on this relatively non-critical aspect of employee development, I wouldn't have had to write this book. After all, the points discussed here are of little consequence to the manager, the employee and their relationship. Development measures should be viewed positively by the employee, unless he/she is "forced" into them. The manager can be an excellent accommodator: "What can I do for you? Is there anything which could help you complete your work even better in future?". Even the problem of equity among team members or department staff is quite easily managed. After all, investment in an employee may be seen as an advantage by his/her colleague. But the significance of an institutionalised discussion between an employee and his/her manager regarding the employee's further development crucially depends on the framework conditions in place. We'll start with the hierarchical view.

Employee re-adjustment

Recently, I once again had the honour of being on the panel of judges at an awards ceremony naming companies for "best employee development". This gave me the opportunity to view many of the application documents submitted by companies. What most struck me was the fact that the majority of companies openly equate employee development with formal training. The higher the relative number of training days per employee, the better the employee development. This at least appeared to be the understanding of many employers. A few also mentioned coaching or mentoring measures. The annual performance appraisal or development talks were repeatedly brought into focus as particularly progressive initiatives, in which development needs and relevant measures are regularly discussed with the parties concerned.

An annual discussion of development measures works very well in a hierarchical world. Individual development targets are set based on overarching requirements, which are communicated top-down to the employees via the manager. The machine metaphor can once again be applied here. The employee is viewed as a single component in a co-ordinated framework – a cog in a greater mechanism. If the framework itself changes, the employee may have to be readjusted to ensure he/she remains employable in future. As the company becomes more international, the employee must improve his/her English skills. The IT system needs to be converted, prompting the employee to be sent off for relevant training.

But development continues to be an issue in hierarchical contexts, even when no changes are imminent. In an extreme case – some HR professionals would even call it an ideal scenario -, the employees and their competencies are classified based on structured processes and specific criteria, and compared with target requirements. Negative deviations between the actual and target profiles are then identified as development needs. In the end, the employee is informed of the development measures planned for him/her by his/her manager. The content of these measures is established in a more or less logical manner. All this is perfectly fine in a hierarchical context, as long as the relevant framework conditions exist.

Working = learning, learning = working

HR development at SAP AG marked one of the first stages of my professional career. At that time, in the early '90s, I was a trainee, and had to follow the instructions of the amazing CEO, Dietmar Hopp, who said: "I don't want institutionalised HR development. Anyone wanting to learn should simply visit the customer". The principle was simple: Go to the customer, and try to understand its plans as best you can. Put these in practice, and get feedback at every opportunity. Solutions are born from ignorance. In between comes the process that we call learning. Or specifically speaking: customer and problem-related learning.

Agile worlds do not distinguish between learning and working. In a hierarchical context, employees are "sent off" for advanced training, in the hope that the skills learned in the seminar will be transferred to practice. Conversely, in an agile world characterised by uncertainty, learning simply means solving a previously unsolved problem, doing something better than before, gaining insights previously unknown. This all happens in groups. People learn from and with one another by tackling the practical challenges, which the team has set as its main task (cf. Senge, 1990). Uncertainty and curiosity are the dominant drivers here. And if the employees in an agile environment consider training appropriate, they organise this themselves.

To understand the significance of the annual "employee development meeting" in an agile model, it is important to understand the differences in learning between a hierarchical and agile environment. Figure 30 compares the two worlds in simplified fashion.

Hierarchical world	Agile world
Individual learning	Social learning
From teacher/manager	From and with others
Off-the-job	On-the-job
Planned	On demand
Formal	Informal
Pre-specified	Self-regulated
Long cycles	Short cycles
Requirements	Curiosity & uncertainty
Transfer of learning	Working = learning

Figure 30:
Learning in a hierarchical and agile environment.

Learning and HR development in an agile environment follow completely different rules to those commonly found in a hierarchical world, though that doesn't mean elements from a hierarchical world play no role here. Agile models can also have long-term development plans which are discussed with employees. They have off-the-job training sessions or long-term requirements which are responded to. But there are other facets which are of much greater significance compared to conventional approaches.

This is largely due to the complex and highly dynamic nature of the tasks. The employees work independently in teams. Annual cycles, in which certain employees' needs for development are reflected on, wouldn't come near to meeting these framework conditions. Employees in an agile world think and act in short cycles. The demand for learning does not arise on an annual basis, but rather at any time – daily, hourly or otherwise. In this respect, the employees primarily learn "on-demand" when relevant knowledge is required to address an acute issue. Teams and employees in an agile world don't know which skills they'll need in six months' time.

In agile environments, teams and their employees define their own targets, or at least play a key role in doing so. As already described on numerous occasions, employees in an agile world work independently and autonomously. It is thus only logical that the employees be the ones to jointly attend to their own learning requirements. They know best what they need.

Talking about development once a year

As mentioned earlier, it can hardly be considered an error if a manager discusses development measures with his/her employee, whether this be in the role of boss, coach, partner or enabler. The approaches, however, differ. A coach will endeavour to ask his/her employee "What would you like to have improved on in twelve months' time?" Which skills do you want to work on?". The results would very likely not be documented or forwarded to the HR department, unless the employee requests this. A company which, despite operating in an agile environment, still sees annual performance appraisals as a central component of its HR development strategy is misjudging key aspects of learning and development. In cases of doubt, the HR department would indicate the unrealistic nature of this. Annual discussions on development are largely unnecessary in agile contexts.

But it is nevertheless possible to have teams in which employees don't wish to leave their development to the mercy of daily dynamics, and instead prefer longer-term prospects. In these cases, the agile environment should be seen as an opportunity to do things virtually unheard of in strictly hierarchical settings. For example, teams can hold orientation sessions, where each member tells the others the areas in which he/she wishes to improve over the next twelve months. The colleagues can in turn respond to this and contribute their views – as feedback and joint recommendations. The ultimate aim is to gear the team members' development around a collective need, and in accordance with individual tendencies and preferences.

In summary

- Annual planning of necessary development measures as part of an annual performance appraisal is never considered problematic.
- In hierarchical worlds, the development needs and measures are based on pre-specified requirements, which are compared with the employees' current skills. Development measures are approved by the respective manager.

- In agile worlds, working equals learning. Needs and measures (usually on-the-job and on-demand) are self-regulated, and defined by the team in short cycles.
- In agile worlds, annual development meetings can be conducted openly and within teams, and provides added orientation for all parties involved.

Offering prospects

In addition to the aforementioned components of identifying short-term learning needs, coupled with an appropriate development plan, development meetings usually also include a discussion on medium-term and long-term development prospects. When we talk of career prospects here, we mean the employee's chances of significantly different, advanced roles or jobs. Prospects may include the opportunity to secure a different job within or outside of his/her own team, promotion to a higher management level, or a switch to another team involving new or different tasks. But they always mean expectations for potential improvement from the employee's perspective.

Where do you see yourself in three to five years?

A common question posed in job interviews is: "Where do you see yourself in five years?". The applicant's response to this question may certainly be relevant if the candidate is to be employed for an entire career, rather than a specific job. In this case, a company should clarify whether an applicant's expectations align with the opportunities on offer. If they don't, for instance because the applicant's expectations are more ambitious than the prospects available, there is destined to be high turnover problems. Completely different problems would indeed arise on the other side of the coin. But how wise is it for a manager to ask this same question at an annual performance appraisal? After all, many companies officially ask managers to discuss professional prospects with their employees as part of formal, annual performance appraisals, and document these in writing (Hossiep, Bittner & Bernd, 2008).

This all sounds very promising in theory. Numerous guidelines on how to conduct an annual performance appraisal read similarly to the quote above. Discussing the employee's prospects can't be a bad thing – at least it doesn't seem so at first glance. But if a manager asks where the employee sees himself/herself in three to five years, the manager must expect all kinds of responses, and it depends on the framework conditions as to whether and how a direct supervisor can react sensibly to them. Here are a number of possible answers:

A desire to move. "I would like a different task or job in my same area or outside of it". The employee may even have specific ideas as to what he/she wants to do next. "I see myself in sales in three years".

- *Disorientation.* "I don't know where I see myself in several years". In this case, the employee doesn't have any current personal prospects. We assume he/she is not totally happy with this disorientation.
- *Satisfaction.* "I'm actually happy with what I'm doing, and don't see any reason to do anything different in future". The employee openly sees no need to think about prospects involving a different task.
- *Lack of prospects.* "I don't see any prospects for myself at this company". While the employee does have a personal career vision, he/she does not believe it aligns with the opportunities offered by the company.

The four scenarios above essentially revolve around two aspects. On the one hand, it's about the employee's *personal career plan*, i.e. his/her personal focus – within or outside of the company. Does the employee know what he/she wants? Does he/she have specific ideas or not? On the other, it's about *concrete opportunities*, jobs or roles within the company. If the employee knows what he/she wants, what does his/her career plan specifically entail? At this point, it is worth asking what a direct manager can do, can't do or shouldn't do, for instance because there is a better authority within the company. We'll start with the concrete opportunities.

Which concrete opportunities?

Should development prospects be covered as formal, stipulated content of an annual performance appraisal? Throughout my career, I have attended numerous workshops where HR professionals have discussed this aspect. On the one hand, it is stated that this aspect is key to any development meeting. Interestingly, however, it is also common to hear the argument of not wanting to create any employee expectations which cannot ultimately be met as a result of broaching this issue. If we look more closely, we usually find that the problem is even more elementary: Many managers cannot offer any concrete opportunities. For example, let's imagine a team leader who manages a specific department's staff at a warehouse (e.g. menswear or consumer electronics). Let's also assume that there are hardly any professional prospects in this area. The employees do what they have to, help each other out, and occasionally rotate their tasks – nothing more, nothing less. Why should the team leader ask his/her employees the aforementioned "where do you see yourself in five years" question? The manager would be at a disadvantage to the employee if he/she were officially urged to not only raise this issue, but also to enter the results in a relevant form.

But let's now imagine a situation in which a manager actually can offer prospects. In a hierarchical world, the following possibilities are conceivable:

- The employee is assigned different or additional tasks within the manager's sphere of responsibility, giving him/her the opportunity to develop further as desired.
- The manager acts as a facilitator in the higher-ranking area. In a strictly hierarchical world, the manager would go beyond his/her immediate manager, and from there arrange a task in a different department or team (see Figure 31).

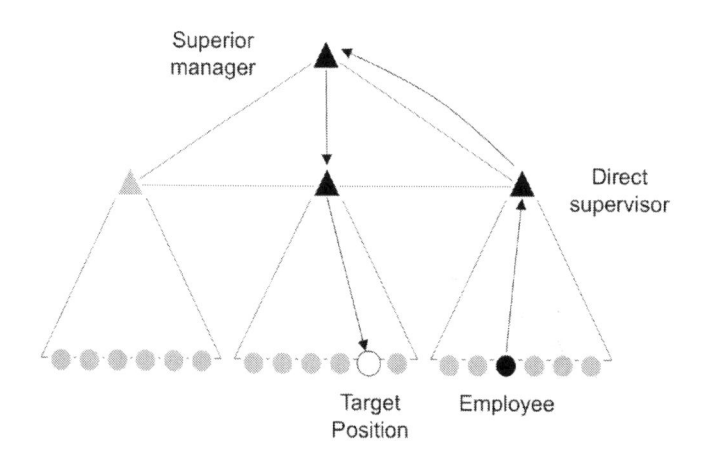

Figure 31:
Facilitating specific career options in a strictly hierarchical world.

If neither approach is feasible, the manager should not broach, nor have to broach, the issue of prospects in a performance appraisal. In any case, he/she should avoid, from the outset, any situations in which the employee could mention career aspirations. This would otherwise end in a farce, and the manager would likely be hopelessly out of his/her depth.

Career coaching

It's a somewhat different story when the issue of prospects is less about concrete career opportunities and more about the employee's professional focus. The employee may not know what he/she wants, and may not be aware of his/her strengths and talents. The employee may not have a specific career dream or a fully thought-out career strategy. While he/she is familiar with the various jobs within the company, he/she is not sure what could work best for him/her in the medium and long-term. In this case, the solution is career coaching. Coaching may also be applied if the employee has ideas about his/her career which do not fit with his/her talents. This includes self-underestimation or self-overestimation.

Career coaching probably happens informally every day. Colleagues speak to each other about their future. They speak with friends, with their spouses or partners. Whether or not this is a professional form of coaching is questionable. In any case, it is a preliminary form. People ask each other questions, and encourage reflection. This happens naturally, without any forms or official instigation. And most importantly, the results are not documented anywhere, least of all in the HR records. Yet these informal discussions are very significant to the parties concerned. They show that people, employees, only talk about their future to those they fully trust, and whom they implicitly attribute with the necessary skills or experience. This role may sometimes be played by the direct manager in very specific situations:

- The employee wants to discuss his/her future with his/her direct manager. Coaching cannot be imposed unilaterally. A manager who approaches an employee saying "It's

January, so it's time for me to coach you again. Give me 2-3 appointment options" has lost from the outset.
- The employee is willing to open up to the manager. This may mean openly discussing strengths, weaknesses, talents and preferences. Under no circumstance should the employee fear his/her answers having negative impacts on his/her salary or career.
- The possible outcomes of career coaching do not conflict with the relationship existing between the employee and his/her manager. The manager does not have to fear the employee leaving or poaching his/her own job: "Boss, after everything I've learned about myself and my career, I have realised your job is the right one for me".
- The coachee is always the customer of the coaching. Confidentiality is top priority for the employee, as coachee. In these cases, the results must remain with the employee, and not be stored by the manager or HR department, assuming anything is documented at all.

All these points collectively show that a manager whose dominant role is that of a boss can never, nor should ever, perform this coaching task. Even if a manager acts largely as a coach or partner, it may be problematic if he/she also takes on the role of career coach. It is generally safer for a company to provide its employees with a neutral career coach if the parties concerned deem this necessary. In this respect, it may be wise to offer this special support to the employee as part of the annual performance appraisal, but without the manager himself/herself adopting the role of career coach.

Employees find their own way

In a hierarchical world, the direct manager plays a key role in an employee's development prospects. In extreme cases, the employee does not get past his/her direct manager. If the direct manager can actually offer an employee realistic career options, it is highly advisable for him/her to discuss these with the employee. It is, however, a completely different story for agile contexts.

Managers and HR professionals operating in a hierarchical world often find it difficult to imagine a strategy of HR development where employees are responsible for their own development – at least that is the impression I have got from many of my own discussions. The argument from a hierarchical perspective is that development is primarily a managerial task, that the company must attend to its employees and their development, that the HR department – along with the managers – is responsible for employee development. All these arguments and views are completely logical from a traditional perspective. Employees and managers accustomed to an agile world, on the other hand, find them very foreign. Their approach is different:

- If employees want to progress, they must do so themselves, using their own initiative. In an agile world following McGregor's Theory Y, it is a given, or indeed a basic assumption, that employees naturally want to drive their own development.
- The company and managers create framework conditions enabling employees to fulfil this responsibility. So it's not a case of doing *nothing*. Key instruments may include internal talent markets or career coaching. As already explained, the latter is only performed by the direct manager on very rare occasions.
- Prospects are generated by personal networks within the company. Advocates of the hierarchical model will dismiss this as "nepotism", but in an agile world, networks are seen as one of the most important foundations of co-operation. Sales staff usually

recognise this immediately. Companies using employee referral programmes as part of their recruitment strategies already acknowledge the professional importance of networks, at least in this area (Berberich & Trost, 2012).

How do employees find new prospects in settings like these? Figure 32 simplifies and illustrates the relevant scenario. It is the exact opposite to the hierarchical approach presented in Figure 31.

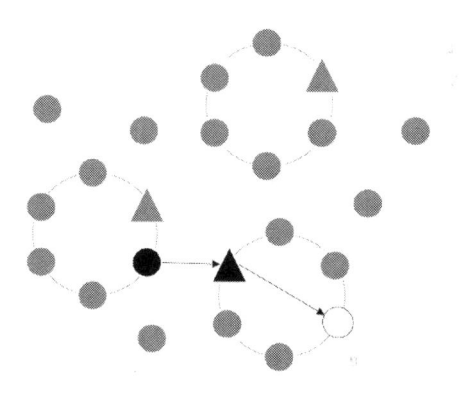

Figure 32:
Prospects in an agile world.

The employees explain and discuss their roles and tasks in a team (agile worlds primarily involve working in teams). At best, managers play a co-ordinating or coaching role here. Once an employee starts seeking challenges at another team, he/she does his/her own research, and activates his/her network accordingly by contacting other team leaders. In other words, the employee moves freely within an internal market of possibilities, so to speak.

So while the manager plays a key role in a hierarchical world, he/she is virtually obsolete in an agile one. In a hierarchical world, the manager discusses prospects with the employee, who is more or less dependent on his/her manager. In an agile world, on the other hand, the employee informs his/her manager of his/her plans and decisions, which can of course be done during a performance appraisal. If, however, this performance appraisal raises the question of where the employee sees himself/herself in three to five years, the relevance of the response varies depending on whether the context is hierarchical or agile. In the former, the manager tries to align the employee's expectations with those of the company, endeavouring to find a solution to suit all parties involved. In the latter, the manager tries to understand the employee's intentions in order to prepare his/her team for possible staffing changes.

In summary

- In a hierarchical world, the annual review requires medium and long-term development prospects, indicating that the direct manager can offer, or at least arrange, specific career opportunities.
- Career coaching is a suitable means of securing an employee for a long-term career path. On very rare occasions, this may be performed by the direct manager.
- In an agile world, the employees themselves are responsible for their long-term development. The company can act as an enabler here if they wish.
- Mandatory career coaching does not work in agile or hierarchical contexts.

Learning through feedback

Employees receive feedback from their managers as part of an annual performance appraisal. When advocates of this tool are asked why this is necessary, they generally say that feedback is important for learning, and learning is a pre-requisite for performance. There is of course a close correlation between feedback and learning. It is indeed difficult to imagine learning without feedback. But is the annual performance appraisal a suitable instrument for providing and receiving effective feedback? Answering this question requires us to examine things more closely.

How do we learn how to present?

In order to better convey the ideas below, we'll start with a simple, familiar example: How do we learn the art of presentation? We learn how to present by presenting. There is basically one main reason why so many presentations are unbearable despite technical facilities like PowerPoint and Keynote: the presenters have rarely received feedback. Feedback must make sense to the person concerned, and results in optimised actions. There can be many different forms of feedback when it comes to presenting.

- At the end of a presentation, the audience's applause is somewhat conspicuous. You don't know whether they're clapping because they enjoyed the presentation, or because they're relieved to have made it through to the end. Or the applause may be interminable, with many attendees paying compliments: "Thanks a lot. I just wanted to say what a great presentation that was".
- A coach, colleague or manager will give the following sort of feedback after a presentation: "You should use fewer slides", "That example was really helpful." "We can understand you very well". "The central theme was not

clear". "The key messages were conveyed very well at the end, because you structured and focused your presentation appropriately". Or people may give themselves feedback by watching their own presentation on video, and are usually surprised at many subconscious behavioural patterns.
- Another form of feedback may look like this: "You don't seem to be self-critical enough when it comes to your presentation style". "Have you ever asked yourself what you could do better?". Or: "I think it's good that you actively obtain feedback after every presentation, and that you openly want to learn for your next presentation". Or: "Don't always be dragged down by failures. Don't take them too personally. Work on yourself, and you'll see how things go better at the next presentations".
- Finally, feedback can also sound like this: "You're a great speaker". "Giving presentations isn't quite your thing". "I admire your charisma".

Attentive readers will have noticed the differences between the four types of feedback. Which type of feedback will be of greatest benefit to someone wanting to optimise his/her presentation style?

Levels of feedback

The impact of feedback on people's performances has been the subject of research for many years (Hattie & Timperley, 2007). One key finding shows that the impact depends heavily on the focus of the feedback. Simply speaking, we can distinguish between four different levels here (see Figure 33).

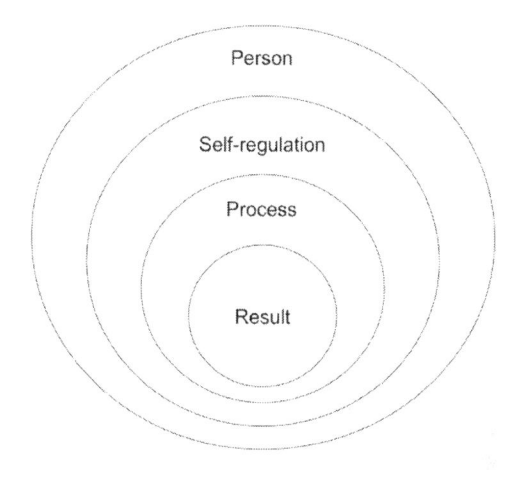

Figure 33:
Levels of feedback.

Employees can receive feedback in terms of target achievement or success in completing a task. This is essentially about *results*. If a sales employee receives feedback on his/her sales figures, these will be the focus. In the scenario above, the applause would be an example of results feedback. If, however, the same employee receives feedback on his/her sales style, e.g. how he/she approaches customers, seals deals or manages relationships, it's about the *how*, the *process*. This is the aim of the second point in the above example (fewer slides, more examples, structure etc.). The third type of feedback relates to *self-regulation*, the person's own way of increasing his/her performance, e.g. how he/she handles successes or failures. Self-regulation refers to the general manner in which someone reflects on, questions or corrects his/her own actions. If a sales employee receives feedback telling him/her to be more self-critical after making a sale, or to be more accepting of successes, the feedback is part of this third level. Finally, employees can also receive personal feedback, which includes aspects such as skills, confidence or relationships with others: "You're a good salesperson", "You're a great speaker".

Scientific studies show that feedback at a process level is the most effective, whereas feedback at a personality level has the least impact (Hattie & Timperley, 2007). This is relevant here, insofar as annual performance appraisals primarily address the *person* and *self-regulation* levels: "You're a good negotiator", "You should approach failures more constructively, and use them as an opportunity for learning", "Don't be dragged down by failure". The *results* are also broached, given that performance evaluations focus on the achievement of predefined targets. The most important feedback level, *process*, is hardly touched on in annual performance appraisals. Negative feedback provided at a process level here seems particularly far-fetched and unforgiving: "Five months ago, you didn't cater properly to the customer's wishes. I've been wanting to tell you that ever since". In any case, one lot of feedback once a year is nowhere near sufficient for generating learning. Feedback at this level only has an impact if provided promptly.

The consequences of one's own actions

From a traditional perspective, the most important feedback an employee can receive is that from his/her boss. Employees in hierarchical worlds virtually internalise this, and live in the knowledge that their work is good if their boss – not the customer - is satisfied. At the same time, providing feedback is often seen as a key managerial task. It doesn't have to be. This notion is actually quite foreign in agile worlds, as demonstrated below. In a hierarchical setting, the employees are distanced from the consequences of their actions. Hierarchies separate employees from their colleagues and customers. Departments divide up the function in the narrowest sense of the word. The individual employee receives is/her orders and instructions from his/her direct manager. The sum of the separate work results ultimately lead to a product with which the customer is more or less satisfied (see Figure 34).

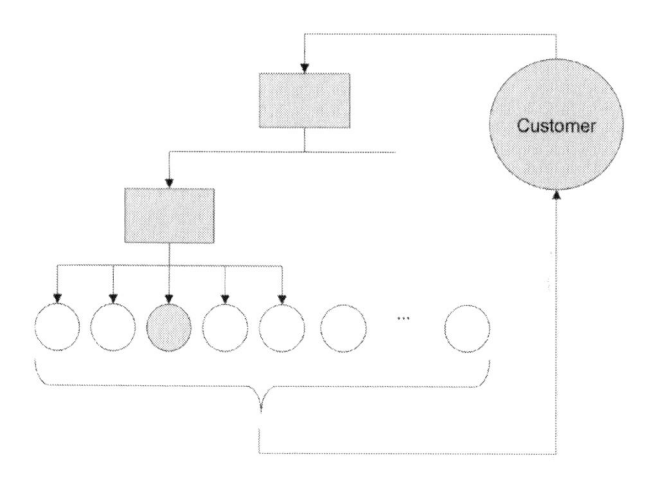

Figure 34:
Feedback in hierarchical systems.

The customer in turn provides its feedback through the hierarchy, reaching the employee from the "top down". There is officially no direct connection between the employee and the customer, nor does a hierarchical system deem this necessary. In this respect, employees in strictly hierarchical worlds must trust that the manager's instructions will result in generally satisfied customers. More specifically speaking, the manager is the employee's customer here. If the manager is satisfied, it means the work is good. In view of this, it is no wonder that the manager is seen as the primary source of feedback, which is then formally reflected by the annual performance appraisal.

Feedback plays a completely different role in agile worlds. It involves two central principles: Firstly, the employees are free to decide how they act. They are the ones responsible for the consequences of their actions. Secondly, there is a direct connection between them and their (internal and external) customers, meaning they see these consequences first-hand. Without this type of direct feedback, self-regulation in an agile world would be inconceivable, and indeed impossible. At best, the manager acts as a facilitator in this context. He/she does not act as a "supervisor", but rather as a "preliminary agent"/"intermediary".

Knowing where you stand

If an employee is employed with a view to successfully performing a specific task over the long-term, it may be a good idea to prepare the employee for this task, e.g. as part of an onboarding programme. Depending on the complexity of the task, this may take a few hours or several years. The former case would relate to simpler, presumably repetitive tasks, while the latter may involve preparing an astronaut for a space mission. Let's stick with that example. Regular reviews will be held with the astronaut-to-be – who may also be the future managing director etc. – to discuss where he/she currently stands. Which strengths need to be further developed, and which weaknesses need to be overcome? What is the level of maturity in relation to the status being aspired to as the long-term goal?

This approach is somewhat reminiscent of the annual performance appraisal. For example, anyone reading a company's internal information leaflets on this topic will no doubt come across the phrase that performance appraisals are an important way of making sure the employee *"knows where he/she stands"*. This sounds good at first. It seems generally good if you know where you stand. Feedback is seen as an element and requirement within a functioning control loop here. Every action is based on a control loop. By grabbing hold of a glass, I am following a control loop in which the feedback relating to the distance between my hand and the glass is a pre-requisite for ensuring I hit the target. But if it's a question of employees receiving feedback on "where they stand", this only makes sense if the reference parameter is clear: where does the employee stand in relation to *what*? What is the target or reference parameter? Where is the glass? If feedback is received in a control loop once a year, the parameter due to be developed, controlled or adjusted here can only be a very long-term one. Our aforementioned astronaut example could fall under this category.

For annual performance appraisals and the desired determination of where the employee stands, the latter is only appropriate if the employee is striving for a long-term status. Flatly requiring managers to use formalised performance appraisals to discuss their employees' standings with their employees would put managers in a rather odd position if they are unsure which reference parameter is to be achieved in the long-term, or what the long-term prospect is. As nice as it may sound to discuss "where the employee currently stands", it may ultimately prove to be pointless and irrelevant in practice.

In addition to the need for a reference parameter, it is also worth noting here the extent to which the direct manager is the authority who can talk to an employee about his/her current situation. Depending on the objective, this may also be a completely different authority. Such is the case for a prevalent practice in talent management. Talent management is usually aimed at guiding selected high potentials into key positions over the long-term (McCall, 1998). The process often lasts several years, and is comparable with the development of elite athletes (Berger & Berger, 2005). In an ideal scenario, a high potential will also be regularly (at least once a year) asked about his/her current standing. This may, but does not have to, be the task of the direct manager. It often tends to be performed by mentors or the talent manager.

Just to reiterate: Meetings or informal discussions about strengths, weaknesses, future, development etc. between any parties, whether between an employee and manager, or between two employees, are a good thing. Joint reflection is helpful. But if an HR manager stands up and expects all managers to formally assess, document and submit their employees' current circumstances, he/she must be sure that all employees are pursuing long-term goals, and that the direct managers are the right contact persons here.

Public image – Self-image

There is an old joke about a motorist driving the wrong way down the highway and listening to the traffic news reporting on a wrong-way driver, whereupon the motorist says: "One? More like hundreds!".

It can be assumed that a psychologically healthy life involves a certain degree of self-reflection. Who am I? How do others see me? If there is a big difference between self-image and public image, this has dysfunctional impacts on more than just the person himself/herself. Before and during my studies, I spent many years working in psychiatric clinics, where I was confronted with severe cases. One patient, for example, was convinced the newsreader on the television was only speaking to him. But the patient could not be treated, because he simply did not accept he was ill – and had not done for over 20 years. The "insane" often believe it is everyone else who is "crazy".

We've seen similar cases in the professional arena. The lonely superstar. The loser who actually isn't. The latently autistic, self-proclaimed nerd. Perhaps it is the high proportion of psychologists in HR departments which make HR professionals feel compelled to attend to this potential conflict between public and self-image (nothing against psychologists in HR – I myself was one). At many companies, all managers are asked by the HR department to evaluate their employees using a standardised, trait-based classification process (cf. Breisig, 2005). Simultaneously, the employees are asked to evaluate themselves using the same criteria. Differences are then discussed. The aim is for the employees to learn through this feedback, reflect, or correct their self-image if necessary. Open-minded managers may even revise their views of certain employees after discussing the results.

But let's examine this method objectively, and consider the extent to which it can contribute to learning through feedback:

- The low degree of objectivity means evaluating an employee's traits and attributes cannot be deemed highly reliable. Evaluations based on these methods say very little about an employee (cf. Becker, 2003).
- A manager's feedback to his/her employee will only be taken as constructive by an employee if the employee accepts the feedback or, ideally, actively requests it.
- As already discussed in the previous chapter, a manager as a boss in the judge's role cannot simultaneously conduct reflective talks with the employee based on mutual openness and trust.

To prevent misunderstandings here, it must be said that open, trustworthy reflections on the employee's attributes and behaviour, requested by all parties, are certainly welcomed. But it remains difficult to understand why so many companies, usually through their HR department, order this kind of across-the-board self-reflection exercise for their employees and managers, with the results then ending up in a system or HR files. A company is not a self-help or therapy group.

This exercise is virtually inconceivable in hierarchical settings due to the relationship between the employee and manager, while in an agile world, it will only work if individually requested by the employee. And even then, results should not be stored by a central authority. It's the last thing that will help with employee learning. Whether or not the direct manager is the right person to be giving an employee feedback on his/her attributes and behaviour is also highly questionable, especially in an agile setting.

In summary

- Feedback may be given in terms of the persons themselves, process, self-regulation and result, with the process level being the most effective. Annual performance appraisals primarily focus on the other levels.
- In a hierarchical world, it is the direct manager who gives feedback (incl. at the annual performance appraisal). In an agile world, it is the colleagues and customers.
- Employees only need to be told where they stand in terms of their development during an annual performance appraisal if the development goal is a long-term one.
- Reflections on public and self-image initiated by the manager can, at best, work in an agile world. And the employee must want this.

Managing companies

Managing companies and employees with objectives is an idea essentially described by George Odiorne (1965), which has been implemented at many companies. It became known as

Management by Objectives (MbO). This approach is based on some key assumptions, one of this is hierarchy. For example, Odiorne writes the following in his ground-breaking book:

> The basic structure of the corporation is the organizational form often called a *hierarchy* [original emphasis]. This is the familiar arrangement of boxes showing the boss in the top box and two, three, or more subordinates in the box one level down. Management by objectives is a system for making that structure work and for bringing about more vitality and personal involvement of the people in the hierarchy (p. 52)

It's as easy as that. Further assumptions are implied. One of which is the notion that the boss, and ultimately the company management, know best what the employee and the company as a whole need to do. Thinking at the top, acting at the bottom. In this context, MbO is nothing more than the lever between hierarchical levels. For example, overarching decisions and objectives are incrementally sent from one level to another as part of the annual performance appraisal, and are further differentiated. Anyone who has been socialised in hierarchical organisations is unlikely to waste a second questioning the principles of this cascading system. Like Odiorne, people naturally assume that is how companies operate. And most organisations do indeed function as per this principle. If it works, that's great. But there is nothing in the Bible, nor is there a law of nature, to stipulate that organisations must work this way. Too many companies and organisations have now proven that other approaches exist (cf. Laloux, 2014). We can envisage many different scenarios of what would happen if an employee came up with an idea.

An idea's path through the organisation

Let's imagine that an employee who is in constant customer contact, is focused on market developments, and is a genuinely recognised expert in his field, comes up with a great product idea. We can assume this idea is of huge strategic importance to the company's future – the company just doesn't know it yet. What will this employee do? How does the life cycle of this idea play out?

For the sake of simplicity, we'll call this employee Robert. After careful consideration and preparation, Robert speaks with his boss, the head of the department, and explains the idea. He doesn't want to invest too much time in his idea, since he hasn't been commissioned to act on it. It's not his job to think about another idea during his paid working time. The head of the department is extremely impressed with the idea, and discusses it with the senior departmental manager, who also views it favourably. The division manager expects a profitability calculation, but still has very little understanding of the idea. A lot has been lost in the "Chinese whispers" from the bottom to the top. The product management department is put in charge of the profitability calculation, and one of the employees there sees this task in his annual target agreement several weeks later. So the matter is officially wrapped up and taken care of from the top. If the profitability calculation yields a positive result, the development division is officially commissioned to work on the idea. Robert will have to wait and see whether he will play any part in implementing the idea. Given his field of activity, it's rather unlikely.

Now let's imagine a different version of that story.

Robert develops the idea behind closed doors. He speaks informally with colleagues from various divisions. They go out to lunch, and meet in the company's tea rooms. The primary aim is to find out what others think about this idea. Where is there interest and potential allies? More and more colleagues appear keen on Robert's idea, which develops further with every conversation. It's a social, creative learning process. Robert involved his boss right from the start, or at least updates him where necessary. He needs his boss as a partner and coach. "Speak to them. Think about this. Focus more on that." Networks show the idea's reach. In this context, Robert is what is known as a "natural leader", which is not the same as an "official leader". Only once the idea has been developed to such an extent that its implementation/further development requires significant resources will people start contending for sponsors within the company, or customers on the market. It pays to be interested in implementation.

Cascading and the role of the performance appraisal

As will no doubt have been obvious, the first story plays out in a hierarchical context, and the second in an agile context. In the former, a company is controlled via a formal hierarchy. Decisions are made at the top, and are then incrementally "broken down". The executive board may decide that profitability needs to rise by 5% the following year. What does this then mean for the production manager, sales manager, HR manager, purchases department and all the others? Only the production manager knows the answer, he/she discusses it with his/her senior departmental managers, who then discuss it with heads of department, who then discuss it with team leaders, who then discuss it with employees. In the end, the aim of the profitability increase finally reaches the bottom. This translation from one level to another is known as *cascading*, whereby the performance appraisal is the central event in which an objective is passed from one level to another. Results, ideas and successes are more or less enacted from the top down. Once the aims have been defined at all levels, target achievement is assessed - from the bottom up (cf. also Kaplan und Norton's Balanced Scorecard approach, 1996). This process generally also goes by the name of *Performance Management* (Gubmann, 1998) in practice.

The key feature of this approach is the fact that employees on all levels each enter into an obligation towards the next level up. They do this in an annual cycle. Once the targets have been agreed on, target achievement is constantly checked *by the direct manager*. Hierarchically socialised readers will see this as a matter of course, and performance appraisals as logical to the point of being indispensable. I dare say most approaches to performance appraisals have been based on this understanding of organisations. Conversely, the descriptions of performance appraisals in literature or practice implicitly or explicitly reflect this notion of organisations.

Self-management in an agile world

In an agile world, company management, and particularly the agreement of targets, follows a completely different approach. At this point, it is important to revisit the specifics of the respective framework conditions. As already mentioned earlier, employees in an agile world always work in interconnected teams, enjoying a high degree of autonomy with great scope for action. The second story about Robert should have demonstrated this.

While external management and cascading through instructions and control dominate hierarchical contexts, an agile world is all about the principle of *self-management*. The teams operate as networks, with an intense customer focus, whether these be internal or external customers. It is from there that the employees and teams are inspired, driven and motivated. As explained in relation to feedback, this self-management includes prompt feedback from the customer's end – a basic requirement for self-managed actions. These teams are supported by internal authorities, such as the IT department, purchases department or HR department (see Figure 35).

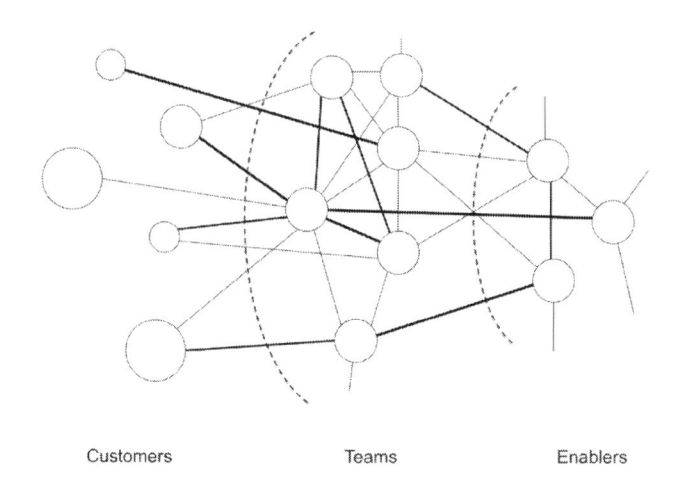

Figure 35:
Customers, teams and enablers in an interconnected, agile world (cf. Pfläging, 2014).

Among the internal enablers are the entities financing a project (sponsors). This all shows that company management operates completely differently in an agile world compared to a hierarchical world. And in any case, it is difficult to formulate so-called "smart" targets in an agile environment.

The employees' commitment

Let's now address the central question of what these two opposing principles of external versus self-management mean for the annual performance appraisal. The employee's commitment is of crucial importance here. More specifically speaking: To whom does the individual employee commit to render a particular service during the course of a year? In order to understand this better, we need to zoom in closer on the organisation and its structure.

If we look at the classic performance appraisal in a hierarchical context, we immediately end up with individual, annual target agreement, which results from overarching goals by way of cascading. No matter how much arrangement, ordering, participation or external influence this process entails, the manager and employee will ultimately agree that the *employee* will render a service which, after twelve months, must bear up under the *manager*'s assessment. That's how easy it is in a hierarchical world. This logic is illustrated on the left side (A) of Figure 36. The solid arrow shows the employee's commitment.

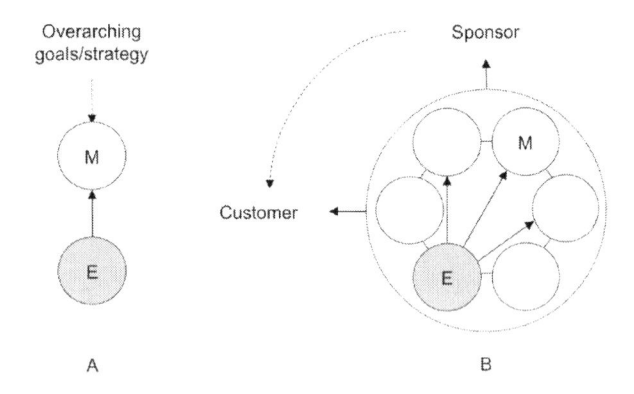

Figure 36:
An employee's commitment in a hierarchical (A) and agile (B) world
(E = Employee, M = Manager).

At first glance, an employee's commitment in an agile world (see on the right-hand side (B) of Figure 36, seems more complex. These employees not only have commitments to their manager, but also to their fellow team members. It is hard to distinguish the individual from the joint performance in this setting. And the manager, playing the role of coach or partner, is also always part of the team. So there is a *joint* commitment. The team as a whole no longer has a commitment to a higher-ranking manager, but rather to the customer on the one hand, and an internal sponsor on the other – if the latter even exists. As shown in the figure above, the assumption here is that the internal sponsor also has an indirect commitment to the customer (based on a positive scenario).

In terms of the annual performance appraisal, these thoughts indicate that it makes little sense for an employee to have an annual commitment to his/her manager in an agile context, and that this can and should not serve as the basis for managing a company in this instance.

In summary

- A cascading, top-down target agreement as part of annual performance appraisals requires a hierarchical structure with thinking at the top and actions at the bottom.
- In a hierarchical world, the employees have a commitment to their respective managers. They agree on targets with the manager, who then evaluates the achievement thereof.
- In an agile world, it is teams – not the individual employees – who have a commitment to their respective customers. Managers act as co-ordinators, intermediaries or enablers here.

Motivating by objectives

Setting targets is one of the key components of annual performance appraisals at most companies, serving many different purposes. Agreed targets may form the basis for a subsequent performance evaluation, clarify mutual expectations in the employee-supervisor relationship, or might help pass company objectives down to the lower levels. Targets are often ostensibly also agreed on to motivate employees, which is probably why annual performance appraisals are commonly known as "motivational interviews". This is the aspect we will now be focusing on.

Commitment and task complexity

Locke and Latham's (1984) goal-setting theory has already been mentioned on several occasions, and is constantly cited as scientific justification for target agreement. Put simply, this theory states that people who have set themselves a specific goal will perform better than those who, completing the same tasks, simply try to "do as well as they can". It revolves around the hypothesis that there is a direct link between a person's performance and the difficulty of the goal: the more challenging the goals, the greater the performance.

At this point, it is worth taking a closer look at the research findings relating to the goal-setting theory, for Locke and Latham don't see it as being quite as simple as that. Commitment and task complexity, among other factors, play a leading, crucial role here. Figure 37 illustrates their moderating effect on the link between goal difficulty and performance.

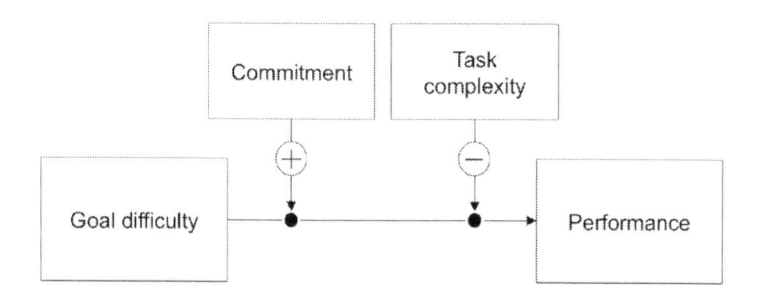

Figure 37:
Commitment and task complexity as moderators.

The links outlined above are as simple as they are obvious. Firstly, goals only result in higher performance if the employees fully embrace them, i.e. intrinsically commit to the goals and give them personal significance. Secondly, there is only a link between goal difficulty and performance when task complexity is low. The implications will be examined in more detail below.

Many guides on how to conduct performance appraisals emphasise the *agreement* part of "target agreement". The focus is on mutual understanding, with no command-like stipulation of goals – essentially intended to strengthen the employee's commitment to his/her goals. The employee may contribute his/her personal development ideas and interests as part of the target-agreement process.

This message is usually and primarily aimed at managers, and rarely at the employees concerned. As long as this is the case, the agreement idea is not truly internalised. If goals have truly been agreed on, all participants (the employee and the manager) operate on equal footing in the target-agreement process. It's not just managers arranging targets with their staff, but also the other way around: Employees arranging targets with their managers.

Only once *employees* – not solely managers – are asked to not only prepare their goals for their manager, but also discuss them with their manager, can we legitimately use the word "agreement". Target *setting* continues to imply the basic notion of calling for more agreement, which is why any conflicts in the "joint" target agreement are generally resolved in a hierarchical manner, as illustrated by an excerpt from a typical policy: "If no […] solution is reached, the matter is resolved by the immediate superior authority". A commission established with equal representation is often also responsible for settling disputes.

True agreement of targets is, however, the key basis of commitment. If targets are not really agreed on, i.e. the employee cannot contribute his/her own ideas in the same way the manager can, target agreement falls short of its aim to motivate employees (Locke, Latham & Erez, 1988). This is particularly the case in a hierarchical context.

Scientific studies have also shown that, when task complexity is high – we refer here to task uncertainty and dynamics -, the link between goal difficulty and performance tends to be weaker (Wood, Mento & Locke, 1987). In this instance, targets do not cause any harm, but don't significantly contribute to higher performance either.

Is it necessary to motivate employees?

When many in-house company brochures advertise performance appraisals by claiming they motivate employees, this implies employees *need* to be motivated. It is an assumption in turn based on a traditional understanding of the importance of work, according to which people work in order to live. We work so as not to have to work for the rest of the time. Work is a burden, a "mild illness" which must be suffered. Employees are forced to do something they wouldn't otherwise do.

However, companies following the agile model have a completely different approach, as described by McGregor (1960) in his Theory Y, which states that employees cannot be motivated. People are intrinsically motivated to "do a good job". At best, they can actually be discouraged, e.g. through limiting structures, rules making little sense to employees, and a lack of trust, coupled with extreme control. In his interesting, well-founded popular scientific book "Drive", Daniel Pink (2009) describes factors responsible for high employee motivation, namely Autonomy, Mastery und Purpose. If employees are able to act independently (Autonomy), recognise the opportunity to become really good at what they do (Mastery), and identify real meaning in what they do (Purpose), there is no need to worry about these employees' motivation levels. This view is consistent with the humanistic ideas expressed decades ago by classic masterminds such as Abraham Maslow and Douglas McGregor.

These ideas are reflected practically in an agile world. The employees have a high degree of autonomy. They operate voluntarily in an agile environment characterised by uncertainty and complexity. Only those wanting this sort of environment, and who tackle the tasks with great intrinsic motivation and curiosity, will "survive" here. Companies working in a highly innovative context know this. In this respect, using a special technique, like target agreement, to motivate employees is simply obsolete in an agile world.

Avoiding lost motivation in teams

Let's imagine five people are pulling as hard as they can on a rope. Let's also assume each person applies an average force of 700 Newtons (the strength needed to lift approx. 70 kg). How much force does the group apply as a whole when jointly pulling on a rope? The answer of "5 times 700 Newtons, i.e. 3,500 Newtons" is incorrect. It is a lot less. This is due to losses in motivation and co-ordination (cf. Latané, Williams & Harkins, 1979). Lost co-ordination happens when not everyone pulls in the same direction. But in the context addressed here, it is the motivation losses, also known as the *free-rider effect*, which are more critical. As the individual performance cannot be identified, each person reduces their personal input. This effect increases per person the larger the group size, and may particularly play a role in agile worlds, where employees always work in teams.

In view of this, teams should consider a way of somehow making each individual team member's performance identifiable, of exposing it. This requires effective methods in an agile, dynamic environment. We can learn a lot from the modern, agile project-management method known as *scrum* (cf. Sims & Johnson, 2011). The term scrum (scrummage) comes from rugby, and describes a situation in which all players (including the opponents) pack closely together with their heads down around a ball in an attempt to gain possession of it. Scrums always occur when play needs to be restarted, e.g. after the ball has gone out of bounds, after an injury break or similar. The scrum as a method for planning and managing projects now primarily plays a role in agile software development, and involves very short, joint consultation cycles in groups. The aim is to quickly and collectively respond to new challenges. The scrum is therefore an alternative to classic, more static methods of project planning and management, which implicitly (and incorrectly) assume that people will know, right from the start of a project, what they want to achieve in each project phase, and what the relevant task sets and their dependencies are (Weltz & Ortmann, 1992). The daily scrum involves the team meeting for 15 minutes every day (standing up), with each team member having to answer questions such as: "What will you achieve today?". At a team level, task sets (backlog elements) are defined every two weeks, and are considered team objectives for this short time frame, which is also known as the sprint.

This has very little to do with the target-agreement method seen in classic performance appraisals. But scrums do clearly show that brief, flexible consultations at a team level are necessary in an agile environment, and that every project member understands, every day, which tasks he/she must perform. The annual performance appraisal comes nowhere near to achieving this. If, however, it comes to reflecting on the importance of goals in relation to motivation, a scrum-based approach is the main way to go in an agile environment. In addition to these methods' great importance for project management, their relevance in terms of motivation is also a key factor here, although the focus is not on how employees can be motivated with objectives. It is instead on how *motivation losses* can be *avoided* through short-term objectives and the definition of individual performances.

In summary

- Annually set targets have a motivating effect if commitment is strong and task complexity is low.
- Depending on the type of task, lost motivation can arise in teams if the individual performances cannot be identified.
- In an agile world, people assume employees don't need to be motivated. At best, they can actually be discouraged.
- Agile teams define performance expectations individually and at a team level in very short cycles.

Retaining employees

An HR manager recently told me his company has been conducting "retention interviews" for some time. These systematic, regular meetings with selected employees not only address their prospects at the company, but also the relevant conditions for ensuring they remain loyal to their company. There's nothing surprising here, for talent shortages have seen employee retention become a serious challenge for many businesses. Estimates indicate that the loss of one single employee generates costs equalling one to three times his/her annual salary (Phillips & Edwards, 2009). What role can the annual performance appraisal play here?

Four lines of argumentation

When it comes to the annual performance appraisal, I am familiar with four lines of argumentation which reflect the assumed importance of this tool in terms of employee retention:

- *Loyalty through trust.* An annual performance appraisal between an employee and his/her manager already has a retention effect on the employee, because the conversation strengthens the interpersonal relationship and the employee's loyalty to his/her manager. This assumption is based on the intention of creating trust through the annual performance appraisal.
- *Retention as a by-product.* If the intended targets discussed in this book are reached through an annual performance appraisal, this indirectly contributes to employees remaining committed to their company. Employee retention thus becomes a positive side-effect of all purposes pursued using the annual performance appraisal. If the employee is motivated by targets, is clear about his/her prospects at the company, receives appropriate

reward for his/her performance, and has people invest in his/her professional development, there is no need to worry about his/her loyalty.
- *Expectations of working conditions.* An annual performance appraisal addresses the working conditions the employee deems relevant to him/her remaining at the company. In essence, it revolves around the jointly discussed question aimed at the employee: "What does the company have to do to ensure you don't leave?".
- *Early detection of employee turnover tendencies.* The issue of employee retention is institutionally integrated into annual performance appraisals. The manager and the employee jointly discuss the employee's future prospects and his/her possible intention to leave the company. From an operational perspective, the manager ticks the relevant box on the performance appraisal sheet if he/she deems there to be a high risk of an employee leaving. In this respect, the annual performance appraisal serves as an early-detection instrument, which is used to initiate the following employee-retention measures.

At this point, we must not attempt to evaluate each of these four lines of argumentation in detail. The objective of creating trust through a mandatory annual conversation was already addressed in a previous chapter, although it did not prove to offer great prospects for success. The second point (retention as a by-product) is certainly important, at least at a theoretical, conceptual level. If the aim of a performance appraisal is to actually help ensure employees are paid appropriately, given prospects, can develop and be motivated by goals, then all these aspects may contribute to a balanced, psychological contract between the employee and his/her employer. The pre-requisite is, of course, that the annual performance appraisal be able to fulfil this role – something which has been questioned in general or in relation to specific framework conditions throughout the course of this book.

The last two lines of argumentation appear particularly worth reflecting on. A detailed examination is required in order to better assess their effectiveness, because, as is so often the case, things are more complex than they may first seem.

The employee's expectations are the main focus

The approach of using an annual performance appraisal to discuss the working conditions relevant to an employee is somewhat of a foreign concept in a hierarchical world, which has always operated on the assumption that employees need to meet the requirements and expectations of the company and respective position. People have become used to job descriptions, job criteria, or standardised, trait-based classification processes. The company's and manager's wish list is the main focus of all HR activities. Let's for a moment imagine an annual performance appraisal like the one in the example below:

> Employee Thomas approaches his manager Dr Piper, and lets him know about the upcoming performance appraisal. "Dr Piper [the manager], the performance appraisal is coming up. Could I please ask you to conduct a few assessments beforehand, and document them on this form?". The form includes criteria on evaluating working conditions, such as work flexibility, workload, co-operation with colleagues, task meaning and identity, prompt feedback, and development opportunities. Thomas [employee] then addresses the various criteria during the appraisal, and gives Dr Piper [manager] his structured feedback on how he himself views the working conditions. "Dr Piper, how do you assess my working conditions in general, and where do you see potential for improving them?". After comparing

Thomas' expectations and ultimate assessments, a plan is developed, stipulating concrete measures to improve working conditions.

Anyone with a hierarchical mindset will struggle with this format, both practically and emotionally. Something isn't right here. Thomas' behaviour seems somehow arrogant. How will we get ahead if we try to please every employee in this way? After all, a company is no picnic.

But retaining employees demands an unconventional perspective. The focus here is not on the company's needs, but rather on the employees' preferences, and the extent to which the employer caters to the employee's requirements. The growing talent shortage has noticeably highlighted this power shift. Particularly in agile environments, companies are increasingly becoming aware that they are more dependent on the employees than the other way around.

Early detection

That leaves us with the fourth line of argumentation, which sees the annual performance appraisal as an opportunity for early detection. This approach must be taken very seriously, and offers realistic options for employers. The idea is once again quite simple: The manager uses an annual appraisal to get a sense of an employee's intentions to stay. If the trust basis permits it, this issue is discussed openly, so as to jointly arrange possible steps to retain the employee.

This, however, is not done with all employees, nor does it have to be. The focus here is primarily on specific internal, critical target functions and selected employee groups (cf. Trost, 2014):

- Employees in *key functions*. Key functions have a particular, strategic importance for the company. Not only

must they be filled with good employees, but also with employees who are considerably better than their counterparts at rival companies. If an employee in a key function is lost, it may noticeably weaken the entire company.
- Employees in *bottleneck functions*. These are functions which, due to labour market conditions, are very difficult to fill, but which involve high quantitative demand. The turnover in bottleneck functions results in significant efforts being made to replace former staff.
- *High potentials*. These are employees deemed to have the necessary potential to successfully fill key positions for the long-term. Companies have often already invested a vast amount of time, energy, money, networking and trust in these people, making the loss all the greater in the event of a resignation.

These sorts of conversations are of course only possible if the mutual trust between employee and manager allows it. In a hierarchical setup, in which a manager acts from a position of power, they can be quite difficult. Even just the suspicion that the employee may leave the company could lead to disadvantages for the employee. In any case, it is likely the employee will at least expect this. Given this, it must be assumed that this approach tends to work better in an agile context, where the relationship between employee and manager (coach or partner) is primarily characterised by trust.

Practical implications

How do these thoughts translate into practice, and what do they mean in terms of an annual performance appraisal? It can generally be assumed that annual, cyclical reflection on this issue is sufficient, since an employee's intentions to stay at or leave a company don't develop overnight. Nevertheless, it is wise to discuss the matter outside of an annual cycle if there is the risk of an acute problem.

In a hierarchical context, it is clear that managements want institutional, mandatory evaluations of the turnover tendencies of critical employees. This would provide an overview of the areas in which the company has an increased turnover risk, to then enable action to be taken "top down", and relevant measures to be initiated. The resulting privacy issues, however, are a completely different kettle of fish. After all, centrally stored information on employee turnover tendencies is highly sensitive, personal data. In the best case scenario, estimations of employee turnover in a hierarchical world are based on the sole estimations of the respective manager, and, as the employee is not likely to be open with his/her feelings due to the existing power relationship, the validity of such estimations is rightly questionable.

The picture is somewhat different in an agile world. Since the relationship here between employee and manager is essentially based on mutual trust, there is a high possibility of potential turnover tendencies being discussed openly – even if it is a constantly challenging issue for both parties. As this context sees the organisation more dependent on the employee rather than the other way around, it is likely the manager will cater to the employee's requirements – and this factor is a basic requirement for conducting such talks. Turnover tendencies are not centrally documented in this setting. This would be tantamount to a breach of trust. Even the mere suspicion that the manager may report an alleged turnover tendency to the HR department or senior management would prevent such talks from succeeding. The only possible outcome of these discussions in an agile world is for the necessary measures to be forwarded to the HR department with mutual consent. Potential measures can include adjusting working hours or salary, or clarifying possible career prospects, though others are of course also feasible.

In summary

- The joint discussion of employee requirements involves adopting an unconventional perspective, placing the focus on the employees' wishes.
- Early detection of turnover tendencies is a particularly good idea when it comes to employees in key or bottleneck functions, or high potentials.
- Discussions relating to turnover tendencies require a high degree of trust and confidentiality – aspects more conducive to an agile world.

Interim conclusion

The sections above critically examined the annual performance appraisal as an instrument for achieving various goals. In each case, this was done in keeping with the differing framework conditions existing in hierarchical and agile worlds. The discussion painted a rather mixed picture overall, making it difficult to draw a comprehensive conclusion. Figure 38 nevertheless cautiously attempts to provide a balanced summary.

Benefit	Hierarchy	Agility
Rewarding the best	****	**
Addressing the weak	***	**
Identifying talent	**	*
Determining internal suitability	***	*
Developing employees	**	*
Offering prospects	*	**
Learning through feedback	***	**
Managing companies	****	**
Motivation through objectives	**	*
Retaining employees	**	*
Summary	**2.6**	**1.5**

Figure 38:
The annual performance appraisal and its prospects of success in a hierarchical and agile world.

Using the very common five-star rating system, Figure 38 evaluates the success of the traditional annual performance appraisal in terms of agile and hierarchical framework conditions, doing so for each of the aforementioned benefits. Five stars mean "The annual performance appraisal works perfectly in relation to the respective benefit", while one star indicates little or no prospects for success. These ratings are based purely on notions of plausibility, as described in previous sections. It must be expressly stated that they are merely hypothetical, and are not founded on empirical evidence. They are simply an attempt to summarise everything outlined above, and are likely to be just as unreliable as a manager's evaluations of an employee's skills. But they should suffice for an interim conclusion.

The process of identifying high-performing employees can work well in a hierarchical setting, even though certain judgements may be dubious. A hierarchical world is generally one involving stable division of labour, where the manager is the boss. Once the framework conditions become more agile, however, the annual performance appraisal fails here for a number of reasons.

When it comes to identifying underperforming employees, it has been found that the annual performance appraisal is, at best, designed as a once-a-year opportunity to name the employees the company wishes to dismiss or whose variable salaries are to be reduced. It serves no other purpose, as it is not sufficiently synchronised with the professional methods for handling underperforming employees. This applies in both agile and hierarchical worlds, though the main reason agile worlds manage without this instrument tends to be because problems are resolved by the teams and employees themselves.

Even in a hierarchical world, it has become clear that, in terms of identifying talent, the direct manager is out of his/her depth in a number of respects, or can wrongly constitute a bottleneck for the career of a talented, motivated employee. If talent is identified in a hierarchical context, it tends to be done so despite, rather than as a result of, the annual performance appraisal. In an agile world, the direct manager, and therefore also the annual performance appraisal, plays a secondary role in identifying talent.

While a stable, work-sharing environment certainly does enable, albeit with difficulty, individual employee suitability to be classified based on standard criteria so as then to be compared with clearly defined and documented requirements, the idea falls completely flat in an uncertain, dynamic world. This is not necessarily perceived as a disadvantage in agile settings; after all, the focus here is more on diverse teams rather than "suitable" individuals.

It is a very similar story when it comes to employee development, where emphasis is placed on future development, based on current suitability. Using the annual performance appraisal as a development dialogue may be a wise course of action here, which is normally viewed non-critically by all parties involved. But even in a hierarchical context, this approach is not easy, nor does it always promise success. In an agile world, employees learn through self-regulation, on-demand, in teams and through networks. The concepts of learning and working are inextricably linked. Working means learning. While an annual, personal discussion of learning requirements with the direct manager cannot hurt, it plays a very minor role in terms of what happens in an agile world overall.

A manager in an agile world is better equipped to talk about an employee's prospects than a manager in a hierarchical world. On the one hand, this is due to the networked structures of agile worlds, where lateral mobility is enabled and managers can act as facilitators. Of more critical importance, however, is the fact that an agile world is more likely to involve a trust relationship between employee and manager, opening up possibilities for career coaching. Conversely, in a hierarchical world, managers are frequently unable to offer prospects, nor can they act as career coaches for their employees, the latter clearly conflicting with the typical leadership role found in a hierarchical context.

An employee is considered successful in a hierarchical world if his/her manager is satisfied with his/her work. Provided an annual performance appraisal does not raise any issues which have already been mentioned and discussed, it can be very helpful for the manager to provide the employee with recapitulative feedback relating to the last twelve months. Feedback in an agile world primarily comes from colleagues and customers, not from the direct manager. The direct manager can nevertheless act as a facilitator in his/her coach's role, albeit usually together with his/her team. Even here, however, the traditional annual performance appraisal soon reaches its limits.

If a company operates in a hierarchical manner, therefore dividing labour, it will not be able to cope without a system of cascading objectives. Whether or not companies do or can function like this in real life remains to be seen. In an agile world, teams – not individuals – primarily see themselves as having a commitment to their customers and internal sponsors, rather than to a higher-ranking management. While personal, annual performance appraisals may help provide individual orientation and focus, e.g. through a target agreement, they hardly have a bearing on managing the company as a whole.

In hierarchical worlds, objectives serve as extrinsic motivation at best. Existing power relationships mean the claim of mutual target agreement is more a theoretical element. While agreeing on targets is certainly a conceivable prospect in agile settings due to employee autonomy, employees do not need to be motivated in the first place. Here, short-term goals serve more to prevent free-rider effects. When it comes to motivating employees, annual performance appraisals are of little relevance in these environments.

Keeping employees loyal to the company is a greater challenge for agile worlds than hierarchical worlds. In the former, the employees have more career options to choose from. On the other hand, agile settings will find it easier to systematically cater to employee needs, as the nature of hierarchical worlds means actions there tend to be dictated by the company's requirements and standards.

However, hierarchical environments do enable systematic, centrally controlled early detection of potential turnover tendencies – an aspect which tends to be impeded in agile contexts due to the trust relationship between employee and manager.

If we use the simplified ratings shown in Figure 38 above to calculate unweighted averages, the annual performance appraisal is awarded 2.5 stars in a hierarchical context and only 1.5 stars in an agile context. These ratings are, admittedly, not very detailed, and purely serve as a summary. The thoughts behind them, however, have been outlined in great detail, and form a key part of this book.

Deeming these ratings to be reliable, we come to the simple conclusion that, in hierarchical worlds, the annual performance appraisal falls *below expectations*, while in modern, agile working environments, it is indeed an actual failure in many respects.

In summary

- Even in hierarchical worlds, only certain aspects of the annual performance appraisal live up to their claims.
- In an agile environment, the annual performance appraisal is largely a failure.

6. Alternatives

The summary in the previous chapter was not very flattering for the annual performance appraisal. In hierarchical worlds, the annual performance appraisal only appears to work, to some degree, for very few benefits, while in agile settings, the traditional annual performance appraisal is largely a complete failure. Criticism of this instrument is nothing new, although various authors have focused on very different aspects. What we are now interested in, however, are the alternatives. Numerous authors who subscribe, at least in part, to the criticism of the annual performance appraisal see no possible alternatives. Well-known management mastermind Edward E. Lawler III hits the nail on the head in one of his blog entries for Forbes, entitled "Performance Appraisals Are Dead, Long Live Performance Management" (Lawler, 2012). He rightly states that talent management without systematic employee evaluation is inconceivable. He also mentions that goals are simply essential when it comes to successfully running any organisation, meaning companies which do not evaluate performance will not cope, whether they like it or not. And that's why these sorts of instruments will continue to exist in the future. End of story.

However, this manner of thinking contains a major flaw, which we addressed very early on in this book. The benefit is being amalgamated with the instrument, the Why with the How. To clarify matters once again: there is no reason to doubt the plausibility of the benefits addressed in this book. Rewarding performance is the right thing to do. Weak performance shouldn't just be identified as such; a suitable solution must also be found for the relevant, underperforming employees themselves. Anyone wanting to systematically promote and encourage talent must identify talent. It is good to know what each employee can do. And the employees themselves particularly need to know this. There are very few companies which can afford not to provide development opportunities for their staff. And yes, it is good to offer the employees prospects, and for the employees to have an idea of their personal career plans. Learning without feedback is inconceivable. In certain circumstances, companies may be managed by objectives, and if these objectives happen to motivate, then so much the better. After all, it must be in a company's interests to retain good employees. The annual performance appraisal shouldn't be assessed based on its intended benefit. It would in fact be a downright blessing if evaluations only took this intended benefit into account. Anyone promising to achieve all targets through the annual performance appraisal will not face any objections; the problem is that a classic annual performance appraisal rarely produces this benefit. That's why it is worth asking how else this benefit may be achieved. This requires new, different ideas which tend to answer the question of *How* more so than *Why*, bringing us to the design.

Successful and effective HR management is impossible without relevant decisions and judgements. The annual performance appraisal provides decisions and judgements. We have already established that these are the actual results of the process. Nothing more, nothing less. This chapter also focuses on decisions and judgements. But instead of identifying alternatives for each benefit, we adopt a more generic approach, in which we discuss the fundamental alternative forms of achieving relevant decisions and judgements. The previous chapter already included several examples of alternative approaches in relation to the various benefits. Four of these, plus one format element, essentially play a role here:

- *Responsibility.* Are decisions and judgements required by a central unit, or are they the responsibility of the affected employees and teams? Who initiates the relevant measures, and who owns the results at the end?
- *Openness and diversity.* What degree of central regulation and standardisation is required for scheduling, content and formats? How much openness is possible? Is the aim for company-wide, statistical comparability or are individuality and diversity permitted?
- *Hierarchy versus networks.* Who makes judgements and decisions? The customers and colleagues or the direct manager? Is the focus on individual employees or teams and networks?
- *A focus on needs.* Are many relevant decisions and judgements made using one single instrument at one single time, always involving the same participants? Or do decision-making and judgement processes revolve around the respective needs and situations?
- *Surrender.* Where can systems, instruments, processes and methods be completely abandoned? This is less about arranging and creating instruments and activities, and

more about simply letting go, doing nothing, and allowing things to flow naturally.

I have long puzzled over and discussed the issue of how to cut to the chase when it comes to design or alternative methods to the annual performance appraisal. I examined how elements such as target agreement, performance evaluation and talent identification could operate differently. Numerous alternatives in general and specifically for agile settings were already outlined in the previous chapter. In the end, it became clear that there is a common denominator. Regardless of the benefit involved, people in hierarchical worlds will try different ways of catering to it compared to people in agile worlds. So it is no surprise that, for example, an environment managed de-centrally requires decentralised instruments, or that a world in which teams and networks play a major role also reflects this in the way decisions and judgements are made – regardless of the benefit sought.

Responsibility

I recently once again participated in an exciting discussion with HR development officers. We talked about competence management and, in this context, also annual performance appraisals. The question of which role IT systems can play here arose. We can see there is now a wide range of system providers offering sophisticated solutions for this. One main sales argument put forward by many of these providers is the high degree of integration. Integration means that information generated in one place may be used in another, e.g. as part of an affiliated HR process. One-off job criteria then re-emerge during the employee evaluation. Skills profiles generated during the employee selection process are retrieved and shown at the annual competence evaluation – to the delight of many companies and HR professionals, who are questioned surprisingly rarely. The big HR machine. But things only got emotional when we started discussing the performance appraisal situation: "Do we really want managers to conduct a performance appraisal with a laptop or tablet in front of them on the desk?". To which the response was a collective, noticeable malaise. So what is the problem? Certainly not the mechanism in itself. The problem is that the talks need to reflect the appropriate confidentiality, except that they simultaneously break this by entering information into a system. This is a very fundamental aspect: who needs and expects the information generated as part of an annual performance appraisal? Once data is entered into a system, the relevant judgements and decisions are clearly no longer just the property of the employee. So who do they belong to then?

This section relates to these sorts of questions. Whenever decisions or judgements are generated in an HR context, we are faced with the issue of whose property they are. Who needs them? Who generates these decisions and judgements? And there are always two sides to the one dimension: the employee and his/her team on the one hand, and the company and HR on the other. This also applies to the question of what the respective judgements and decisions focus on: is it the employee or the company?

A central authority versus the employee

As part of his/her annual performance evaluation, an employee receives a tick in the box entitled "Meets expectations". It's the middle box. Not bad, but nothing exceptional either. Who needs this information? This question is comparatively simple, but crucial. And there are two extreme answers to it: Firstly, *HR* or *the company management* need this information to initiate any necessary measures. Secondly, the *employee* needs the information so he/she "knows where he/she stands". We could ask this question for all benefit types. Who needs objectives? Who needs feedback? Who needs an assessment of employee potential? Who needs prospects? The two possible answers are based on two opposing philosophies, which were already addressed in an earlier chapter about the customers of performance appraisal: "Central planning" on the one hand, and "Enabling and personal responsibility" on the other.

In the case of central planning, the HR department is the focal point. HR needs decisions and judgements in order to fulfil its responsibility. Based on potential assessments, employees are assigned to a central talent pool managed by HR. Skills profiles are used to allocate suitable jobs to the employees as part of a centralised personnel placement plan. Development requirements are noted in order to plan and initiate the appropriate measures. Objectives are cascaded in order to achieve over-arching goals. The best need to be identified in order to ensure they are specially and centrally recognised. The weak must be identified to ensure HR keeps these on its radar. The list could go on, and many traditionally socialised HR professionals will have thought: "What else?".

Here is the alternative: The employee or his/her team sets goals for their own guidance. The employees within the team determine each other's needs for development, and attend to the respective development measures in order to ultimately improve on the whole. Employees want feedback in order to learn – from their customers and their colleagues. They obtain feedback when they need it. They tell their team their expectations regarding working conditions so as to strike a better work/life balance. An employee who feels he/she has a higher calling will take the initiative to participate in an internal talent programme or fight for the opportunities he/she needs in order to develop. The employee identifies a need for learning, and actively seeks out solutions. This list, too, could go on and on. So where does this leave HR? The role of HR is to enable the employee to do this, insofar as it is possible and necessary.

Compatibility between different philosophies

Is it possible to combine both philosophies? Can you give employees responsibility and still call for judgements/decisions as a central authority? Are these mutually exclusive approaches? Do these two extremes apply equally to all benefits? Do you apply one or the other for all benefits? Once again, things are much more complex than first thought. Here are a few rules and basic assumptions:

An employee can only be enabled to take personal responsibility if he/she wants to do this himself/herself. Some HR professionals argue it is important for the employee to receive an annual performance evaluation from his/her manager. Fuelled by this notion, they demand this evaluation, and often note that the employee doesn't even want it, meaning this approach can be deemed a failure from the word go.

In some scenarios, HR cannot ask for certain judgements of decisions as a central authority, nor should it even attempt to do so. For example, managers primarily acting as coaches will evade any central requirements for a documented performance evaluation. Teams truly seeing themselves as such will view target agreements as an inherent inconsistency in the system. Further examples were sufficiently addressed in chapters 4 and 5. In general, I would go so far as to say that HR can demand more in hierarchical worlds than in agile worlds.

HR can ask for decisions and judgements from a central authority if there is an express or unspoken partnership agreement between HR and the employees regarding this. The central recording of individual development needs and plans to better enable HR to offer relevant measures such as training is a simple example. Or individual, annual working time regulations may be discussed, as is the case at the Germany's Trumpf corporate group. Every two years, employees can decide how many hours per week they wish to work. HR can and must, of course, be advised this information in such cases, and the employees will not have any problem with it if it has been agreed on in advance.

Things may differ depending on the benefit. While HR may likely be dependent on information relating to relevant employees when it comes to analysing potential in the context of a centrally run talent development programme, this may not be the case when assessing development prospects.

There are a lot of factors in favour of applying a case-by-case approach to decide which method to adopt when it comes to institutionalised decisions and judgements.

Who owns the results?

During the presentations, seminars and part-time Masters courses I run, I often ask the question: "When was the last time you checked your goals in the HR system"? Or: "When was the last time you looked at your personal skills profile?". The answers range from complete irritation, "What sort of question is that?" to "Why should I?" to "During the last performance appraisal". Most employees are rarely interested in this information during the year, deeming it to be of little relevance. When I ask HR professionals the same questions, the answers are naturally different, although I do still see a lot of pensive expressions. The annual performance appraisal is conducted one way or another, documented in a form, and the matter then forwarded to HR, thereby completing the process. "That's a matter for the HR department. What does it have to do with me?".

This is admittedly a lopsided, bleak portrayal. Behind it lies the aforementioned question of who can lay claim to the judgements and decisions resulting from an annual performance appraisal. The answer should be based on relevance: who needs these judgements and decisions? HR? The respective manager? The team? The employee? This requires absolute rigour, which is often lacking in many HR instruments – not just the annual performance appraisal. To clarify things, let's take a simple example which doesn't directly relate to a performance appraisal, but ties in particularly well with the discussion to follow: upward appraisal. There is generally no problem with employees conducting structured evaluations of their managers. Feedback is good. Comparability has its advantages. But *who* receives the results, and *why*? Here, again, there are two extreme answers: Firstly, the manager receives the results in order to optimise his/her leadership. Secondly: HR or the company management receives the results so that a decision can be made as to whether the respective manager is suited to his/her role. These cases are mutually exclusive. Telling managers and their employees something is feedback, only to then use the results as an instrument for assessing suitability will never work. It would be utterly disingenuous.

If a manager gives an employee feedback, this feedback should be the employee's property. HR plays no role here. If a team's employees evaluate each other in a confidential setting, the results belong to the team, and particularly to the respective employees. If employees independently define their own objectives, HR doesn't need to know. In practice, however, there are unfortunately only very few examples of decisions and judgements being handled independently in this context; in any case, they only appear very rarely in the HR literature.

One clear, relevant example is the current self-tracking movement, which obviously has very little to do with HR, but which can provide a learning curve for companies. People set themselves sport and health goals, and track their development using relevant technical devices and apps – "The Quantified Self". They measure their daily calorie consumption, their mileage on their daily run, and the changes in their own body weight, sharing their results with their community on a daily basis. The results belong to those for whom they are relevant. HR is far removed from such approaches, although this sort of enthusiasm would certainly come in handy here. In the long-term, we will be referring to so-called "quantified employees".

Putting the employee first?

HR management has always been characterised by needs-based attitudes. We see it in many textbooks and reference books, and it is also reflected in HR approaches and processes. It's all about the right employee in the right place at the right time – but for whom? Organisational units and managers issue quantitative and qualitative workforce requirements at short notice or as part of regular HR planning. HR is consequently assigned the task of meeting these requirements. Skills profiles are devised to help determine individual development needs. And it's a similar story when it comes to employee recruitment and selection, where candidates are compared against set criteria. Wherever we look in HR management, we see this approach, whereby the primary objective is to meet the company's needs. It's all about the company.

At the same time, I also see many businesses claiming to "put the employee first". What does this mean? The company gears itself around the employee's needs when creating the working environment. Every effort is made to ensure employees are given what they need in order to be successful. It's a matter of playing to their strengths, rather than eliminating their weaknesses. It's about trying to understand the employees' talents so as to facilitate a setting in which these can be developed. It's a case of being guided by the awareness that it's the employees who make the company successful – not the managers.

When I see businesses which essentially adopt a needs-based approach to their HR management yet still claim that "we put employees first", I don't initially believe the second part. While a corporate, HR-based focus on needs can operate alongside an employee-focused approach, there is a considerable risk of neglecting one while concentrating on the other. The annual performance appraisal in its traditional form is clearly geared around needs. It serves to get employees where the company wants them to be, whether in terms of performance, skills or motivation. So when judgements and decisions are made – e.g. during an annual performance appraisal – do they focus on the requirements (needs) of the manager and company or those of the employees?

Classic employee *surveys* tend to be geared around the employee. Employees evaluate working conditions which are assumed to have not only influenced their performance, but also their satisfaction. It is critical to note here, however, that merely conducting an employee survey is certainly no guarantee that the focus will be on the employee. This will only be evidenced by the clear consequences derived from the results. If the employee's working conditions are discussed at an annual performance appraisal, with the focus being on his/her requirements, we can say this is employee-oriented. If the employee's satisfaction with his/her manager, and not the manager's satisfaction with the employee, is addressed, we can say this is employee-oriented. "Employee-oriented" can mean that the employee conducts the meetings and documents them – in his/her office.

I recently discussed the issue of leadership with some operations managers from Bavaria. When it came to talking about annual performance appraisals, a young master electrician who employed

17 staff at his company piped up, saying "I conduct that sort of performance appraisal every year, the day before my birthday. During this appraisal, every employee must tell me ten things which he/she believes are going like shit [his words] at our shop. We then talk about how we can change these". I finally had a perfect practical example of an employee-oriented performance appraisal.

In summary

- HR-relevant judgements and decisions can either be made by a central authority (HR, company management) or by the employees and their teams.
- If applicable, the relevance of the results should be used to clarify who these ultimately belong to, and where they are stored/documented.
- Employee-oriented means focusing on the interests of the employees and their teams. These often differ from the interests of the company.

Openness and diversity

When companies think about introducing leadership, planning, control or other management systems, they envisage a uniform system which applies to everyone affected. An approach developed based on the premise of "laissez-faire" is unlikely to operate as a system, or at least would not be called a management system. For this reason, there are usually stipulated content, rules, formats and responsibilities which are created and implemented centrally by the system owner. This logic can be found in almost all areas of life. So it would be odd, for instance, if every person completed a tax return based on what they deem to be correct. But it's not just a case of black and white here. Depending on objective and framework conditions, there are some sensible intermediate stages between consistent uniformity and openness. To use another analogy from public life: In most countries, the meaning of and adherence to traffic-light signals are governed by standard rules. "Just as well", most of us would say. Otherwise how would we manage? In other cities around the world, like Shanghai, this is not the case. Traffic-light signals are simply a recommendation here.

But what about for judgements and decisions normally made in the context of the annual performance appraisal? How many rules does the company/system manager need to set? How much openness is permitted/strived for in an attempt to achieve the benefits usually pursued through annual performance appraisals? This section will not just be looking at the operational standardisation or openness of a tool or system, but also its result. Standardised tools can generate standardised results. Is that what we want? Open systems encourage the much-lauded diversity.

Charming openness

Both the literature and discussions among managers and HR professionals constantly raise the very charming suggestion of reducing the annual performance appraisal form to a particularly simplified version (see Figure 39). This variant consists of just one page, a single sheet of paper with two questions: What do I want to be proud of in 12 months' time? And: What areas do I want to improve in over the next 12 months?

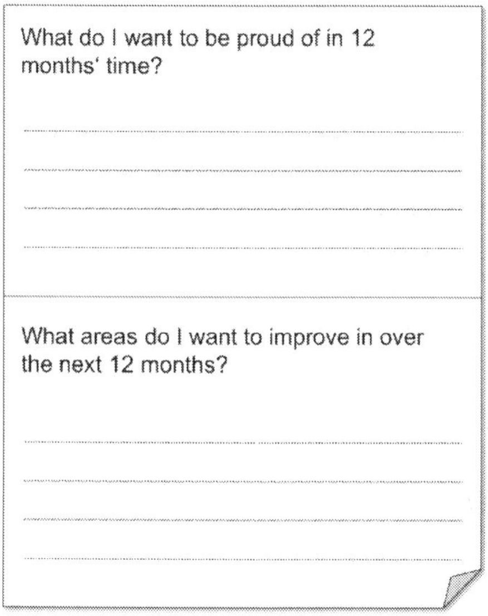

> What do I want to be proud of in 12 months' time?
>
> ....
> ....
> ....
>
> What areas do I want to improve in over the next 12 months?
>
> ....
> ....
> ....

Figure 39:
A very simple form for the annual performance appraisal.

The simplicity of this approach is almost unbelievable compared to the bureaucratic, tedious monster forms commonly found in practice. Content is formulated openly here. In actual fact, I would recommend every person – not just every employee – to answer these two questions for themselves at the start of each year. No one conducts an annual performance appraisal with me, but I willingly do this exercise.

At this point, however, it should be less about the number of questions or simplicity in itself, and more about the qualitative character of the judgements and decisions. If, for example, we are talking about assessing a particular skill, there are two extreme variants: the qualitative version and the quantitative, structured version. To demonstrate, let's take the skill of team-working ability. A fictitious evaluation could be as follows:

Overall, you're a team player, but with some limitations. For example, I have often seen you in situations where you intensively and successfully strive to achieve a consensus within the team, as was the case recently. [insert example] At the same time, you also pursue your own interests, particularly if you are 100% convinced of an idea. That's ok, but I think you would be doing yourself and the team a favour if you found a better balance here. Etc.

The other variant sounds something like: "In terms of team-working ability, I see you as being a level 4" (on a scale of 1 = weak to 5 = very strong).

So what is the more sensible option? When choosing a format, the first crucial factor is to determine who receives the result and which format usually benefits this recipient. When it comes to compiling reports based on judgements and decisions which ultimately end up on the senior management's desk, quantitative formats are the preferred option. This is simply due to the fact that quantitative, closed formats are better suited to statistical analyses. If, however, it's a question of increasing benefit for the employee, qualitative formats are preferred, since they are more informative.

The consequences resulting from a judgement or decision similarly play a key role. Examples here include school grades or the awarding of marks in competitions like figure skating. While qualitative judgements can help with learning or training, quantitative judgements (grades) from a central authority serve to make clear decisions: who will move up to the next year of schooling? Who passed the examination? Who won the competition? It once again becomes clear here that it's all about the benefit. Is the focus on particularly rewarding the best or more on learning through feedback? Just to name two. Depending on the answer, people will tend to go for openness or structure.

Forced distribution – good or bad?

Another area which has for years been controversially discussed both in practice and academia in relation to performance evaluation relates to the question of whether *forced distribution* as a special form of standardisation makes sense. Forced distribution (also forced ranking) requires that employee evaluations ultimately match a predefined distribution. It features particularly prominently in performance evaluations. So instead of evaluating employees absolutely, they are assessed relatively to one another, e.g. so that the distribution always produces 10% C-players, 70% B-players and 20% A-players. Forced distribution is even applied when the different performance levels have specific meanings, as demonstrated in Figure 40.

Performance level	Presetting
Performance is well above expectations	10%
Performance is above expectations	15%
Performance meets expectations	60%
Performance is below expectations	10%
Performance is well below expectations	5%
Total	**100%**

Figure 40:
Example of forced distribution for a performance evaluation.

If a company identifies all underperforming employees every year in order to sever ties with them, rankings may play an important role. In fact these scenarios are the only time rankings make total sense. Studies show that international top managers in particular appear to be fond of this method (Axelrod, Handfield-Jones & Michaels, 2002). The idea is quite simple: The average overall performance is gradually increased by continuously capping the bottom end of the performance distribution, and replacing the relevant employees with average or better employees. Simulations, at least, have shown that this effect exists in the first few years, but that it then becomes increasingly difficult to increase performance in general (Scullen, Bergey & Aiman-Smith, 2005; Grote, 2005).

Another main argument in favour of forced distribution is the avoidance of inflationary positive judgements. The managers have virtually no choice but to also deliver negative evaluations within their team, resulting in the evaluations losing their absolute meaning. On average, a national football team would be evaluated in the same way as a local seniors' team in a small village. As has been scientifically proven, this does not provide more valid results (cf. Breisig, 2005).

Companies focused on lateral co-operation and social learning (learning from one another) should show particular restraint when it comes to forced distribution, as it tends to spark competition amongst employees. If there are only limited positions available for A-players, employees will do all they can to boost themselves and – more importantly – weaken others within the company. In certain situations, internal competition can be good, and can motivate employees to perform better. In agile settings, however, where networks are of key significance, it is advisable to avoid such internal competition.

There is only *one* feasible reason to use forced distribution: when the evaluation criteria are associated with concrete measures for which limited resources have been defined. If, for example, a company decides to reward all A-players with a cruise, but the budget only allows for a limited number of places, the number of A-players should be restricted right from the outset. In a functioning talent-management system, this means not all employees who demonstrate a high level of performance, and who are deemed to have high potential, can be included in a development programme. Companies which do this may find they have more talent in their development programmes than key positions which need to be permanently filled, resulting in unmet expectations among the best and most talented. It is instead advisable to think of talent management in terms of long-term needs, and thus support enough talent to ensure sufficient, mature candidates are available at all times – nothing more, nothing less (cf. Conger, 2010). A hierarchical world caters to this much more easily than an agile one, or it at least tends to be assumed that future needs can be quantified. Whether or not this eventually works is another matter entirely.

Uniformity

Another aspect relating to openness and diversity involves the issue of *uniformity*. Uniformity in HR processes, methods and relevant content across all company divisions is seen by many companies as being particularly desirable. In my work as a consultant and trainer, I am constantly coming across clients complaining about a lack of uniformity: "We have no *uniform* understanding of the necessary skills", "there is no *uniform* understanding at our company as to what performance means", "we lack *uniform* standards when selecting employees" etc. Uniformity reduces complexity. There is less need for adjustment, and things run more smoothly, when everyone at the company thinks the same and acts in accordance with the same standards. This particularly applies when complex systems are being managed and co-ordinated. HR departments, as central authorities, often operate from this perspective.

The ideas raised in this book, on the other hand, have shown that HR processes and instruments should be geared around the existing framework conditions. Not only does this result in different companies needing different approaches due to differing framework conditions; differing framework conditions often even exist within individual companies. Can a performance evaluation in an environment of highly repetitive tasks be conducted following the same pattern as applied in an environment involving projects with maximum task uncertainty? Should the Research and Development division adopt the same approaches as the accounts department or service hotline?

Diversity as an attitude

The issue of openness is thus also raised when it comes to criteria used for decisions and judgements, whether it be when evaluating skills, potential, performance, development needs etc. Companies can operate in small, separate units here, or in a more open, general manner. Agile environments tend to prefer the openness option.

This aspect includes the important issue of *diversity* – a key feature of agile organisations. Many versions of the annual performance appraisal stipulate specific skills based on which employees are evaluated annually by their direct managers. The underlying message is: "That's how we (the company) want our employees to be". The more specific and narrow these skills requirements are, the more diversity is institutionally prevented. Companies which have realised this are increasingly making the switch to phrasing employee requirements in an extremely generic, general manner. One example of this is Google, which only focuses on four very general criteria for its employee selection process: Role-related knowledge, general cognitive abilities, leadership, googliness.

In the end, diversity is not expressed in pie charts illustrating a variation in gender or age, but rather in the internalised attitude of appreciating the freedom of individuality. The potato example is helpful here. If someone has picked a certain variety of potato for many years, e.g. medium-sized and round, and now tries to pick a range of different potatoes, they have two options. Either add certain different types of potatoes (small, gnarled) to the existing medium-sized, round ones in order to systematically change the composition of the harvest, or accept the potatoes as they are. Both approaches result in diversity, but only the second is characterised by an internal attitude of permitting individuality.

In summary

- Decisions and judgements can either be generated openly and qualitatively, or in a structured, quantitative manner. The right variant in each case depends on which benefit is to be achieved for which party.
- Forced distribution results in massive disadvantages. It particularly prevents successful co-operation in and between teams.
- Detailed, structured categories, particularly when assessing skills, may impede diversity. Diversity is not expressed in statistics, but is rather an internal attitude of permitting individuality.

Networked thinking

How does an employee ultimately know that he/she has done a good job? I would advise any CEO to pose this question to randomly chosen employees when the opportunity arises. The answers vary greatly, but two possible ones are worth noting: "If my *boss* is satisfied, it means I've done a good job". Or "If my *customers* are satisfied, it means I've done a good job". If the first answer predominates at a company, the company has a hierarchical structure. The second answer dominates at more agile companies. I would then like to ask the respective CEO which answer they prefer, for this would have important implications for the design of many HR processes.

Many employees will instinctively mention the customer, since numerous presentations, signs and seminars have taught them that a customer focus is supposedly a good idea. Deep down, however, employees will always be thinking of their boss, particularly in hierarchical systems. "Will he/she be happy with what I'm doing?". In hierarchical systems, customers can rarely directly reward or punish the employee, or decide his/her future at the company. The direct supervisor, however, can. Employees in these systems know this, and act accordingly.

Social and collaborative approaches

In recent years, there has been a trend towards social or collaborative forms of performance evaluation (Mosley, 2013). This is known as "Social Performance Review" in international contexts. It is a development whose roots lie in the changing working world and associated agilisation. Knowledge-intensive contexts in particular see employees primarily working in teams of sometimes highly specialised experts. The success of these teams is in turn based on a dynamic, close co-operation between all team members. What's unique about this is the fact that the managers here usually have less of an idea of what the employees do than the employees themselves. The complexity of the work content and the increasingly rapid shift in relevant knowledge simply do not permit anything else. Even if a manager works 100 hours a week, he/she will not be able to bear up against the employees' professional development. He/she shouldn't even bother trying. Chapter 4 already examined this in detail, and it became clear that a manager in these environments can only play the role of coach, partner or enabler. He/she is really not qualified to professionally evaluate an employee's performance. So it is only logical for employees already working in networked, customer-oriented teams to be evaluated by customers and other colleagues (peers). Consequently, an employee is only successful if his/her customers and colleagues deem this to be true. Evaluations and feedback thus do not occur vertically (top-down) via the manager, but rather horizontally. Two real-life examples will illustrate this:

- Every year, a computer game manufacturer in Frankfurt gives every employee ten points to award to colleagues at his/her discretion. Each point thus constitutes a special form of collegial recognition. At the end of the year, the individual bonus is determined by the number of points received by other colleagues.
- An American airline gives its frequent flyers the opportunity to award points to cabin crew for special service and friendliness in the form of vouchers.
- At an internationally managed music-streaming service provider in Sweden, employees evaluate each other daily through an internal Facebook of sorts.

So-called Employee Recognition Systems are clearly also on the rise. Employees have access to a kind of internal Amazon, from which they can give gifts to selected colleagues. Each employee has a certain budget for this, proportionate to his/her base salary. In addition to the official effects of direct, personal recognition, these systems are also a way of analysing which employees receive gifts, and what the total value is. This, in turn, can be used as a valid indicator of performance.

Instant feedback

A typical feature of peer-to-peer evaluations is the fact that the evaluation/feedback occurs directly, and is a natural part of daily co-operation and communication. If a Facebook user posts something today at 2pm, whether it be a video, text or image, he/she expects feedback from his/her "friends" within a few minutes or hours. The post is considered old and out-of-date by the time 24 hours have passed. Bloggers who publish a new entry hope to receive an appropriate response within a few hours or days. These expectations have basically been hard-wired into the consciousness of the entire Internet community – and by no means just among young people. The only notable factor when it comes to younger generations is that they know no different.

This form of instant feedback contrasts sharply with annual feedback, e.g. given as part of an annual performance appraisal. What's critical here, however, is not just the fact that modern, socialised people want instant feedback, but rather that this feedback is provided horizontally by other people, regardless of their hierarchical position.

Gamification

Gamification is a further advanced variant of this approach, and may be illustrated using a fictitious example: John works in the sales department of a large vehicle manufacturer. Like his colleagues, he too has noticed that customers buying medium-sized vehicles are hard to convince when it comes to selling the benefits of a sunroof. More by accident than anything else, he developed an effective technique. When customers take a seat in a car with a sunroof, the first thing he does is cover the sunroof. He does not uncover it until the customers are sitting in the car, allowing them to experience a real Wow moment – an irresistible sense of space.

John posted this effective technique in an internal knowledge portal for salespeople, and was highly commended for it by his colleagues. More than 50 colleagues liked the idea (50 likes). A badge is awarded for 25 likes, and John is only three badges short of going from silver to gold status. All employees who achieve gold status are invited to a "Sales Hero Conference" once a year, where they not only celebrate with the executive board, but are also each given the chance to prominently present their ideas. Those who do so acquire internal followers within the company more easily (similar to Twitter), which in turn makes it easier to earn more badges.

This story makes John's work sound like a kind of game. And based on the ideas of gamification, that's what it should be. The principles of game design are applied to encourage employees to do things which are intrinsically boring, such as documenting ideas in a knowledge portal. It should once again be pointed out that John and his colleagues are not evaluated by their direct supervisors, but by peers.

In this context, it is worth revisiting the aspect of forced distribution in employee evaluations. Forced distribution is ideal for preventing precisely this form of knowledge exchange. Because which employee would be interested in strengthening the position of his/her colleagues if it means he/she runs the risk of not ending up in the top 10% of the performance distribution?

In summary

- Decisions and judgements can either be made vertically through the hierarchy (top-down) or vertically based on networks.
- In an agile world, the manager alone does not decide (top-down) whether an employee has been successful at his/her job, but rather the colleagues and customers (vertical). Social approaches of performance management are increasingly being adopted here.

- Instant feedback from customers and colleagues to almost everything is a central element of lateral collaboration in agile environments.
- Gamification is a far-reaching, modern approach designed to encourage lateral collaboration, feedback and peer-to-peer evaluation.

Sorted formats, content, times and players

If the HR department announces it's time for the annual performance appraisal, many employees and managers think: "how has a year gone by so quickly?". It's a constant cycle. At most companies, the annual performance appraisal is a familiar event occurring once a year. Many HR managers in fact appear to emphasise the uniqueness of this one-off discussion as a positive. "It's important for the managers and their employees to take time out of their hectic everyday routine *once* a year to talk about *all* the important issues at *one* time". That's how it usually goes. In most cases, it is the same HR managers who, when asked if feedback *once* a year is good, then instinctively admit: "No, feedback is important the whole year round. Not just once a year".

There is a clear need to sort content, times, players and formats more clearly here. What kind of time frame is appropriate? Should relevant judgements and decisions be combined, i.e. made "at once", or distributed better? When should decisions and judgements be made if they are needed?

Why once a year?

If we now look at the various benefits mentioned in chapter 3, the obvious question is how often relevant decisions and judgements should be made during the year, and how planned this process must be, in order to achieve maximum benefit. When it comes to the annual performance appraisal, there is an implied assumption that *once* a year is a suitable interval for *all* benefits. Even just scratching the surface causes initial doubts. The great inventor of Management by Objectives (MbO), George Ordiorne, himself writes this in his groundbreaking book:

> There is no special significance in managerial performance being reviewed annually. The underlying value of performance appraisal is the opportunity it affords to feed back results against goals in order to improve performance. This does not necessarily have to take place at year's end, as if it magically coincided with the rotation of the earth on its axis, like a pagan holiday. It is merely convenient for some purposes. (1965, p. 235).

When feedback is given annually, it can only be as a form of cumulative feedback. And anything that hasn't already been said during the year should certainly not be mentioned in an "annual review". "No surprises in the annual review", as Odiorne succinctly puts it. Learning requires prompt feedback. Apart from spontaneous, one-off bonus payments, decisions regarding salaries should be made no more than once a year. The need for learning often arises acutely, and must be met immediately – daily, sometimes even hourly. Questions about long-term career prospects, on the other hand, should not be asked daily. Things can vary greatly when it comes to the matter of agreeing on and setting goals. Strategic goals should be adjusted annually, while operational goals in uncertain environments are adjusted continuously.

If we now look at the various benefits, from rewarding the best, to identifying talent, to retaining employees, and duly examine the question of how often per year it is advisable to make relevant decisions and judgements, the results will differ greatly, depending on the framework conditions and benefit. And we will commonly find that "once a year" is certainly not the best answer. The three main possible results are:

A   Relevant judgements and decisions should be made precisely *once a year,* if possible at a fixed time.
B   Relevant judgements and decisions should be made *more than once a year*, if possible at set times (e.g. always at the end of a quarter).
C   Relevant judgements and decisions should be made *as necessary*, whenever they are warranted or required, meaning they can occur at any random time and at varying intervals.

It is difficult to make general recommendations here. How often judgements and decisions should be made ultimately depends on who is making them and how. But we can assume some basic tendencies. An agile world, for instance, can be expected to prefer the needs-oriented variant (C), due to its high degree of task uncertainty and personal responsibility. Depending on the intended benefit/objective, it may also be wise to favour certain methods. Learning through feedback is one example. Feedback must be given promptly in order to be effective. The overview in Figure 41 provides a rough estimation, though serves as a guide only. We must remember here that, as already demonstrated, certain benefits have varying degrees of importance in different settings.

	Hierarchy			Agility		
Benefit	**A**	**B**	**C**	**A**	**B**	**C**
Rewarding the best	X				X	
Addressing the weak			X			X
Identifying talent	X				X	
Determining internal suitability	X					X
Developing staff	X					X
Offering prospects	X			X		
Learning through feedback			X			X
Managing companies		X				X
Motivating by objectives	X					X
Retaining employees	X			X		

Figure 41:
Frequency based on various benefits and work environments
(A = once a year, B = more than once a year, C = as necessary).

If an HR department introduces a new HR instrument at a company, the common trend is for this to be assigned all kinds of different purposes, based on the mindset of: While we're at it, let's also include this or that. This logic has already been discussed in detail in an earlier section in chapter 3, where we saw that the instrument is often initially open to addressing all ideas, and not the intended benefit. Hardly any other instrument reflects this trend as clearly as the annual performance appraisal. As a result, the manager discusses performance, goals, skills, potential and prospects with his/her employee, gives feedback, clarifies development needs etc. once a year, as part of a one-off event. All at once. This approach has a number of advantages, the most important of which probably being that many judgements and decisions are interdependent, and should be treated as a unit. The goals are used to derive necessary skills, and the skills used to determine needs for development, which are in turn based on the relevant employee's performance in recent months. Everything somehow ties in. It is therefore understandable to want to deal with the entire matter outright, in one go. All of this takes time to prepare, execute and follow up, which is why no one wants to think about having to do it several times a year - better to do it once and get it right.

Times and players

But anyone who thinks in terms of benefit, and works on the basis of relevant judgements and decisions, should ask themselves *who* makes these and *how often* they are required in order to achieve the intended benefit. Companies which think this exercise through logically will find that the manager is not always the most suitable player, and a year is not always a suitable interval. Figure 42 shows the results of such an exercise – for the annual performance appraisal and a fictitious alternative.

| | Annual performance appraisal || Alternative ||
Judgements and decisions	Who	How often	Who	How often
Identification of A-players	Manager	Annually	Team	Annually
Identification of C-players	Manager	Annually	Manager	As necessary
Feedback on skills	Manager	Annually	Customers/ Peers	As necessary
Definition of learning needs	Manager	Annually	Employees	As necessary
Target agreement	Manager	Annually	Team	Quarterly

Figure 42:
Players and frequency based on various judgements and decisions for a fictitious company.

Whether or not certain content can be treated separately or jointly in the same instrument is initially determined by the necessary intervals. This is a matter of time synchronisation. Judgements and decisions requiring a varying degree of frequency cannot be made jointly. Different content may also need different players, which once again calls for separate treatment.

One particular aspect was already discussed in earlier chapters in relation to rewarding the best and addressing the weak. A-players are traditionally identified "all at once", like the C-players. The performance continuum used is more or less indicative of this approach. The considerations outlined in the previous chapter showed, however, that it is better not to identify A or C-players in one single process.

Artificial separation

In practice, however, attempts are often made to artificially separate content in order to suggest the independence of various aspects to employees. Based on my observations, many companies have already adopted the approach of separating meetings about salary from meetings about performance. The thinking behind this is as simple as it is obvious: once things become directly about money, employees are no longer open-minded enough to discuss their performance in a self-critical manner and accept negative feedback. That's why performance is addressed first, and any pay rises tackled later on. This initially sounds clever and even empathetic to a degree. The critical point, however, is not the chronological congruence with which performance and pay are addressed, but rather the common fact that feedback is given by the same person who ultimately also decides on the employee's salary and future. Here, again, we see the conflict of roles between judge and coach, which McGregor was so quick to point out even in 1960. The employee does not mind whether there is a time gap between the performance appraisal and salary assessment. He/she knows that the judgments from one will influence decisions in the other. Anything else would be naïve. If we want to separate judgements and decisions on one matter from those relating to another, we first need to separate the players. Feedback comes from customers or colleagues, while salary is decided on by the manager. Feedback comes from the manager, and the salary is decided on by the superior manager.

Letting go

In an extended conversation with a very experienced and extremely reflective HR manager from a large IT company, I recently took the liberty of asking what would happen if the annual performance appraisal were abolished at his company overnight. His response astonished me: "Nothing". Having barely had time to digest this radical answer, I dug deeper: "So why don't you abolish it then?". "Because we spent a lot of time and effort introducing it many years ago. We trained all our managers, implemented extensive communication measures, and finally convinced the workers' council. We can't do away with it all now".

Companies lay the annual performance appraisal to rest

The media is reporting of an increasing number of companies which are simply laying the annual performance appraisal to rest. Like Microsoft, which was always known for its well-though-out, progressive HR management approaches (Bartlett, 2001). One element of these was the annual performance review with forced distribution. It took many years for the company to realise that this damages the internal co-operation so vital to innovative businesses. Steve Balmer finally abolished this practice in 2013[4].

In 2011, Donna Morris, Senior Vice President for People Resources at Adobe, was so dubious of the practices in place at the time that, following intense discussions with staff, she took the decision to abolish the annual performance appraisal.

> We came to a fairly quick decision that we would abolish the performance review, which meant we would no longer have a one-time-of-the-year formal written review. What's

---

[4]The original message to all employees can be read here:
http://www.theverge.com/2013/11/12/5094864/microsoft-kills-stack-ranking-internal-structure (last viewed on 31/12/2015)

more, we would abolish performance rankings and levels in order to move away from people feeling like they were labelled[5].

It is worth noting here that, in some cases, the aforementioned companies replaced the abolished methods with more agile alternatives, like those described in the previous sections – but only in some cases. The question of whether certain instruments can be gotten rid of without replacement is indeed a relevant one. Systems can operate independently, so to speak, and often do this better if they are not being specifically manipulated. This aspect of self-regulation relates to the concept of resilience.

Resilience through self-regulation

The concept of resilience comes from systems theory. Resilience describes a system's ability to handle disruptions, whereby it generally strives for stability. This aspect of agility, which has been intensively addressed in this book, may be viewed as a prerequisite for resilience in this context. A good example I often use in my presentations to illustrate resilience and self-regulation is a simple pendulum. If a freely hanging pendulum is pushed by an outside force, it swings back into a stable position on its own. It does this best when left to do so itself – i.e. we do nothing (see Figure 43).

---

[5]http://www.hreonline.com/HRE/view/story.jhtml?id=534355695 (last viewed on 31/12/2015).

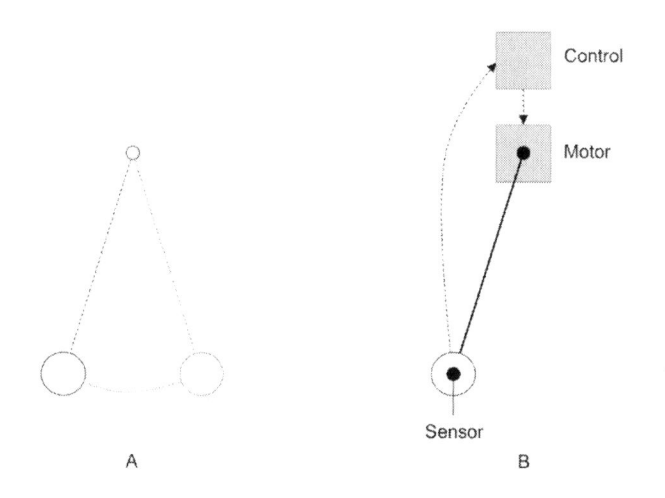

Figure 43:
The resilient pendulum and the centrally controlled pendulum.

In contrast to this (A), there is another possible type of pendulum. The free-hanging chain or string is replaced with a static rod (B), and the pendulum itself is fitted with a sensor which measures the pendulum's current position in relation to the stable one. Deviations are continuously or cyclically reported to an overarching control centre, which then sends a corresponding impulse to a motor, which in turn corrects the pendulum's position.

The latter variant reflects what is simply known as management – the separation of thoughts and actions. The situation at the bottom is reported "up", where decisions are made to ultimately establish a target condition "down below" – a combination of target agreement, performance evaluation and corrective management decisions. This is a recipe for inaction or incorrect decisions, e.g. due to insufficient feedback or inappropriate responses.

This pendulum analogy is of course highly simplified, designed to illustrate that the best approach is often to not actively intervene in systems, and to instead leave things to run their natural course.

Under no circumstances, however, should it be misconstrued as meaning that management systems are fundamentally harmful.

The idea of self-regulation can, for example, be easily applied to HR development or, in particular, talent management. When examining the question of who the customer of the annual performance appraisal is, it was already mentioned that a company generally has three extreme methods at its disposal when it comes to HR development: central planning (by HR), own responsibility, and employee competence or "Darwinism". Allowing things to run their natural course means Darwinism here. The best will find their own way – without any management systems or annual performance appraisals. This is probably a very common approach. I know of many companies which are extremely successful despite not having HR management systems. They don't worry about specifically enabling their employees to take personal responsibility, nor do they have a central HR unit active in all HR matters. These companies often end up introducing the annual performance appraisal as a management system at some point, but this doesn't always improve things.

Motivation and intelligence

To get a better idea, let's take a look at Peter's scenario. Peter and his team work in the product management division at an automotive supplier. They are responsible for the planning, development and market positioning of drive components primarily used in car seats.

Who is best qualified to rate Peter's performance? Who can best describe Peter's professional preferences and potential prospects? Who has the greatest interest in ensuring Peter's ambitions are met? Who can best assess Peter's strengths and weaknesses, and who is most curious about these? Who is in the best position to determine Peter's acute and long-term learning needs, and who is most intent on ensuring Peter meets these? Who has the greatest interest in making sure Peter receives feedback, and who is best equipped to give this to him? Who is best suited to setting realistic, sensible goals?

In an extremely hierarchical world, the response to almost all these question is: Peter's *manager*. Because he/she is the one with the responsibility. Because he/she, as a manger, can/should be able to. Because it's his/her job. This responsibility is often shared with HR or other authorities. But the alternative response to any question could also be: the *employees* themselves, i.e. Peter and his team. As the above questions already suggest, the issue initially revolves around two simple yet central aspects – ability and will. Who is most capable of making relevant judgements and decisions? Who is most motivated to do so? Depending on the type of judgements and decisions, this may be the employee himself/herself, his/her team, his/her manager, colleagues, customers, certain experts, mentors, the senior management or HR. The matter is too complex for across-the-board trends to be identified or general recommendations to be made. It instead requires careful, case-based examination and evaluation.

If, however, it is concluded that it is the employees and their teams who have the highest degree of motivation and ability when it comes to certain judgements and decisions, a third, obvious aspect comes into play: permission. Only then will teams stop being told when and how to set targets, where these must be documented, and whom they must be forwarded to. Only then will people stop stipulating when and based on which criteria employees must be evaluated, and by whom. It will be left to the employees and teams to identify their own development needs, and independently seek the help they require. Never again will we see people succumbing to attempts to motivate employees. They will instead rely on the employees' intrinsic motivation, and do away with various processes, instruments, KPIs, reports, scorecards and systems so as not to get in the way of this.

In summary

- More and more companies are abolishing their traditional annual performance appraisal, or parts thereof. This is frequently being replaced by agile approaches.
- Systems often operate best when left to their own devices, i.e. without any active intervention.
- If employees and teams are those best equipped to make certain judgements and decisions, and want to do this, they should be allowed to do this. In some cases, certain HR instruments can be completely done away with.

What now?

This book has attempted to illustrate that the starting point for introducing any HR instrument should always be the intended benefit: What do we want to achieve for whom? Only after detailed and considered examination of the framework conditions do we address the question of the most suitable tool, so as to then ultimately focus on possible relevant designs and formats. The latter were discussed in this chapter, whereby it was demonstrated that agile contexts in particular offer options different to those conventionally associated with annual performance appraisals.

The initial situation

However, companies rarely find themselves in the oft-cited "green pastures" in this respect. Their history is instead one of different, more or less established approaches. In practice, it is thus much more common to hear the question of how things could be done *differently* in future, rather than how they should be *set-up from scratch*. Almost all companies I have had dealings with in recent years have an annual performance appraisal, albeit displaying certain differences in content or format. These companies often operate in hierarchical worlds, but are increasingly asking themselves how they can shift towards greater agility. The past is primarily seen as a hurdle or challenge here. It is as if many HR managers wish they could start over again, clear away the sometimes painful experiences associated with previous approaches, and re-sort and re-focus their processes, instruments and systems.

When attempting to achieve more agile conditions and approaches, however, it is not just the existing systems for which so many HR professionals and managers have fought, but also the attitudes and culture at the company, which often make change so difficult. Both aspects must be taken into account here when it comes to altering HR approaches. Figure 44 shows a simplified diagram of the various initial situations and objectives.

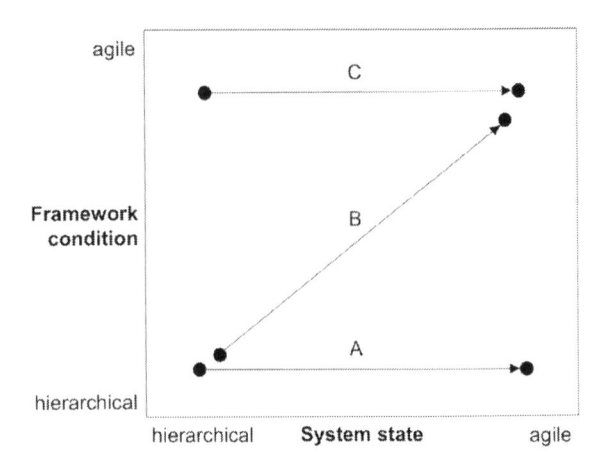

Figure 44: Initial situation and intended target state.

Figure 44 initially distinguishes between two dimensions: the framework conditions and the state of the respective system. The framework conditions are the very aspects addressed in this book. A distinction is made here between hierarchical and agile framework conditions, which are contrasted with the state of the respective HR system. This covers the annual performance appraisal or alternative approaches, which can themselves be more hierarchical or agile. In many cases, the two dimensions match, e.g. hierarchical systems will dominate under hierarchical framework conditions, while agile worlds are more likely to feature agile approaches. This is no surprise; on the one hand, the HR systems have been developed based on the respective framework conditions. On the other, HR systems can also determine or reinforce existing framework conditions. But it doesn't have to be so. I know of numerous companies which, despite having agile framework conditions, have tried to establish systems of a clearly hierarchical nature.

Apart from these two dimensions, the figure above also contains arrows showing a company's initial situation in relation to the framework conditions and current systems, as well as to the intended target state. The former is indicated by the start of an arrow, and the latter by the end. This simple representation helps identify where companies are in terms of their status quo and desired state, producing very different practical implications depending on the results. One common thread is the fact that the hierarchical system is always striving to become an agile one. While other scenarios are certainly conceivable, the three shown above (A, B and C) appear to be the most common. In recent years, I have not come across a single company pursuing a hierarchical objective from an agile initial situation. These three scenarios will be examined in more detail below. We'll start with scenario A.

More agile systems in an unwaveringly hierarchical environment

My personal network contains many highly respected HR professionals who, at deeply hierarchical companies, have taken on new challenges, often involving great responsibilities, e.g. as HR directors. Some of them have previously worked at extremely agile companies. So it is no surprise that they make well intended attempts to implement agile systems for their new employers. They do this out of inner conviction, and because their approaches resulted in primarily positive experiences with their former employers. They feel confident here, and are often able to fulfil their role as innovators. The fact that they are sometimes also perceived as troublemakers or rebels is something they see more as recognition rather than criticism.

But it's not just about the lateral thinkers brought in from external sources. I know equally as many HR professionals and managers who have implemented and run hierarchical systems in a hierarchical context for a number of years. Many of them were indeed actively involved in introducing the annual performance appraisal. Several years later, they realised that even a hierarchical instrument like the traditional annual performance appraisal could only achieve limited success in a hierarchical environment. Over the years, the internal pressure from managers and employees grew, with increasing doubt as to the effectiveness of existing approaches. In their search for appropriate alternatives, even these highly regarded colleagues often turn to agile methods for their long-awaited salvation.

The situation in such instances is pretty clear. Establishing agile methods in a hierarchical environment is very likely doomed to fail. We see the common phenomenon whereby whenever formal systems collide with culture, culture is always the winner. An environment characterised by external control will not accept approaches revolving around personal responsibility. When it's bosses who are required, coaches have no chance. When job-specific criteria are the main focus, the employees' individual preferences don't matter. I dare say this scenario is the most hopeless of the three.

Moving towards an agile world

The second scenario (B) describes what is known as agilisation. A hierarchical company as a whole sets about becoming more agile. In their initial form, the HR systems are usually cast in a similarly hierarchical mould. This intended change may be driven by a number of different motives. One such example are companies which have been built up by their founder, run in an often patriarchal fashion for decades, and have now been taken over by the son or daughter. These younger successors, often holding MBAs from leading international business schools, strive to manage the company differently, more openly, in a more modern manner, with employees and teams taking greater personal responsibility. They want to break down internal boundaries, and become quicker and more flexible in every respect – with greater agility. In these cases, organisations are frequently scrutinised from scratch.

I know of many companies where the senior management was aware its company no longer appeared attractive to young people. It is worth asking how these can remain attractive, including for future generations. This discussion revolves around a specific image of young generations. People who think in networks, who are searching for meaning, whose values have definitively shifted towards greater self-fulfilment. People who are at home on social media, know no formal boundaries, and reject rigid hierarchies.

Other companies, in turn, are growing increasingly concerned about their own competitiveness. They can sense the threat on the market from small, agile businesses which are able to develop disruptive technologies and successfully position them on the market breathtakingly quickly. We have seen entire industries completely transform themselves within the space of just a few years. We have seen reputable, long-established, seemingly impregnable companies lose all prominence overnight because they were evidently not agile enough. One such company was Kodak which, although capable of offering digital photography early on, was ultimately too stubborn and rigid to get onboard with it in time. Mail-order companies are another example – having originally been indispensable on the market, they were suddenly and completely squeezed out. These cases must make senior managements scared, and they do. So it is no surprise that many decision-makers are asking themselves the burning question of how they can change their companies to ensure they can cope with the increasingly complex, dynamic, fast and uncertain markets of the future.

The issue of agility is thus a hot topic in management circles, cropping up more and more on agendas and in informal conversations. Work groups are being formed. And sooner or later, questions will be asked as to what all this means for HR. This is about far more than just the annual performance appraisal. It's about flexible work structures, new forms of management, altered skill requirements, values as a whole, the manner in which future decisions are made, etc. But it does also include the annual performance appraisal. At this point, HR should fundamentally scrutinise existing processes and practices following the methods described in this book. In any case, it should ensure its established processes do not impede this development.

The central idea of the four-phase scheme, on which the structure of this book is also based, should serve as a guide here. We start with the issue of benefit in order to define suitable instruments, having assessed relevant framework conditions. The annual performance appraisal should be critically examined in this context; only then can there be discussions and decisions about appropriate instrument design. From a methodological perspective, this approach initially appears to be very simple. You start by testing out the annual performance appraisal in its current form. What did we want to achieve with it? For whom? What did we achieve? How will relevant framework conditions change in future? What will we achieve with the current approach under future framework conditions? What won't we achieve? Based on this, where are changes needed? What can be "thrown out the window"? The list of relevant questions could go on and on. What is important in this phase is unmitigated openness and honesty. It is also crucial at this point to involve relevant stakeholders, who usually include employees, managers, the workers' council, and management representatives. This phase ultimately results in an overview of the areas requiring change, future intended benefits, and beneficiaries. Only then can the design phase begin, taking into account relevant format aspects. Everything else is classic change management using agile methods: Communication, training and involvement based on a clear understanding of what is changing for whom, and which opportunities and risks this entails for the affected parties.

As already mentioned, this approach initially sounds simple and obvious. In practice, the change process is very complex – professionally, systemically and politically. The biggest challenge, however, lies in the fact that a hierarchical attitude cannot produce agile thinking. If the essence of agility has not been understood, attempts will be made to implement agility using hierarchical means. I see real-life examples of this everywhere I turn. Personal responsibility is stipulated top-down and upheld, instead of just being permitted. There can be a customer-focus, but only under supervision. Employees must give each other feedback, which is then reported to the superior manager. Employees request decisions "from above". The patriarchs' successors frequently hear: "Things were better before. Everyone knew where they stood. Today people are trying to shift responsibility onto us employees". Trust and freedom are not always welcomed.

If a company originally operates in a hierarchical manner, it still has the useful opportunity to decide on structural changes top-down. Numerous examples have demonstrated this. I know of CEOs who have cut their working-time recording system overnight. Others have simply abolished a number of management layers, committees etc., and deemed that departmental heads, teams and employees should and can immediately start making the majority of necessary decisions. I know of companies which have thrown the entire budgeting process out the window. I myself have witnessed many management meetings where it is no longer the CEO who stands at the front and speaks, but rather the customers or employees. These were and are all decisions which managing directors can make and enforce, insofar as the company still operates according to a strictly hierarchical structure. The annual performance appraisal, or at least parts thereof, can be handled in a similarly radical manner, provided formal framework conditions permit it. In Germany, it is a well known fact that workers' councils have a big say in matters relating to annual performance appraisals.

Adjusting foreign matter

Employer-branding projects usually involve examining the question of what makes an employer so special in the eyes of its relevant target groups (Trost, 2014). What are the particular strengths? What can a company offer that its competitors on the job market cannot (or not to the same extent)? I recently addressed these kinds of questions while working as an advisor for a company. The special features often require deeper examination, but in this case, things were comparatively obvious. The company I was involved with appeared to be highly agile. Its employees enjoyed incredible freedom, worked very independently in teams and networks, and set their own goals. There were never any set working hours, or even any everyday things like travel allowances. No manager at this particular company would have thought to act like a boss towards the employees. Trust existed at every level, even though some internal discussions – and a lot was discussed there – would cut straight to the chase.

More in passing, and personally motivated by my professional involvement, I asked a group of employees about the annual performance appraisal. "Do you have anything similar?". The responses initially astonished me. The annual performance appraisal had obviously been introduced a few years prior – in its most traditional, hierarchical form. A new HR manager had apparently been appointed at that time, and had been commissioned by the executive board to raise the HR management systems at this company to a more professional level. HR software had also been introduced, requiring, or at least allowing for, an instrument like the annual performance appraisal. It surprised me that a company highly agile by nature would implement a hierarchical approach. Less surprising, however, were the employees' comments that this instrument would not really take off. One of them hit the nail on the head when he smiled and simply said, "the annual performance appraisal is not relevant".

Agile companies are often somewhat chaotic. Many people are working together on things they define themselves. The notion of "anyone can do whatever they like here" is not always viewed positively. Agile companies allow mistakes, which are seen as opportunities for learning. At companies like these, employees and teams whose projects have failed are much more valuable than those who haven't dared to do anything – because they at least have experience. But a company and its management must then actually be able to cope with self-regulation, learning from mistakes, and failures. So it is no wonder that agile establishments sometimes think about implementing an instrument to provide a little more structure, albeit consistently re-iterating that its culture of openness and agility must not be affected. It is with an element of naivety that people think there can't be anything bad about structured feedback, clear goals, and reflecting upon performance and skills. Nor can it do any harm to document results in some way. And just like that, a company adopts an HR instrument which, given its framework conditions, it would have been better off avoiding.

I'm talking about scenario C in Figure 44 above: An agile company with a hierarchical HR instrument. What happens if this company tries to makes its instrument more agile? This scenario is the easiest of all those described here; rather than framework conditions being adjusted to systems, it's the other way around. So it's no wonder that companies like Adobe or Microsoft, which have always been used to agile framework conditions, abolished their performance review overnight and replaced it with more agile methods. This doesn't require any elaborate change management which employees just have to "go along with". If a hierarchical instrument is abolished or replaced at an agile company, the employees tend to actually welcome this. I wouldn't be surprised if SAP is the next to follow in Adobe's and Microsoft's footsteps and scrap its annual performance appraisal.

In summary

- There seems to be more companies shifting from hierarchical to agile structures rather than the other way around.
- Implementing agile methods in a constantly hierarchical environment is virtually hopeless.
- Adjusting the annual performance appraisal as part of a shift from hierarchical to agile structures requires careful, self-critical, open consideration and needs-based change management.
- Agile companies with hierarchical instruments find it comparably easy to abolish and replace these instruments overnight, because this change tends to be welcomed by employees.

7. Conclusion and final remarks

This book started off with the simple idea of managers discussing the basics with their employees away from everyday work as part of annual performance appraisals. It soon became clear that what initially comes across as a harmless meeting is actually a complex, integrated and institutionalised system consisting of target agreement, evaluation of performance, skills and potential, and much more. Experience has shown that the employees and managers involved do not always view this meeting favourably. The system sometimes even meets with fierce resistance, which some HR professionals often attribute to the relevant players' supposed management incompetence. The aim of this book was to show that this resistance or lack of understanding should be taken seriously. There is a very high risk of the annual performance appraisal as a system conflicting directly with the existing or desired framework conditions. While it has chances of surviving at strictly hierarchical organisations, it remains well *below expectations* in a modern, agile work environment.

It is naïve to think it is possible to motivate employees, encourage learning through feedback, distinguish between performance strengths and weaknesses, identify talent, manage the company, retain employees, develop employees, determine internal suitability, and illustrate career prospects with just one single instrument, regardless of the company's framework conditions. And even if the expected benefits of an annual performance appraisal are reduced to a more modest number, there is still a big risk that this instrument will have more toxic, rather than favourable, effects, given the existing framework conditions. This statement will come as a surprise, considering any meeting between a manager and its employee can't do any harm per se. As shown in this book, however, this toxic effect arises due to the fact that most of these meetings are ordered from the "top down", and their results are centrally documented.

The benefits usually expected of an annual performance appraisal are discussed in detail here in the context of two different worlds. A concise, simplified distinction is made between hierarchical and agile environments, with an implied assumption that more companies will shift from a hierarchical to an agile setup in future – something they will be forced to do in view of changing markets and challenges. Although this assumption was not the main focus of the book, it does underline the magnitude of the conclusions drawn here. While the annual performance appraisal was only able to achieve some of the intended goals even in a hierarchical world, it fails almost completely in an agile context. The goals in themselves were not questioned. But when it comes to achieving them, and asking which instrument is most suitable for this, companies should consider alternatives. At the very least, they should carefully scrutinise their approach in terms of key design and format elements. The latest trends show that more and more companies are doing just this.

The many HR professionals and HR departments are doing themselves a huge favour in the process. This profession continues to strive for recognition at its respective companies. In view of the ideas raised in this book, however, I don't think HR will be taken seriously by other departments until it stops trying to naively integrate over-the-top instruments like the annual performance appraisal into their organisations regardless of the framework conditions.

Many of the statements made in this book are bold or ambitious. A number of the ideas and conclusions are of a hypothetical nature. In most cases, plausibility or common sense prevails over empirical, scientific validity. Extensive research has already been conducted in numerous aspects of HR management, whether it be the relevance of assessment centres or the impact of variable incentive systems on employee motivation. But the question of whether and how the annual performance appraisal will measure up in a modern work environment is definitely not one of them. Although some passages in this book may appear arrogant, it is in fact with great humility that I myself respond to its content. From a scientific perspective, there is too much uncertainty surrounding the questions addressed in this book. Over the coming months and years, we will witness further intensive and controversial discussions on these matters, coupled with several scientific studies. I particularly look forward to the latter. Parts of this book may well have to be rewritten just a few years from now. What is most important, however, is that these discussions do, in fact, take place. I naturally hope this book has at least provided some sort of food for thought.

Any author wants his/her book to remain relevant for a long time or indeed forever. When I consider the relevance of this book's content from a present-day perspective, it would appear to be high, otherwise I wouldn't have written the book, nor would it have been published. But in terms of the future, I in fact hope it becomes irrelevant. Many years down the track, people may even smirk at its content. Was that really necessary? Did annual performance appraisals truly exist in the form described here? Did people actually think one instrument could achieve all the things mentioned here? It will be a source of amazement, and that's precisely what I look forward to.

8. Bibliography

Argyris, C. (1960). Understanding organizational behavior. Homewood/Ill.: Dorsey Press.

Axelrod, B., Handfield-Jones, H., & Michaels, E. (2002). A new game plan for C players. In Harvard Business Review, January, 81-88.

Bartlett, C. A. (2001). Microsoft. Competing on Talent (A). Harvard Business School.

Bartlett, C. A., & McLean, A. N. (2006). GE's Talent Machine: The Making of a CEO. Boston: Harvard Business School Publishing.

Becker, F. (2003). Grundlagen betrieblicher Leistungsbeurteilungen. Stuttgart: Schäffer-Poeschel.

Berberich, M. & Trost, A. (2012). Employee Referral Programs. BoD.

Berger, L. A., & Berger, D. R. (2005). Management Wisdom From the New York Yankees' Dynasty: What Every Manager Can Learn From a Legendary Team's 80-Year Winning Streak. San Francisco/CA: John Wiley & Sons.

Bernardes, E., & Hanna, M. (July 2008). A theoretical review of flexibility, agility and responsiveness in the operations management literature. International Journal of Operations & Production Management, p. 30-53.

Breisig, T. (2005). Personalbeurteilung: Mitarbeitergespräche und Zielvereinbarungen regeln und gestalten. Bund-Verlag.

Buckingham, M., & Vosburgh, R. M. (2001). The 21st Century Human Resources Function: It's the Talent, Stupid!. In Human Resource Planning, Vol. 24 Issue 4, p. 17-23.

Cappelli, P. (2012). Why good people can't get jobs. Wharton.

Christensen, C. M. (1997). The Innovator's Dilemma. Boston, MA: Harvard Business School Press.

Coens, T., & Jenkins, M. (2000). Abolishing Performance Appraisals: Why They Backfire and what to Do Instead. San Francisco CA: Berrett-Koehler Publishers.

Conger, J. A. (2010). Developing Leadership Talent: Delivering on the Promise of Structured Programs. In R. Silzer & B. E. Dowell (ed.): Strategy-driven Talent Management, p. 281-312. San Francisco, CA: Jossey-Bass.

Conner, D. R. (1992). Managing at the speed of change. How resilient managers succeed and prosper where others fail. New York/NY: Villard.

Culbertson, S. S.; Henning, J. B.; Payne, S. C. (2013). Performance appraisal satisfaction: The role of feedback and goal orientation. In Journal of Personnel Psychology, Vol 12(4), 2013, p. 189-195.

Culbert, S. A. (2010). Get rid of performance review! How companies can stop intimidating, start managing and focus on what really matters. New York: Business Plus.

Deci, E.L., Koestner, R., & Ryan, R.M. (1999). A Meta-Analytic Review of Experiments Examining the Effects of Extrinsic Rewards on Intrinsic Motivation. In Psychological Bulletin 125, p. 627–668.

Dowell, B .E. (2010). Managing Leadership Talent Pools. In R. Silzer & B. E. Dowell (ed.): Strategy-driven Talent Management, p. 399-438. San Francisco, CA: Jossey-Bass.

Eichel, E., & Bender, H. E. (1984). Performance Appraisal. A study of current technique. New York: Research and Information Services, American Management Association.

Fiske, S.T., & Taylor, S.E. (1991). Social cognition. New York: McGraw-Hill.

Forsyth, D. R. (2014). Group Dynamics. Cengage Learning.

Fulmer, R. M., & Conger, J. A. (2004). Growing your Company's Leaders. How great Organizations use Succession Management to sustain competitive Advantage. New York: Amacon.

Gallup (2013). Gallup Engagement Index. http://www.gallup.com/strategicconsulting/158162/gallup-engagement-index.aspx (last viewed on 30/9/2014).

Grote, R. C. (2005). Forced ranking: making performance management work. Boston MA: Harvard Business School Press.

Gubmann, E. L. (1998). The Talent Solution: Aligning Strategy and People to Achieve Extraordinary Results. Mc Graw-Hill.

Gunderson, L. H., & Pritchard, L. (ed.) (2002). Resilience and the Behavior of Large-Scale Systems. Washington DC: Island Press.

Hattie, J. & Timperley, H. (2007). The Power of Feedback. In Review of Educational Research, Vol. 77/1, p. 81–112.

Hinrichs, S. (2009). Mitarbeitergespräch und Zielvereinbarung. Betriebs- und Dienstvereinbarungen. Frankfurt/M.: Bund-Verlag.

Hossiep, R., Bittner, J. E., & Berndt, W. (2008). Mitarbeitergespräche. Motivierend, wirksam, nachhaltig. Göttingen: Hogrefe.

Huselid, M. A., Beatty, R. W., & Becker, B. E. (2005). A Player or A Positions? A strategic Logic of Workforce Management. In Harvard Business Review, Dec 2005, p. 110-117.

Illgen, D. R., & Feldman, J. M. (1983). Performance appraisal: a process approach. In B. M. Staw (ed.). Research in organization behavior (Vol. 2). Greenwich CT: JAJ Press.

Jenewein, W., & Heidbrink, M. (2008). High-Performance-Teams: Die fünf Erfolgsprinzipien für Führung und Zusammenarbeit. Stuttgart: Schäffer-Poeschel.

Joch, W. (1992). Das sportliche Talent. Talenterkennung, Talentförderung, Talentperspektiven. Aachen: Meyer und Meyer.

Katzenbach, J. R., & Khan, Z. (2008). Leading outside the lines. How to mobilize the (in)formal organization, energize your team, and get better results. San Francisco CS: Jossey-Bass.

Kaplan, R. S., Norton, D. P. (1996).The Balanced Scorecard: Translating Strategy Into Action. Boston MA: Harvard Business School Press.

Kettunen, P. (2009). Adopting key lessons from agile manufacturing to agile software product development - A comparative study. In Technovation, p. 408-422.

Laloux, F. (2014). Reinventing Organizations. Brussels: Nelson Parker.

Latané, B., Williams, K., & Harkins, S. (1979). Many hands make light the work. The causes and consequences of social loafing. Journal of Personality and Social Psychology, 37, 822-832.

Lawler III, E. (2012). Performance Appraisals Are Dead, Long Live Performance Management. http://www.forbes.com/sites/edwardlawler/2012/07/12/performance-appraisals-are-dead-long-live-performance-management/ (last viewed on 30/9/2014).

Lepper, M. R., Greene, D. & Nisbett, R. E. (1973). Undermining children's intrinsic interest with extrinsic rewards. In Journal of Personality and Social Psychology, 28/1, 129-137.

Locke, E. A., & Latham, G. P. (1984). Goal Setting: A Motivational Technique That Works!Prentice Hall

Locke, E. A., Latham, G. P., & Erez, M. (1988). The Determinants of Goal Commitment. Academy of Management Review, 13 (1), 23-39.

Luhmann, N. (2000). Vertrauen. Ein Mechanismus der Reduktion sozialer Komplexität. Stuttgart: UTB.

Malone T. W. (2004). The Future of Work: How the New Order of Business Will Shape Your Organization, Your Management Style, and Your Life. Boston/Mass.: Harvard Business School Press.

Markle, G. L. (2000). Catalytic Coaching. The End of the Performance Review. Westport: Quorum.

McCall, M. W. (1998). High Flyers: Developing the next Generation of Leaders. Boston/Mass.: Harvard Business School Press.

McCoy, T. J. (1992). Compensation and Motivation. Peterimizing Employee Performance with behavior-based Incentive Plans. New York: Amacon.

McDermott, R., Snyder, W., & Wenger, E. (2002). Cultivating Communities of Practice: A Guide to Managing Knowledge. Berkshire/UK: McGraw-Hill.

McGregor, D. (1960). The human side of enterprise. New York NY: McGraw-Hill Professional.

Michaels, E., Handfield-Jones, H., & Axelrod, B. (2001). The war for talent. Boston (Mass.): Harvard Business School Press.

Morgan, G. (1997). Images of Organization. London: Sage.

Mosley, E. (2013). The Crowdsourced Performance Review: How to Use the Power of Social Recognition to Transform Employee Performance. New York/NY: McGraw-Hill.

Murphy, K. R., & Cleveland, J. (1995). Understanding Performance Appraisal: Social, Organizational, and Goal-Based Perspectives. London: Sage.

Neuberger, O. (1980). Rituelle (Selbst-) Täuschung. Kritik der irrationalen Praxis der Personalbeurteilung. In Die Betriebswirtschaft, 1, p. 27-43.

Odiorne, G. S. (1965). Management by Objectives. A System of Managerial Leadership". New York: Pitman.

Phillips, J. J., & Edwards, L. (2009). Managing Talent Retention. An ROI Approach. San Francisco CA: John Wiley.

Pink, D. (2009). Drive. The surprising truth about what motivates us. New York NY: Riverhead Books.

Phillips, J. J., & Edwards, L. (2009). Managing Talent Retention: An ROI Approach. San Francisco CA: Pfeiffer.

Pfläging, N. (2014). Organize for Complexity: How to Get Life Back Into Work to Build the High-Performance Organization. BetaCodex Publishing.

Robinson, K. (2009). The Element. How finding your Passion changes everything. New York: Viking.

Rothwell, W. J. (2005). Effective Succession Planning. Ensuring Leadership Continuity and building Talent from within. New York: Amacon.

Scullen, S. E., Bergey, P. K., Aiman-Smith, L. (2005). Forced Distribution Rating Systems and the Improvement of Workforce Potential: A Baseline Simulation. In Personnel Psychology 58/1, p. 1–32.

Senge, P. (1990). The Fifth Discipline. The Art & Practice of The Learning Organization. New York/NY: Doubleday.

Silzer, R. F., & Church, A. H. (2009). The pearls and perils of identifying potential. In Industrial and Organizational Psychology: Perspectives on Science and Practice, 2(4).

Sims, C., & Johnson, H. L. (2011). The Elements of Scrum. Foster City CA: DyPetericon.

Taylor, F. W. (1911). The Principles of Scientific Management. Harper & Brothers.

Trost, A. (2014). Talent Relationship Management. Competitive Recruiting Strategies in Times of Talent Shortage. Heidelberg: Springer.

Vester, F. (1988). The biocybernetic approach as a basis for planning our environment. In System Practice, Dec. Vol. 1/4, p. 399-413.

Weltz, F., & Ortmann, R.G. (1992). Das Softwareprojekt: Projektmanagement in der Praxis. Frankfurt/M.: Campus.

Wood, R. E., Mento, A. J., & Locke, E. A. (1987). Task Complexity as a Moderator of Goal Effects: A Meta Analysis. Journal of Applied Psychology, 72 (3), 416-425.

Zimbardo, P. G. (2007). The Lucifer Effect. How good people turn evil. Random House.

About the author

Born in 1966, Professor Armin Trost lectures and researches at the HFU Business School in Furtwangen, Germany, focusing primarily on talent management, employer branding and the future of work. He previously also had a professorship at Würzburg University of Applied Sciences, and was head of worldwide recruiting at SAP for many years. He is a long-time trusted advisor for companies of all sizes and industries in matters relating to strategic Human Resource Management. Not only is Professor Trost known as the author of numerous articles and books, he is also a trend-setting speaker at reputable conferences.

www.armintrost.de

mail@armintrost.de

Twitter: @armintrost

About the translator

A native English speaker from Australia, *Emily Plank* has been working as a freelance translator since 2007. Having studied French and German from an early age, she has always been passionate about foreign languages, and has been fortunate enough to travel extensively throughout Western Europe on numerous occasions, including a stint in Spain studying Spanish and teaching English. After graduating from the University of Western Australia with a Bachelor of Arts in French, German and Linguistics in 2006, she completed a Certificate of Translation (Spanish to English) and set about establishing her own business, E-Translations, with an international client base. Her career has since gone from strength to strength, and her work has been featured in numerous publications and websites. In 2015, she became a certified member of the UK-based Institute of Translation & Interpreting. Emily Plank prides herself on her ability to translate in a wide range of fields and registers, and her clients have come from industries as diverse as tourism, law, medicine, commerce and HR.

Printed in Great Britain
by Amazon